The Essentials of Instructional Design

Second Edition

The Essentials of Instructional Design

CONNECTING FUNDAMENTAL PRINCIPLES WITH PROCESS AND PRACTICE

Abbie Brown

East Carolina University

Timothy D. Green

California State University–Fullerton

Boston Columbus Indianapolis New York San Francisco Upper Saddle River
Amsterdam Cape Town Dubai London Madrid Milan Munich Paris Montreal Toronto
Delhi Mexico City São Paulo Sydney Hong Kong Seoul Singapore Taipei Tokyo

Senior Acquisitions Editor: Kelly Villella Canton
Editorial Assistant: Annalea Manalili
Senior Development Editor: Shannon Steed
Vice President, Director of Marketing: Quinn Perkson
Senior Marketing Manager: Darcy Betts
Photo Research: Annie Pickert
Project Manager: Renata Butera
Operations Specialist: Renata Butera
Creative Art Director: Jayne Conte
Cover Designer: Suzanne Duda
Cover Image: Getty Images, Inc.
Full-Service Project Management: Aparna Yellai, PreMediaGlobal
Composition: PreMediaGlobal
Printer/Binder: R.R.Donnelley/Harrisonburg
Cover Printer: R.R.Donnelley/Harrisonburg
Text Font: Minion 10/12

Credits and acknowledgments borrowed from other sources and reproduced, with permission, in this textbook appear on appropriate page within text.

Photo Credits: Shutterstock, p.2; iStockphoto, p.21; Bob Daemmric, p.40; iStockphoto, p.56; Shutterstock, p.70; Shutterstock, p.88; iStockphoto, p.100; Shutterstock, p.114; Bob Daemmrich, p.136; Shutterstock, p.160; Bob Daemmrich, p.180; iStockphoto, p.196; Abbie Brown, p.202.

Library of Congress Cataloging-in-Publication Data

Brown, Abbie.
The essentials of instructional design : connecting fundamental principles with process and practice / Abbie Brown, Timothy D. Green. — 2nd ed.
p. cm.
Includes bibliographical references and index.
ISBN-13: 978-0-13-508422-9 (alk. paper)
ISBN-10: 0-13-508422-9 (alk. paper)
1. Instructional systems—Design. I. Green, Timothy D., 1968- II. Title.
LB1028.38.B76 2011
371.3—dc22

2010031395

10 9 8 7 6 5 RRD-VA 14 13

www.pearsonhighered.com

ISBN-10: 0-13-508422-9
ISBN-13: 978-0-13-508422-9

Dedication

To Paul: the dog's favorite gorilla and my best friend – AB

To J, B, and H. Thank you for your support! – TG

BRIEF CONTENTS

CONTENTS

PREFACE

The intention of this book is to provide a foundational overview of instructional design (ID) activities; to explain the essential principles of instructional design; to describe the processes used to put these principles into practice; and to offer examples of their practical application in a manner that transcends any single ID model or approach.

NEW IN THIS EDITION

This second edition provides more details and updated information about the instructional design process:

- Each chapter that addresses one of the instructional design processes begins with brief cases that illustrate the challenges instructional designers face with regard to that specific process. Each case is revisited at the chapter's midpoint and end, illustrating the process in action.
- Chapters have been reorganized into five parts: Before you begin designing instruction; Examining the Situation: Needs, task, and learner analyses; Creating instruction: Planning, designing, and implementing the intervention; Evaluation: Determining the effect of the intervention; and Media Production: Managing the media development process. The reorganization aligns the chapters with the most common presentation of the content in college courses.
- The chapters on how people think and how people learn from the first edition have been synthesized and updated to form a single chapter in the second edition. The single chapter approach allows instructors to assign the reading on thinking and learning more efficiently.
- A new chapter on visual design has been added to help students understand how best to present instructional media.
- All references have been updated, and newer instructional design-related information (e.g., brain-based research) has been added.
- Chapter 3 through 12 each include a new section on how the chapter information directly relates to the instructional design process.

THIS IS A BOOK FOR BEGINNERS

This book is not intended to replace or compete with such texts as Dick, Carey, and Carey's *The Systematic Design of Instruction;* Smith and Ragan's *Instructional Design;* or Morrison, Ross, and Kemp's *Designing Effective Instruction.* These texts and others like them form the core of any instructional design professional's library. Each provides valuable information about a single model or a specific approach to instructional design (ID) that is worth detailed study by students at the intermediate and advanced levels.

This book is designed to introduce the essential elements of instructional design to students who are new to ID, providing an overview of the fundamental principles, processes, and practices that currently shape and define the field. In the chapters that describe the essential elements of instructional design, we begin by articulating the principle (e.g., task analysis) and then describe, compare, and contrast the processes of applying the principle established by leaders in the field. Finally, we offer practical examples of how to apply the principle.

No matter which established model one refers to, there are generally three phases to the ID process: examination of the situation (needs, task, and learner analyses); creating instruction (planning, creating, and implementing the intervention); and evaluating the effect of the instruction. Once an individual understands these phases, he or she is ready to study and experiment with various methods of putting them into practice. This book explains the component parts of each of these phases, making reference to the most popular models and approaches and describing, comparing, and contrasting the strengths of each approach. This book also includes examples and recommendations for practical application.

THE FIVE PARTS OF THIS BOOK

Although the ID process can be articulated as having three major phases, this book is divided into a total of five parts. The first part we call "Before you Begin Designing Instruction"; this part contains information that is necessary for every ID professional but is not a traditional component of the ID process. Part 1 includes chapters that review the discipline of instructional design and what is known about thinking and learning.

Parts 2, 3, and 4 are the generally agreed-upon, principle phases of ID, examining the situation, creating instruction, and evaluating the instruction's effect.

Part 5 deals with production issues. In this part, we have provided a chapter on **project management** and a chapter on **visual design**. We have included these at the request of a great many of our colleagues. The chapter on project management deals with practical issues of producing instructional media. The chapter on visual design explains basic visual design principles and methods of creating effective and pleasing visual displays. Although this may not always be part of every instructional designer's job, it is often a part of an instructional design student's experience. The production management chapter also contains information on communication and conflict resolution that has proven helpful to students working on ID projects.

PROFESSIONALS IN PRACTICE SECTIONS

To provide even greater breadth to this text, we asked instructional designers from a number of professional settings to provide descriptions of how their organizations put the various ID principles and processes into practice.

Throughout the text, we share our own experiences as instructional designers and teachers as well as the experiences of a number of other professional instructional design specialists in sections we call "Professionals in Practice." We hope these reports from the field help students better understand how these processes are applied in business and education settings.

Our goal in writing this text is to provide students with an introduction to the principles and processes of instructional design without placing undo emphasis on any single ID model while at the same time offering practical advice on how to design, develop, and evaluate instruction. We hope the practical examples and suggestions we have included will help novice instructional designers understand the issues that surround ID in practice and that the descriptions of the processes and the practical examples presented will help emergent instructional designers apply these principles and processes to their own projects.

—Abbie Brown and Tim Green, authors

ACKNOWLEDGMENTS

We would like to express our appreciation to everyone at Pearson Allyn & Bacon/Merrill, with special thanks to Shannon Steed and Gregory Erb for their help during writing and production.

We would also like to thank the reviewers of this edition for their valuable feedback: John H. Curry, Oklahoma State University; Kendall Hartley, University of Nevada–Las Vegas; Cheri Toledo, Illinois State University; and Cheryl A. Wissick, University of South Carolina.

Our appreciation also goes out to those who contributed to the "Professionals in Practice" sections. We would thank Kara Andrew, Kursat Cagiltay, Jona Titus, Lisa Hansen, Erik Novak, and Jody Peerless for providing us with insights into how they practice the principles of instructional design.

ABOUT THE AUTHORS

Abbie Brown, Ph.D., is an associate professor at East Carolina University in the Department of Mathematics, Science and Instructional Technology Education. He is an award-winning teacher and scholar, helping educators in K–12, college, government, and corporate settings understand and apply the instructional design process to their work. Dr. Brown is the editor-in-chief of the journal *TechTrends* and author of numerous books and articles related to teaching, instructional design, and educational technology. He received his Ph.D. in Instructional Systems Technology from Indiana University.

Tim Green, Ph.D., a former elementary and middle school teacher, is a professor at California State University–Fullerton in the Department of Elementary and Bilingual Education, where he teaches primarily in the educational technology graduate program. Dr. Green conducts research and has published numerous works related to instructional design, online teaching and learning, and the integration of educational technology into teaching and learning processes. He was formerly the director of distance education for California State University–Fullerton. He received his Ph.D. in Instructional Systems Technology from Indiana University.

The Essentials of Instructional Design

Part I

BEFORE YOU BEGIN DESIGNING INSTRUCTION

Chapters 1 and 2 provide background information that you will find useful as you begin your study of instructional design. Chapter 1 is an overview of the history, traditions, and current state of the instructional design discipline.

Chapter 2 describes how people think and learn. This chapter introduces and reviews cognition and the basic cognitive functions as well as the most popular description of what learning is and how it occurs.

Chapter 1

The Discipline of Instructional Design

People have been instructing each other since people have existed. Showing an infant how to speak; explaining to an apprentice how an axe head is forged; guiding a daughter's hands as she attempts to make a clay pot—humans have been teaching each other for a long time.

Instruction can be a casual event. It can be as simple as answering a question such as, "How did you do that?" Instruction can also be carefully planned. It can encompass a course of study that concludes with students receiving a diploma or certificate marking the achievement. It is the history and current state of instruction brought about through careful planning—the discipline of instructional design—that we will examine in this chapter.

GUIDING QUESTIONS

- What is an instructional designer?
- How did the discipline of Instructional Design develop?
- What is an instructional design/development model?
- How has general systems theory affected instructional design?
- How does the historical and philosophical postmodern approach affect instructional design?

KEY TERMS

ADDIE model *7*
behaviorist *13*
educational psychology *4*
general systems theory *3*
positivistic *15*
postmodernism *13*
rapid prototyping *16*

CHAPTER OVERVIEW

Taking a logical and structured approach to the process of developing, delivering, and evaluating instruction and instructional materials has been popular among scholars and practitioners for almost a century. A number of models have been developed to help explain the processes of instruction as well as the process of designing and developing materials for instruction. This chapter provides an overview of instructional design from its beginnings in the late nineteenth century, through its blossoming in conjunction with the development of **general systems theory**, up to a present-day postmodern look at how instructional design (or ID) continues to develop. This chapter also describes the essential processes of instructional design as they are articulated through traditional ID models and examines the potential of nontraditional models, describing rapid prototyping in particular as an innovative ID approach.

A Historian's View of Instructional Design

No particular event or date marks the beginning of a modern science and technology of instruction. Yet it is clear that at the beginning of the twentieth century there occurred a series of related events that together might be interpreted as the beginning of a science of instruction.

William James (1842–1910), for example, in his book, *Talks to Teachers on Psychology*, makes one of the first distinctions between the art and the science of teaching, calling for a scientific

> approach to instruction. Similarly, also in 1901, John Dewey (1859–1952) interpreted a method of empirical science in educational terms, viewing the classroom as an experimental laboratory. In 1902, Edward Thorndike (1874–1949) offered the first course in educational measurements at Columbia University and became the first to apply the methods of quantitative research to instructional problems. G. Stanley Hall (1846–1924) published his *Adolescence* (1904), a landmark in the scientific study of the child. The French psychologist Alfred Binet (1857–1911) and Théodore Simon, his collaborator, published *A Method of Measuring the Intelligence of Young Children* (1905). Moreover, a true science of behavior, and especially of learning theory, began to emerge, no longer based primarily on metaphysical or philosophical speculation. This new science and learning theory would eventually be applied to a technology of instruction.
>
> — Paul Saettler, *The Evolution of American Educational Technology* (1990, p. 53)

WHAT IS INSTRUCTIONAL DESIGN?

"The purpose of any design activity is to devise optimal means to achieve desired ends."

— *Charles Reigeluth, 1983*

The ritual dance around the fire at the front of the cave depicting the hunt and kill of a large animal may be one of mankind's earliest forms of designed instruction. The hunters of the group had to find ways to teach other potential hunters the process of stalking and bringing down a large animal. Creating a dramatic display that describes the procedures for the hunt in a ritualized fashion captures the group's attention and provides them with a stylized presentation of how hunting works. This type of instructional design—based on inspiration and creativity—remained prevalent for millennia. But the *science* of instructional design is relatively new.

Throughout history, a number of individuals gave careful thought to the design of instruction. For example, the scholar Comenius (1592–1671) was among the first to plan for the use of visual aids in teaching. Comenius's *Orbis Sensualum Pictus* (*The Visible World Pictured*) was the first illustrated textbook designed for children's use in an instructional setting (Heinich, Molenda, Russell & Smaldino, 1996). Until the late 1800s, however, there was no organization that gathered this kind of work together, offered like-minded individuals a forum for discussion on the topic, or sought to continue its development.

At the beginning of the twentieth century, John Dewey—one of our most influential educators—called for a linking science between what is known about how people learn and the practice of delivering instruction. At the time, this was a radical thought. Before the mid-1800s, there was no educational science with which to link.

There had been no organization devoted to the study of how people learn or how to study methods of delivering instruction. Although there had been scattered attempts to improve instruction throughout history, no specific discipline had emerged to guide these efforts. Education-oriented organizations existed to protect and direct the curriculum and content of the instruction, but very little attention was paid to how instruction might be made more effective. The psychology of education—how the learner learned—was a school of thought in search of an organizing body. With the formation of the American Psychological Association in 1892, the discipline of **educational psychology** began.

In the late 1800s and early 1900s, education was still very much the province of those with religious backgrounds and training (Berliner, 1993). It is important to keep in mind that teachers were originally members of the clergy and that, prior to World War I, one of the main purposes of education in the United States was to ensure that people could read passages from the Bible. It was not easy to convince those who believed education to be a moral and philosophical endeavor in which scientific methods might be employed to improve educational processes. With the establishment of the discipline of educational psychology, however, educators interested in improving instructional practice through scientific means found both a home organization and like-minded fellows to report to and hear from.

With the formation of the land-grant universities in the late 1800s (each state was entitled by the federal government to form its own university within the state's borders) and the subsequent need to determine what constituted college readiness on the part of an individual, educational psychologists were called on to develop valid and reliable tests and measures of academic achievement. For example, the Scholastic Achievement Test (or SAT, now known as the Scholastic Aptitude Test) was first offered in 1901 and is to some extent an indicator of a trend toward the scientific testing of the learner to determine the appropriate next course of action in his or her education.

By 1915, the application of scientific methods to the solution of educational problems had won out among the leaders in American education, setting the stage for the development of Dewey's linking science, which scholars such as Snellbecker (1974) suggest is the discipline of instructional design. Educators began to develop an experimental view of instruction. Along with testing students to see what they knew, the newly organized discipline of educational psychology devised tests for the purpose of discovering whether the instruction worked. The traditional approach had been for an educator to focus completely on the information that should be included in the lesson; instructional design demanded that the educator add to that some consideration for how the information was to be organized and presented based on what is known about the learners and their abilities.

As the century progressed and more scholars focused their attention on the science of designing instruction, educational psychology blossomed into university departments and international organizations that reported and discussed research in the field. The discipline of instructional design is directly descended from educational psychology. Although some scholars argue that it is not actually a field of its own but rather a subactivity within educational psychology, instructional design can point to its own university departments and international organizations as indicators that it is now indeed a separate and distinct discipline.

As a linking science, instructional design is a discipline that constantly looks to the findings of other disciplines (e.g., cognitive psychology, communication) to study and improve methods of developing, delivering, and evaluating instruction and instructional practices.

According to Smith and Ragan (2005), instructional design may be currently defined as "the systematic and reflective process of translating principles of learning and instruction into plans for instructional materials, activities, information resources, and evaluation."

The Applied Research Laboratory at Penn State University is attributed with developing a four-part definition of instructional design (University of Michigan, 2003):

> **Instructional Design as a Process**
>
> Instructional Design is the systematic development of instructional specifications using learning and instructional theory to ensure the quality of instruction. It is the entire process of analysis of learning needs and goals and the development of a delivery system to meet those needs. It includes development

of instructional materials and activities; and tryout and evaluation of all instruction and learner activities.

Instructional Design as a Discipline

Instructional Design is that branch of knowledge concerned with research and theory about instructional strategies and the process for developing and implementing those strategies.

Instructional Design as a Science

Instructional design is the science of creating detailed specifications for the development, implementation, evaluation, and maintenance of situations that facilitate the learning of both large and small units of subject matter at all levels of complexity.

Instructional Design as Reality

Instructional design can start at any point in the design process. Often a glimmer of an idea is developed to give the core of an instruction situation. By the time the entire process is done the designer looks back and she or he checks to see that all parts of the "science" have been taken into account. Then the entire process is written up as if it occurred in a systematic fashion.

An instructional designer's job is to create something that enables a person or group of people to learn about a particular topic, develop or improve a set of skills, or encourage the learner to conduct further study. The "something" created can take many forms: a lecture, a multimedia presentation, the curriculum for a year's study, a piece of computer software, an in-person demonstration, or a test-preparation booklet. The list is almost endless. However, everything an instructional designer creates has something in common with all other instructional designs: The designer has identified a need for instruction and decided on a method for delivering that instruction. Most instructional designs (the best ones, we would argue, and the ones that follow the precepts of the discipline as it is currently defined by its governing organizations) also have a strategy for evaluating whether the instruction produced and delivered achieved the desired effect as well as how the design might be improved.

Instructional design advocates making use of the available research on how people think, how people learn, the technologies available for communication (information technologies), and methods of analysis. An instructional design is the practical application of this knowledge to create a situation where learning is most likely to effectively occur.

As scholars and practitioners have examined the process of developing, delivering, and evaluating instruction, they have devised a number of models to explain the process; these models are intended to help instructional designers perform their job better. It is important to be aware of the more popular models and to be cognizant of special cases that are currently a topic of discussion within the instructional design community. It is perhaps even more important to understand the big picture of designing instruction for a particular situation in terms that go beyond the application of any one instructional design model or adherence to any one instructional design theory. To become a well-rounded instructional designer today, one must be able to take a broad view of the ideas and practices that define the field.

Probably the most popular approach to designing instruction is to follow some variation of what is essentially a three-step process:

1. Analyze the situation to determine what instruction is necessary and what steps need to be taken to deliver that instruction.
2. Produce and implement the instructional design.
3. Evaluate the results of implementing the instructional design.

One of the most popular descriptions of this process is **ADDIE**, an acronym that divides the three steps described above into five actions: Analyze, Design, Develop, Implement, and Evaluate. ADDIE is not really a specific instructional design/development model but an illustration of the conceptual components of many instructional design/development models. See the section "A Special Case: ADDIE" later in this chapter.

Another view of the instructional design process in general is David Merrill's "first principles of instruction" (2002). Merrill suggests there are five basic principles that hold true for the design of any instruction. The first principles of instruction state learning is promoted when:

- Learners are engaged in solving real-world problems.
- Existing knowledge is activated as a foundation for new knowledge.
- New knowledge is demonstrated to the learner.
- New knowledge is applied by the learner
- New knowledge is integrated into the learner's world. (2002, pp. 44–45)

As practitioners of a linking science, instructional designers have become adept at examining and making use of ideas developed by a wide variety of specializations. Students of instructional design learn from other disciplines, sometimes borrowing development models created for activities that are similar to designing instruction (for example, software development, which shares the common purpose of creating something of use and usable to people). There is a tradition within the discipline of instructional design of taking a systematic approach and following accepted protocols for development. However, at this point in time (what many refer to as the postmodern world), the instructional designer may also take an eclectic approach, borrowing ideas and strategies from a variety of unconventional sources.

Models of Instructional Design/Development

Models by definition are a reflection of reality—temporary stand-ins for something more specific and real. Models are helpful in explaining things that may be difficult to describe. However, it must be remembered that any model is just a shadow or reflection of the *real* thing. A model may describe commonalities among a number of similar items; a model may illustrate a process; a model may be a representation of something:

- A "model home" in a new housing development will not be exactly like every home, but the model serves to give the potential buyer a pretty good idea of what is available for sale.
- Participation in a "model Congress" and "model United Nations" activities give students an opportunity to better understand how the real organizations work, even though they are not the same as participating in the actual UN or congressional meetings.

- Hobbyists build model trains, automobiles, and planes. These models are usually significantly smaller and do not operate in exactly the same way as the original item.

In a professional setting, good models can be helpful tools. They offer guidelines and can ensure a level of quality and uniformity by providing a means of comparison. Well-considered models of instructional design and development can perform this task, helping to explain in general the instructional design process in a way that can be applied to a number of specific situations.

Several well-established and respected models for instructional design/development provide guidelines and procedures that can be applied to a wide variety of specific situations. Using these models to design and develop instruction can help to significantly reduce costs in training and education (Nixon and Lee, 2001).

We have selected—and next describe—two of the most famous models of instructional design/development with which every instructional designer should become familiar: Dick and Carey's systems approach model and Kemp, Morrison, and Ross's plan. These models are intended to guide the instructional designer through the ADDIE process—analysis, design, development, implementation, and evaluation—which is discussed after the two models.

THE SYSTEMS APPROACH MODEL FOR DESIGNING INSTRUCTION Dick and Carey's systems approach model (see Figure 1.1) is a classic example of performing an instructional design task systematically. At the time it was developed, taking into consideration components of the instructional context—such as the learners and the environment in which the instruction was to be offered—was a significant departure from the more traditional approach of presenting information through some combination of lecture, textbook reading, review, and testing. With the traditional approach, the burden is placed squarely on the learners to do the best they can with the content, and little thought is

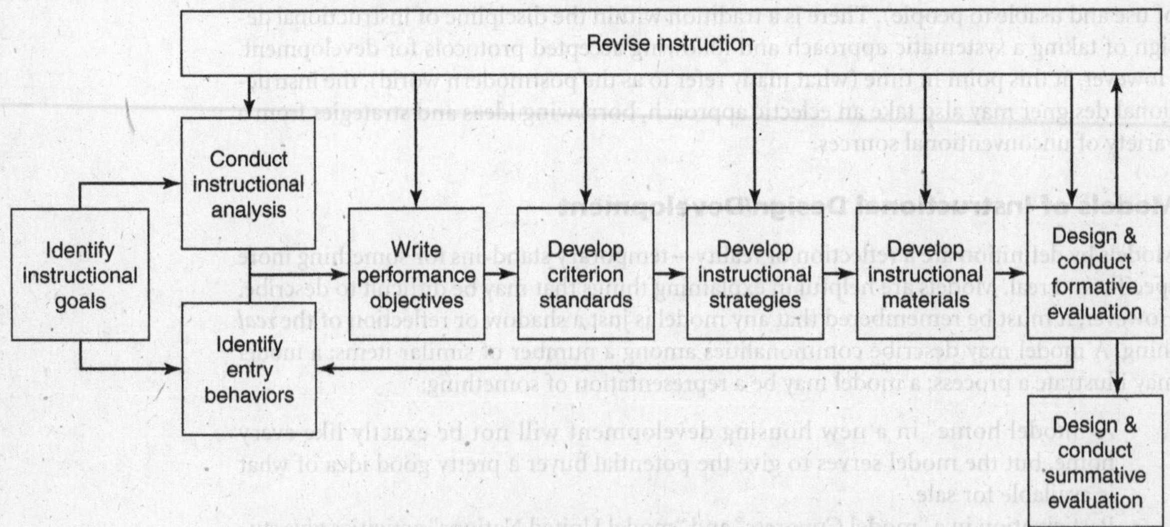

FIGURE 1.1 Dick and Carey's Systems Approach Model for Designing Instruction *Source:* Dick et al., The Systematic Design of Instruction, "Instructional Systems Design Model," p. xxiv, © 2009. Reproduced by permission of Pearson Education, Inc

given to adjusting or improving the instruction itself. Dick and Carey's model was designed to emphasize the importance of examining and refining the instruction and provides guidance for making improvements. (Dick, Carey & Carey, 2009).

KEMP, MORRISON, AND ROSS'S INSTRUCTIONAL DESIGN PLAN The Kemp, Morrison, and Ross plan (see Figure 1.2) is expressed as nine elements:

1. Identify instructional problems and specify goals for designing instruction.
2. Examine learner characteristics that will influence your instructional decisions.
3. Identify subject content, and analyze task components related to stated goals and purposes.
4. Specify the instructional objectives.
5. Sequence content within each instructional unit for logical learning.
6. Design instructional strategies so that each learner can master the objectives.
7. Plan the instructional message and develop the instruction.
8. Develop evaluation instruments to assess the objectives.
9. Select resources to support instruction and learning activities. (Morrison, Ross & Kemp, pp. 7–8)

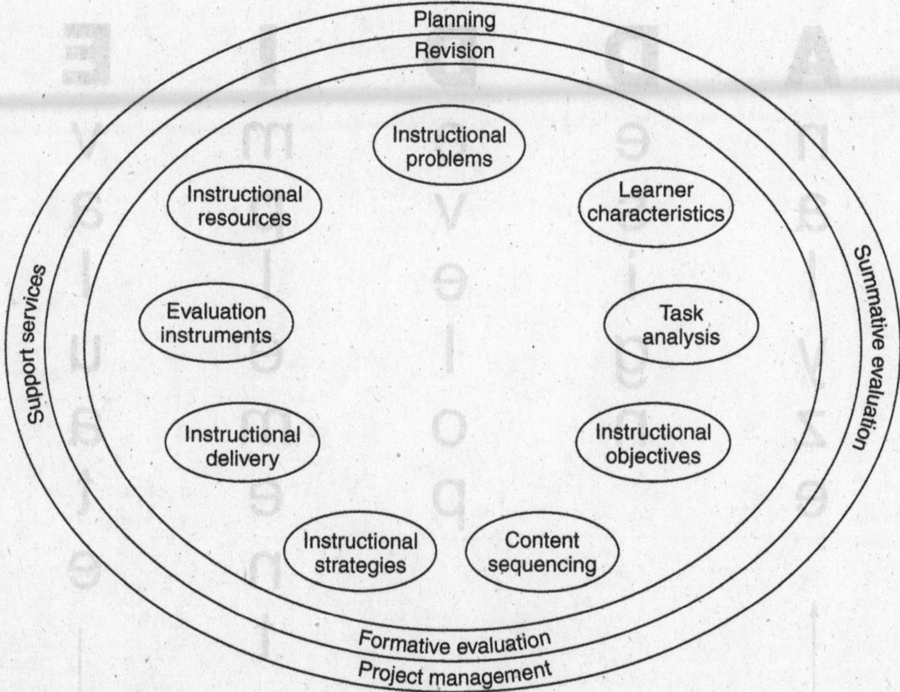

FIGURE 1.2 Kemp, Morrison, and Ross's Instructional Design Plan *Source:* Morrison et al., Designing Effective Instruction, "Components of the Instructional Design Plan" p. 12, © 2007. Reproduced by permission of John Wiley & Sons, Inc

One interesting aspect of this design plan is that it is not illustrated as a specific sequence. According to Morrison et al. (2004), each of the nine elements of development are presented in an oval pattern without lines or arrows pointing the way because each element may be addressed at any time while developing the instruction.

A SPECIAL CASE: ADDIE One of the most commonly used descriptions of instructional design/development is ADDIE. ADDIE is an acronym for Analyze, Design, Develop, Implement, and Evaluate (see Figure 1.3). Although many ID practitioners use ADDIE as a prescriptive model for developing instruction, it is actually a means of describing the essential components of *any* instructional design model (Molenda, 2003).

Scholars generally agree that ADDIE is an illustration of the essential steps of the instructional design/development process (Molenda, 2003; Reiser & Dempsey, 2002). ADDIE is particularly useful as a framework for comparing and contrasting more formally and completely developed instructional design/development models.

CAVEAT The two models and ADDIE are intended to guide individuals through the process of creating and evaluating instruction. Each model articulates the steps involved in creating an instructional intervention differently, and these are only a few of many

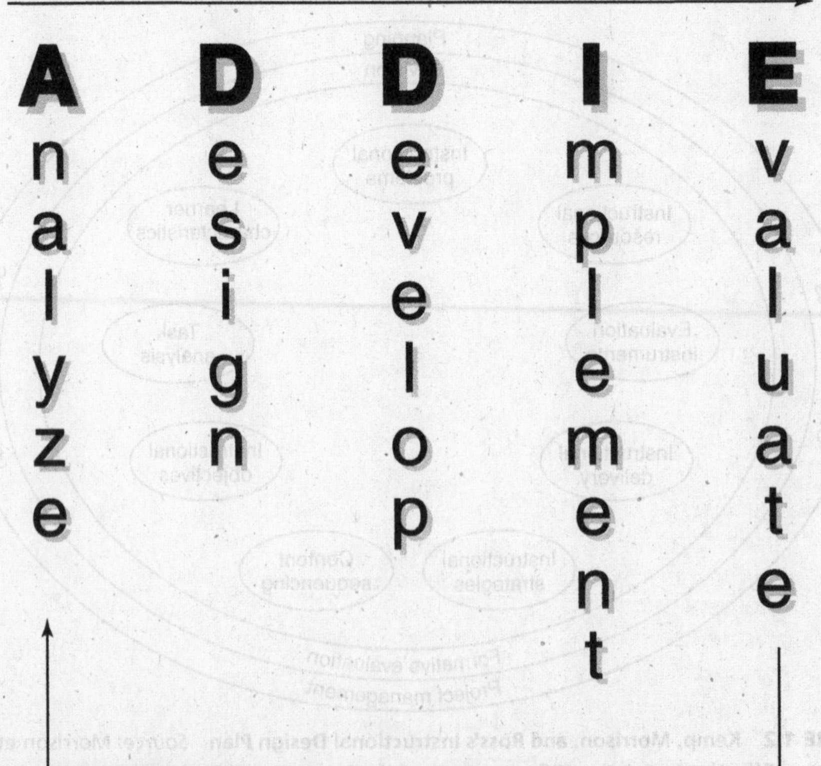

FIGURE 1.3 The ADDIE Process

instructional design models scholars have created through the years. Often, an instructional designer makes use of a particular model because it is popular within his or her professional setting. However, you should bear in mind that these are *models* of instructional design/development; no single model should be considered the only correct way to design instruction.

PROFESSIONAL INSTRUCTIONAL DESIGN PRACTICE

Deciding how to design and develop instruction often depends on the organizational setting in which the instructional design professional finds him or herself. Organizations that have established traditions of delivering instruction may demand that certain forms be followed. For example, universities in North America and Europe traditionally require that for each course offered, a syllabus be created beforehand and students receive evaluation in the form of letter grades (an evaluation strategy developed at Cambridge University in the early 1800s). University courses traditionally require weekly three-hour meetings (or semiweekly 1.5-hour meetings). These requirements necessarily affect the way college professors design their instruction.

K–12 environments are under different but similar constraints. Designers who create instruction for K–12 school settings (this would include teachers, textbook writers, educational software manufactures, etc.) must work within the constraints of a system that has a specific timeframe (in the United States, typically 182 days of school, with approximately seven hours of instruction each day beginning with the first grade), assigned curriculum (established by state and local authorities), and evaluation procedures that include the awarding of letter grades and promotion to grade levels.

Nonacademic organizations have their own traditions and requirements for instructional design. For example, the U.S. military has a tradition of using specific theories and development models to guide instructional design activity. During the twentieth century, the U.S. military offered instructional designers numerous opportunities to contribute to the knowledge base of the discipline: Military actions that required the massing of troops from a civilian population also required that those troops receive training for their new roles. In peacetime, military personnel must receive training on a variety of highly technical, demanding, and dangerous tasks for which public school and college has not prepared them. These models continue to be used as protocols, allowing designers to develop instruction efficiently and (it is hoped) effectively.

Traditional Approaches (Analyze, Develop, Evaluate)

What are generally considered traditional approaches to instructional design are in fact based on relatively recent developments in the theory of how people think about the way the world works. In the 1950s, the basic concepts and principles of a general theory of systems were established by scholars (notably Ashby, Bertalanffy, Boulding, Fagen, Gerard, Rappaport and Weinner) who were, at the time, pioneers of a new method of thinking about how people and things operate (Banathy, 1996; Banathy & Jenlink, 2004). One critical argument was Bertalanffy's observation that modern science was becoming increasingly specialized and that people therefore perceived science not as an integrated realm but rather as a series of small specializations that operated using their own premises, techniques, and structures. The goal of general systems theory (GST) is to explain the common elements of the theoretical constructions of the various scientific disciplines.

General systems theory is similar to the search for a unified field theory in physics. Currently in the scientific discipline of physics, there are theories that seem to successfully explain how the universe works at the submicroscopic level (electromagnetic forces), and there are theories that seem to successfully explain how the universe works on a larger level (gravitational forces). However, the two sets of theories cannot be put together into one logical theory that explains how the universe works on every level. The unified field theory is what physicists hope will explain the fundamental interactions of the physical universe, both electromagnetic and gravitational. Work on the general systems theory (GST) is in some ways the social scientists' version of a unified field theory; the GST is what they hope will explain—in general—how systems work, regardless of the specific setting.

The quest for a unified field theory can also be used as an example of how little is known about the world. In physics, various theories are used for practical purposes to explain and predict phenomena, but physicists are still working to discover "the truth" about how the physical world works. Like physicists, educators use a variety of theories to explain and predict how learning and instruction work. However, no educational theory is universally accepted, and no one knows "the absolute truth" about instruction and learning environments.

The academic community was deeply influenced by the ideas put forth by systems theory. That influence continues to this day; most people take for granted the concept that much of what occurs in the world is influenced by—and in turn influences—actions and events that may not seem at first related to each other. One more modern and extreme example is chaos theory, which was popularized by the idea that a butterfly's wings beating in the Amazon has an effect on the amount of rainfall Newfoundland receives in a year (Gleick, 1987):

In examining a systems approach to designing instruction, Hoban (1977) wrote:

> In any system, everything is related to everything else, sooner or later and in one way or another. This means that every essential element, factor, or component, and some seemingly inconsequential ones, can seriously affect the final product, outcome, or output of the system. What media people do or don't do not only affects other people in the system but the quality of the output of the entire system. This follows from general systems theory. (p. 71).

Systems theory caused educators to examine how the various factors that influence learning interact to create a complete instructional experience. How the learner thinks, what the learner knows prior to the instructional event, what motivates the learner, how the teacher teaches, what the consequences of evaluation are, and many other factors became objects of consideration. This once-innovative approach to instruction has become the modern standard.

Nontraditional Approaches

A systems approach to instructional design is the modern approach. The word "modern" in this case refers to the period in history called the "modern age" (the age of approaching problems logically and scientifically; solving those problems systematically using new and innovative technologies). One school of thought argues that the current era is a postmodern age (Hlynka, 1995; Hlynka, 2004). It is *post*modern because scholars can identify and describe the reasons for "modern" approaches. Whether experts agree or disagree with the approaches and the reasoning behind them, once they are identified and described, they are relegated to a specific time period; the current generation is outside of that time period—hence, the term "postmodern."

The discipline of instructional design blossomed at a time when systems thinking was a dominating force in the scientific and academic community. For this reason, it is often referred to as "instructional systems design" or "instructional systems technology." Instructional systems design is used primarily to teach adult learners and is based on a mastery approach (a student may move on to the next task only after he or she has mastered the previous one). This approach is **behavioristic** in that it works only for instruction that is immediately measurable (the ability to perform a task) and requires that the instruction follow from a specific behavioral objective (for example: "At the end of the instruction, the student will be able to take apart and put together a carburetor").

> The ISD [instructional systems design] model begins at the curriculum level with analysis of content, definition of overall objectives, delineation of sequences and subsequences of the curriculum. It proceeds with the selection of instructional methods and media, designing individual lessons to enhance learner mastery of the objectives, developing delivery systems for the individual lessons, and ends with evaluation of the lessons and the entire instructional system. Evaluation in ISD emphasizes measurement of observable target behaviors. (Alessi and Trollip, 2001, p. 18)

Instructional systems design has been criticized as generating models that are too complex to use effectively and focusing too much on strictly observable (behavioral) outcomes without addressing the more subtle aspects of learning that include reflection, retention, and motivation (Alessi & Trollip, 2001). Having shifted from placing all responsibility on the learner without regard for the design of the instruction, teaching had shifted to a point where the learner was becoming an overlooked portion of the instructional design process.

In the 1980s and 1990s, instructional design theorists began to develop models that include approaches that diverge from the strictly behavioral. Cognitive and constructive approaches became topics of discussion and research (Reigeluth, 1999; Alessi & Trollip, 2001).

Eclecticism and Postmodern Approaches

We have offered a general definition for the term "postmodern": after the historical period referred to as "modern." However, the guiding principles of postmodern thought are far more difficult to define. **Postmodernism** is concurrently an historical epoch, an intellectual movement, and a general social condition (Hylnka, 2004; Solomon, 2000).

A postmodern approach to instructional design recognizes that the instructional designer must take four societal factors into account:

1. Society is past the point where there are a limited number of authorities available to a classroom student. The modern classroom had two authoritative sources: the teacher and the textbook. This situation no longer exists because students have access to many other sources, including the Internet, television, and, in some cases, friends and family who are more educated than the teacher is (Hlynka, 1995).
2. No longer can there be an agreed-upon, single type of well-educated individual. Determining a curriculum and including all important artistic and scientific works that would be appropriate for all individuals is impossible.

3. The currently popular cognitive paradigm—constructivism—does not recognize or advocate a traditional, linear educational sequence. With information available from a variety of sources outside the classroom, learners will inevitably deviate from a linear instructional model by observing and reacting to other examples, non-examples, and divergent examples of the concepts they study in school.
4. No single, objective truth exists. Truth is a construct that is based on an individual's personal interpretation or on the consensus of a group of people for their purposes. The truth—also known as "the right answer"—may change depending on the context and the individuals involved.

Professionals in Practice

Where do the roots of my ID philosophy come? The first one comes from my undergraduate study of mathematics. I believe that many concepts of mathematics are helpful for instructional technologists. I am particularly under the influence of the concepts of chaos theory while working on any ID project. Unfortunately, I am not the inventor of this idea. This connection between chaos theory and ID was already realized by other researchers in our field (e.g., You, 1993; Jonassen, 1990). Why is chaos theory important for me, and why is it a part of my ID approach? Here is a quick summary:

Several researchers agree that the traditional systems approach to problem-solving has a reductionist nature, and it tends to solve a problem by fragmentation—one stage at a time (Finegan, 1994; You, 1993; Jonassen, 1990). This approach may work for some small-scale and well-defined situations. However, the systems associated with human activity are complex and not well-defined. According to Jonassen (1990), "simple systems behave in simple ways, and complex systems behave in complex and less predictive ways. The behavior of a system cannot be examined accurately by analyzing its components" (p. 34). As an alternative to a linear, reductionist, and deterministic approach, chaos or the dynamical systems approach is proposed. In a complex system, "the components are related and interlock with one another such that a change in one component invariably affects another part of the system, or eventually even the entire system" (Murnare, cited in Chieuw, 1991, p. 25). Gordon and Greenspan explain chaos as the study of disorder, and it appears in nonlinear systems (as cited in King, 1991). Because Chaos deals with nonlinear and disorderly systems, many disciplines—including technological, social, and economic—are appropriate for applying its principles. As stated by Highsmith (2000), "from physics to biology to chemistry to evolution, complex adaptive systems theory began to help explain occurrences in the real world that the linear approximations of the old science could not" (p. 10). According to King (1991), for many different disciplines, chaos gives new data, suggests innovative approaches to old ideas, and reaffirms certain approaches. Before proceeding further, in order not to cause a misunderstanding, it is better to state that nonlinear systems are not completely disorderly systems. As stated by Chieuw (1991), such systems have an interconnected nature, and a subtle order is always present.

Actually, instructional systems design (ISD) is inherently a complex process, which some instructional designers have already noted. For example, Appelman (2000) states that in real life, when experts implement the ISD process, they realize that the linear approach does not work. He says, "It appears to be almost a random pattern of attention being focused on different steps of the process out of order" (p. 137). So, it is not wrong to say that ISD is a chaos-based system.

— Kursat Cagiltay,
professor at Turkey's Middle East Technical University in Ankara,
Department of Computer Education and Instructional Technology

Postmodernism may also be referred to as "postpositivism" because the "modern" approach was **positivistic**. In a positivistic worldview, any problem has only one correct answer; postpositivism suggests that any one problem may have a number of different correct answers depending on the worldview of the person attempting to derive the answer.

According to Solomon (2000), a postmodern philosophy of instructional design has the following tenets at its core:

> - The philosophical core of postmodern instructional technology is a belief in pluralism, which can be described as respect for difference and resistance to single explanations.
> - Knowledge, truth and reality are constructed by people and groups of people.
> - Criticism is an appropriate method for inquiry in instructional technology.
> - Systems are interpreted as highly complex entities with adaptive qualities. (p. 423)

According to the postmodern approach, completely isolating the learner or the instructional event may not be possible. Furthermore, isolating the process of instructional development to apply a traditional instructional design/development model in the way it was originally intended may not be possible.

Postmodernism in instructional design does not necessarily reject the more traditional systems approach. To some extent, postmodern thought suggests only that the system may be far more complex than anyone had originally thought.

Postmodernism coincides with the proliferation of computing tools that allow individuals a greater degree of freedom in creating sophisticated printed work and interactive software. Before the proliferation of desktop publishing and multimedia authoring programs, creating high-quality instructional media was the province of specialists. The ubiquity and popularity of programs such as Microsoft's PowerPoint attest to the fact that everyone now considers him or herself competent to create and deliver media that is adequate for professional presentation and distribution. Prior to the mid-1980s, an individual had to rely on a trained specialist with access to esoteric tools to create materials such as handouts, brochures, slide presentations, videos, and interactive software.

Instructional designers became aware of the limitations of a systems approach around the same time they came into control of tools that would allow them to design and create instructional media without having to entirely rely on those who specialized in the development and production portion of the instructional design/development process. Access to these new computing tools meant the process of creating mockups, prototypes, and finished products became less costly and time-consuming. One concern about all this newfound flexibility in creating instructional media is that it can lead to slipshod development.

> Experienced designers and typographers were appalled that so many people (including some of their longtime clients) could be hoodwinked into thinking that the results of "dumping text" into page layout templates and "copying and pasting" clip-art were synonymous with expert design. Although professionals tacitly knew that quality design and illustration were not just a "click" away, very few of them could characterize their expertise in ways that nondesigners could appreciate. (Schriver, 1997, p. 43).

This awareness that a person might not have to follow a systems model to the letter and that an individual had the power to create the necessary media with his or her laptop computer leads instructional designers to experiment more with nontraditional approaches. It can easily lead them to take an eclectic approach, picking and choosing the better aspects of any number of design procedures and recommended practices.

An eclectic approach allows the designer to choose specific elements from a variety of sources. This approach can be viewed both as "taking the best there is to offer" and "taking things out of context." It is easy to see why this approach might make scholars of instructional design uncomfortable; if not carefully considered, articulated, and evaluated, the linking science that so many worked to create might be seen as changing to a less rigorous, less scientifically sound activity.

However, just as some well-established, dedicated educators were dismayed at the advent of a science of instructional design at the end of the nineteenth century, some well-established, dedicated instructional designers are dismayed at the advent of a change in the science of instructional design at the beginning of the twenty-first century. A heightened awareness of the greater complexity of systems and the new, increasingly ubiquitous, computer-based media production tools have created a situation in which instructional designers must adapt their views and practices.

EXAMPLE: RAPID PROTOTYPING **Rapid prototyping** is a different approach to the design and development of instruction. It represents a relatively recent paradigm shift in instructional design because it does not strictly follow the traditional systems process of design and development. Part of the conversation among instructional designers for more than a decade, rapid prototyping is a development approach used in a variety of professions and has been found particularly useful in engineering-oriented activities (e.g., automobiles are designed by creating a series of testable prototypes). The essential idea behind rapid prototyping is to arrive at a final product through the creation of a number of prototypes. Each prototype is evaluated by some combination of experts and end users; each successive prototype is more like the final product; that is, the fidelity of the prototypes increases with each new one until a working product is achieved.

For example, a typical set of prototypes developed in the process of creating a working piece of instructional software might include:

- Rough pencil sketches
- Refined pencil sketches
- Computer-generated printouts (a paper mockup)
- A computer-based prototype with little or no interactive programming
- A computer-based prototype programmed with appropriate interactions and navigation
- The final product

A rapid prototyping approach requires that the design environment allow for the relatively quick and easy creation of instructional materials (Tripp & Bichelmeyer, 1990). The current availability of computing tools that facilitate the creation of instructional media (including word-processing, image-editing, and software-authoring software) greatly increases the attractiveness of the rapid prototyping approach.

As Rathbun, Saito, and Goodrum (1997) pointed out, "the intermediate prototypes become an important means of getting feedback; the design and development process become intertwined" (p. 291). This method is different from traditional instructional design approaches in which the design process and the development process are separate.

In traditional instructional design models, once the design has been prepared, no critical feedback about the design is offered during the development process. When instructional design is accomplished by a large group of specialists, separating the design and development has a certain utility: "Make the product according to the specifications that an expert has provided; send the finished product to experts for evaluation." An underlying assumption of this approach is that an expert in a specific area oversees each stage of the instructional design process. The traditional process focuses on creating an effective end product without much regard for the efficiency of the process, which is time-consuming and costly (Nixon & Lee, 2001; Tripp & Bichelmeyer, 1990).

Traditional theatrical production may be considered a form of rapid prototyping for artistic purposes. A time-honored approach to preparing a theatrical presentation is the process of rehearsal and criticism. The play begins as an idea that a writer puts down on paper. The successive prototypes include: a *read-through*, where the actors speak their lines to each other without any staging or costumes or lighting; a *walk-through*, a performance with actors in their street clothes; a *dress rehearsal*, with sets, costumes, and lighting (but no audience); and a *preview*, with sets, costumes, lighting, and an invited audience that is aware the production is a work in progress. At each point in this process, the actors and designers receive feedback from the director as well from the other actors and designers (and, in the last stage, the preview audience). This incremental feedback is used to improve and refine each new performance until opening night, when the play is considered a completed artwork. Even after the work is considered complete, the director, cast, and crew continue to monitor performances to evaluate their success and determine what (minor) changes might be necessary.

Rapid prototyping may be seen as an example of a new way of viewing the instructional design process. The traditional approach to instructional design is based on the underlying assumption of the objectivity of science and the scientific method. With rapid prototyping, the scientific method is not rejected, but a more constructive (as opposed to objective) approach to the problem can be taken by incorporating more opportunities for everyone involved in an instructional design project (the clients, the designers, the producers, the learners) to participate in evaluation, problem-solving, and revision. Rapid prototyping is a popular way of thinking about and approaching instructional design problems, but it is not a perfect solution. We end this section with an admonition from Tripp and Bichelmeyer (1990):

> "The main disadvantage of prototyping can be summed up in one complaint that is easy to imagine: it has a tendency to encourage informal design methods which may introduce more problems than they eliminate. . . . Prototyping can lead to a design-by-repair philosophy, which is only an excuse for lack of discipline. . . . Prototyping may lead to premature commitment to a design if it is not remembered that a design is only a hypothesis." (p. 42)

This warning should serve as a reminder that a "Let's try it and see what happens" approach is no substitute for careful planning and evaluation.

Summary

Instructional design is the linking science that applies logic and scientific methods to the problems involved in designing and developing instruction. Instructional design developed from the discipline of educational psychology that came into being at the turn of the twentieth century. Instructional design became particularly popular with the articulation and acceptance of a general systems theory around the 1950s. One problem instructional design faces is its long association with strictly behavioristic approaches to teaching. Instructional design scholars have produced models of instructional design/development that describe the process of analysis, design, development, implementation, and evaluation (ADDIE).

Recent approaches to the instructional design process include breaking from the tradition of systems models in favor of more eclectic approaches that combine the five processes of instructional design instead of formally separating them. Two critical factors that foster this type of approach are a postmodern approach to solving a problem and new and relatively easy-to-use, computer-based multimedia production tools. A particularly popular postmodern approach to instructional design is rapid prototyping, which suggests that the final product should be taken through a series of mockups that can be evaluated and refined, with each new mockup getting closer to how the final product will look and operate. A potential pitfall of rapid prototyping is an informality that may produce an undisciplined approach to the instructional design problem. For any instructional design problem, careful planning and evaluation are always recommended.

Connecting Process to Practice

1. After reading the chapter, how has your thinking about education and designing instruction changed?
2. How would you describe the field of instructional design to a friend who is not an instructional designer?
3. As a novice instructional designer, which aspects of developing instruction do you consider to be inherently artistic? Which aspects of developing instruction do you consider inherently scientific?
4. Which model of instructional design/development would you most likely follow? Why do you suppose that model is particularly appealing to you?
5. Do you consider your view of the world to be positivistic or postpositivistic? How might your feelings about positivism affect your approach to instructional design?
6. Would you consider rapid prototyping to be an eclectic approach to instructional design? Why or why not?

Recommended Reading

Gagne, R. M. (1985). *The conditions of learning and theory of instruction.* Holt, Rinehart and Winston.

Kearsley, G. (2009). *Theory into practice (TIP).* Accessed on January 7, 2010, from http://tip.psychology.org.

Reigeluth, C. M. (1983) *Instructional design theories and models: An overview of their current status.* Hillsdale, NJ: Lawrence Earlbaum Associates.

Reigeluth, C. M. (1999). *Instructional-design theories and models: A new paradigm of instructional theory, volume II.* Mahwah, NJ: Lawrence Earlbaum Associates.

References

Alessi, S. M. & Trollip, S. R. (2001). *Multimedia for learning: Methods and development, 3rd edition.* Boston: Allyn & Bacon.

Appelman, R. (2000). An iterative development model: A genesis from pedagogical needs. *International Journal of Engineering Education and Lifelong Learning, 10*(1-4), 136–141.

Banathy, B. (1996). 3. Systems inquiry and its application in education. In D. Jonassen (Ed.), *Handbook of research for educational communications and technology* (pp. 74–92). New York: Macmillan.

Banathy, B. H. & Jenlink, P. M. (2004). Systems inquiry and its application in education. In D. Jonassen (Ed.), *Handbook of research for educational communications and technology, 2nd edition*, (pp. 37–57). Mahwah, NJ: Lawrence Earlbaum Associates.

Berliner, D. (1993). The 100-year journey of educational psychology, from interest, to disdain, to respect for practice. In T. K. Fagen & G. R. VandenBos (Eds.), *Exploring applied psychology origins and critical analysis: Master lectures in psychology*. Washington, DC: American Psychological Association.

Bichelmeyer, B. A. (2003). Instructional theory and instructional design theory: What's the difference and why should we care? *IDT Record.* Retrieved from http://www.indiana.edu/~idt/articles/documents/ID_theory.Bichelmeyer.html.

Bloom, B. S. (Ed.) (1956). *Taxonomy of educational objectives: Cognitive domain.* New York: David McKay.

Chieuw, J. (1991). *An alternative approach to educational planning based on a conceptual framework of the educational system as dynamic: A theoretical study.* Unpublished Doctoral Dissertation. Florida State University, Tallahassee.

Dewey, J. (1900). Psychology and social practice. *The Psychological Review, 7*, (pp. 105–124).

Dick, W. & Carey, L. (1996) The systematic design of instruction. In D. P. Ely & T. Plomp (Eds.), *Classic writings on instructional technology, volume II.* Englewood, CO: Libraries Unlimited.

Dick, W., Carey, L. & Carey, J. O. (2009). *The systematic design of instruction, 7th edition.* Columbus, OH: Allyn & Bacon.

Finegan, A. (1994). Soft systems methodology: An alternative approach to knowledge elicitation in complex and poorly defined systems. *Complexity International, volume 1.* (pp. 232–241).

Gleick, J. (1987). *Chaos: Making a new science.* New York: Viking.

Heinich, R., Molenda, M., Russell, J. D. & Smaldino, S. E. (1996). *Instructional media and technologies for learning.* Englewood Cliffs, NJ: Merrill Prentice Hall.

Highsmith, J. A. (2000). *Adaptive software development: A collaborative approach to managing complex systems.* Dorset House Publishing: New York.

Hoban Jr., C. F. (1977). A systems approach to audiovisual communications. In L. W. Cochran (Ed.), *Okoboji: A 20 year review of leadership 1955–1974* (pp. 67–72). Dubuque, Iowa: Kendal/Hunt. Reprinted in D. P. Ely & T. Plomp (Eds.), *Classic writings on instructional technology, volume I.* Englewood, CO: Libraries Unlimited.

Hlynka, D. (1995). Six postmodernisms in search of an author. In G. J. Anglin (Ed), *Instructional technology: Past, present, and future* (pp. 113–118). Englewood, CO: Libraries Unlimited.

Hlynka, D. (2004). Postmodernism in educational technology: Update 1996–present. In D. Jonassen (Ed), *Handbook of research for educational communications and technology, 2nd edition* (pp. 243–246). Mahwah, NJ: Lawrence Earlbaum Associates.

Jonassen, D. H. (1990). Thinking technology: Chaos in instructional design. *Educational Technology, 30*(2), 32–34.

King, J. W. (1991). *Chaos, communication and educational technology.* Paper presented at the annual meeting of AECT, Orlando, Florida.

Merrill, M. D. (2002). First principles of instruction. *Educational Technology Research and Development, 50*(3), 43–59.

Molenda, M. (2003). In search of the elusive ADDIE model. *Performance Improvement, 42*(5), 34–35.

Morrison, G. R., Ross, S. M. & Kemp, J. E. (2004). *Designing Effective Instruction, 4th edition.* John Wiley & Sons.

Nixon, E. K. & Lee, D. (2001). Rapid prototyping in the instructional design process. *Performance Improvement Quarterly, 14*(3), 95–116.

Rathbun, G. A., Saito, R. S. & Goodrum, D. A. (1997). Reconceiving ISD: Three perspectives on rapid prototyping as a paradigm shift. *Proceedings of selected research and development presentations at the 1997 national convention of the association for educational communications and technology.* Washington, DC: AECT. 291–296.

Reigeluth, C. M. (Ed). (1983). *Instructional design theories and models: An overview of their current status.* Hillsdale, NJ: Lawrence Earlbaum Associates.

Reigeluth, C. M. (ed). (1999). *Instructional-design theories and models: A new paradigm of instructional theory, volume II.* Mahwah, NJ: Lawrence Earlbaum Associates.

Reiser, R. & Dempsey, J. (2002) *Trends and issues in instructional design and technology*. Upper Saddle River, NJ: Merrill Prentice Hall.

Saettler, P. (1990). *The evolution of American educational technology.* Englewood, CO: Libraries Unlimited.

Schriver, K. A. (1997). *Dynamics in document design.* New York: John Wiley & Sons.

Smith, P. L. & Ragan, T. J. (2005). *Instructional design, 3rd edition.* New York: John Wiley & Sons.

Snellbecker, G. (1974). *Learning theory, instructional theory, and psychoeducational design.* New York: McGraw-Hill.

Solomon, D. L. (2000). Toward a post-modern agenda in instructional technology. *Annual proceedings of selected research and development papers presented at the National Convention of the Association for Educational Communications and Technology.* Bloomington, IN: AECT. 415–428.

Tripp, S. D. & Bichelmeyer, B. (1990). Rapid prototyping: An alternative instructional design strategy. *Educational Technology Research and Development, 38*(1), 31–44.

University of Michigan (2003). Adapted from "Training and Instructional Design," Applied Research Laboratory, Penn State University. (1996). The University of Michigan. Retrieved from http://www.umich.edu/~ed626/define.html.

You, Y. (1993). What can we learn from chaos theory? An alternative approach to instructional systems design. *Educational Technology Research and Development, 41*(3), 17–32.

Chapter 2

Understanding How People Think and Learn

Discussions on how individuals think and learn have taken place throughout history. As a result, various perspectives—influenced by philosophy and psychology—have developed and continue to be developed. Successful instructional designers have a clear understanding of the major perspectives and how they influence the design and implementation of instruction. This chapter provides an overview of the most common perspectives on thinking and learning that influence instructional design.

GUIDING QUESTIONS

- Why is it important for instructional designers to understand how people think?
- How have historical and current perspectives on thinking and the thinking process in instructional design been influenced by philosophy and educational psychology?
- What point of view do instructional designers typically have with regard to thinking and the thinking process?
- What is learning?
- Why is it important for instructional designers to understand how people learn?
- What are two of the most common theories on how people learn that instructional designers make use of in their work?
- What different types of learning are there?

KEY TERMS

behaviorism *26*
classical conditioning Model *29*
cognition *23*
cognitive abilities *24*
cognitivism *27*
constructivism *27*
eclecticism *28*
executive abilities *24*
memory *23*
mental power *24*
metacognition *24*
operant conditioning model *30*
scholasticism *25*

CHAPTER OVERVIEW

Take a moment to reflect on what your definition is for "thinking." If you struggled to come up with what you believe is a clear definition, do not anguish over it because you are not alone. In *How We Think*, John Dewey wrote: "No words are oftener on our lips than *thinking* and *thought*. So profuse and varied, indeed, is our use of these words that it is not easy to define just what we mean by them" (1910). The words that Dewey wrote a century ago still ring true. Thinking remains a complex concept that is often used in a variety of contexts to indicate very different things; therefore, understanding what is meant by thinking at any given time can be quite a challenge.

Despite the challenges inherent in understanding thinking and the thinking process, having knowledge about how people process, store, and retrieve information—in other words, *think*—is crucial for an instructional designer. This understanding can help him or her better comprehend how people learn because thinking and learning are very much interconnected. An instructional designer who has a solid grasp on thinking and learning is able to design and develop efficient, effective, and meaningful instructional interventions.

The goal of this chapter is to provide you with a framework for understanding how people think and learn. Our intention is to simplify—if possible—how thinking and learning have been conceptualized historically and in more modern times. The opening section of the chapter is organized around two major topics. The first is how instructional designers typically view thinking and the thinking process. The second is a discussion on thinking from various historical and contemporary perspectives. The second half of the chapter takes a look at two major psychological perspectives of learning—behaviorism and cognitivism—and describes how each conceptualizes the learning process.

COGNITION AND BASIC COGNITIVE FUNCTIONS

Before beginning a discussion on how instructional designers typically view thinking and the thinking process, an important concept to understand is **cognition**. How people go about the process of thinking is often referred to as cognition. Cognition is the mental process of knowing, including aspects such as awareness, perception, reasoning, and judgment. In essence, cognition includes all the brain's mental input and output. Cognition encompasses basic activities—such as using language and math functions during a trip to the hardware store—to making complex decisions—such as selecting between two job offers—to writing a creative story and being able to understand another person's perspective.

"Cognition" and "thinking" are terms that can be used interchangeably. This may not resonate well with some; however, this book is not the place for a debate over the intricacies of cognition and how thinking may or may not be synonymous. It is important to realize as an instructional designer that cognition and thinking can and are used, in essence, to refer to the same thing.

Basic Cognitive Functions

There exists numerous technical terms related to cognition. Making sense of these is not an easy task. There are hundreds of terms for specific components of cognition, with many having the same or very similar meanings. What makes it difficult in dealing with these components of cognition is that they can mean different things in different settings. Some of the differences may reflect important scientific or theoretical nuances, but many are simply jargon-specific to a particular discipline or profession.

The important thing to remember is that cognition and the components of cognition are important to understand because, as mentioned earlier, understanding how people think helps to understand how they learn. Understanding how people learn will help you as an instructional designer assist your clients in developing effective and efficient instructional interventions. However, you do not have to be a cognitive scientist to have an adequate understanding of how people think.

Let's review some important concepts related to cognition.

MEMORY **Memory** is much more than just a passive storage system of knowledge. Memory is a set of active processes that encode information. Memory places information into "packages" or "packets," making information easier to recall and allowing it to be associated with related items already in memory. Memory also involves storing information.

Part of this process is the constant rearranging of what has been stored in order for that new knowledge to be integrated with what has already been stored. Additionally, it provides for the locating and retrieving of information as it is needed.

MENTAL POWER **Mental power** is the basic energy that supports mental activity. It refers to how much mental work can be performed during a specific period of time. Power can be used to sustain something simple like using a television remote control or something more complex like operating a computer. With either case, the central issue focuses on having enough power on hand to complete the task. In the cognitive domain, power refers to arousal level, concentration span, channel capacity, and mental stamina.

SPECIFIC COGNITIVE ABILITIES These functions refer to an individual's stored supply of knowledge and skills. This includes items such as reading, writing, comprehension, motor skills, and visual-spatial skills.

EXECUTIVE ABILITIES **Executive abilities** encompass a very large category of cognitive functions. Executive abilities include such higher-order thinking skills as being able to anticipate future needs and planning accordingly, the ability to set priorities, and being able to self-correct and regulate actions. In essence, these are the capacities that allow an individual to use his or her mental power and specific **cognitive abilities** to meet social, professional, and psychological needs.

METACOGNITION **Metacognition** is the ability to control one's own cognitive processes. It is often referred to as the practice of "thinking about thinking." In using metacognition, an individual takes an introspective look at the thought process that he or she has gone through. It allows him or her to critically consider how he or she arrived at certain ideas, concepts, and thoughts. Metacognition is a reflective process that helps improve an individual's control over his or her own thinking process and learning (Bleiberg, 2001; Flavell, 1979; Ormond, 2009; Sternberg, 1986; Woolfolk, 2004).

A HISTORICAL PERSPECTIVE ON THINKING: A BRIEF HISTORY

Historically, thinking was consigned to the realm of philosophy. Possibly the earliest theory about how the mind works was offered in the 4th and 5th centuries B.C. by Greek philosophers, such as Empedocles, Democritus, and Epicurus. These philosophers believed that the mind perceived images given off by objects. These perceived images were then copied as sense impressions and stored into memory. "Knowledge then becomes a matter of knowing these mental copies, and the earliest copy theories suggested that the mind knew directly what the sensory nerves brought to it" (Herrnstein & Boring, 1965, as cited in Driscoll, 2004).

A very different perspective—suggested by Plato (and much later by Kant) and generally known as "idealism"—states that the mind does not directly comprehend reality or copy it. With this perspective, reason is considered to be the primary source for understanding and knowledge. The major proposition behind this perspective is that all data coming from the senses is interpreted by the mind according to the mind's innate tendencies (Collinson, 1978; Driscoll, 2004).

Philosophy followed this theme (with numerous slight variations) up until the influence of the Catholic Church shifted philosophical thought around the 9th century. This influence lead to what was called **scholasticism**, a philosophical perspective based on a mixture of Aristotelian and Church writings and thought. Scholastic philosophy was built around a highly organized system of truths, which were distinct from Church doctrines but were not in opposition to them. Scholastic philosophers, such as Thomas Aquinas, believed that human intellect was incapable of acquiring knowledge of intelligible things without illumination from God. Individual interaction and participation with the Word of God was necessary if knowledge was to be gained. Thinking was directly related to what God provided to individuals through his inspiration (or "illumination") (Nichols, 2003).

Another shift in the view on thinking began with the dawn of the Renaissance and continued into the seventeenth and eighteenth centuries. A movement began that shifted attention away from the belief that truth was divinely inspired by God and that the individual was incapable of discerning what is real or what is truth. Philosophers, such as Descartes and Locke, believed to be true what they saw with their own eyes and experienced with their senses. Rather than assuming God played the key role in the universe, humans began to be the standard for judging what was real and what truth was. Human intellect was deemed capable of discriminating between truth and error. Certain defined methods for discovering truth and evaluating evidence came to be considered reliable and sufficient for discovering truth. Thinking focused more on observation, experience, rational thought, and the scientific-method rather than solely on God and tradition (Almog, 2002; Sorell, 2001; Locke, 1996).

A MODERN VIEW ON THINKING: THE SHIFT FROM PHILOSOPHY TO PSYCHOLOGY

While philosophy continues to play a role in how thinking and the thinking process is conceptualized, the emergence of psychology (especially educational psychology) in the mid- to late nineteenth century has had and continues to have the most significant influence on how instructional designers view thinking. Educational psychology, which originated as a separate branch of psychology in 1892 (Berliner, 1993), has provided a concentrated look at thinking and learning through a more scientific perspective—one based on research and which includes a focus specifically on how thinking and learning are interconnected.

Two Major Perspectives

Two major perspectives, with several variations, emerged from psychology and have dominated the way instructional designers view how people think—and, in turn, how people learn. Provided in this section are brief explanations of these two distinctly different perspectives—behaviorist and cognitivist—with mentions of key individuals who have had an influence on how these perspectives have developed.

As an instructional designer, it is important to keep in mind that neither perspective is inherently better than the other. Each perspective offers important contributions that help us understand how individuals think and how people learn. Although most instructional designers tend to feel more comfortable with one perspective over the other, instructional designers will use principles and practices from both as they design and develop instructional interventions. It is also important to remember that these two perspectives are two of out of many that exist. They are described here because they are two of the most influential perspectives.

POSITIVISM AND INTERPRETIVISM Before we begin the discussion of behaviorist and cognitivist perspectives, it is important to provide a brief description of two contrasting philosophical perspectives. We include this information because it helps explain how many people come to understand how people think and learn.

Positivism and interpretivism are often seen as a dichotomy for describing individual approaches to how knowledge is generated and verified. Positivism presumes that there are only two sources of knowledge: logical reasoning and empirical experience. Logical knowledge includes mathematics, which is reducible to formal logic. Empirical knowledge includes such areas as physics, biology, and psychology. Experience is the only judge of scientific theories—and, therefore, knowledge. Interpretivism is based on the view that knowledge is a matter of perspective. In order to understand the world, an individual must interpret it. Schwandt (1998) wrote: "What we take to be objective knowledge and the truth is the result of perspective. Knowledge and truth are created, not discovered by the mind" (p. 167).

As you will read shortly, behaviorist and cognitivist perspectives draw from positivist and interpretist philosophies.

THE BEHAVIORIST PERSPECTIVE The behaviorist perspective, known as behaviorism, dominated psychology for the first half of the twentieth century (Brandt & Perkins, 2000). **Behaviorism** includes a group of theories that share several common beliefs—"the generalizability of learning principles across species, the importance of focusing on observable events, and the 'blank slate' nature of organisms" (Ormond, 2004, p. 48). According to behaviorists, mental processes are invisible and therefore cannot be studied scientifically. What can be observed is outward behavior; therefore, rather than speculating on internal causes for why things take place, focus should be placed on how organisms respond to different stimuli (Brandt & Perkins, 2000; Ormond, 2004; Woolfolk, 2004). From a behaviorist perspective, the human mind is malleable, capable of being shaped and formed into producing desired responses and behaviors if specific conditions and circumstances are accounted for and controlled.

The early foundational work of behaviorism was carried out by individuals such as Pavlov (1800–1950), Thorndike (1874–1949), Watson (1878–1958), and Guthrie (1886–1959). Their research was most notably conducted using animals—typically, rats, pigeons, cats, and, in the case of Pavlov, dogs. Examples include the experiments conducted by Pavlov related to salivation in dogs. He observed that a dog's behavior could be conditioned in such a manner that if provided with a specific stimulus (e.g., the ringing of a bell), a particular behavior (e.g., salivation) would take place. Pavlov conditioned a dog to associate the ringing of a bell with eating, which was done by the repeated ringing of a bell and then immediately feeding some meat to the dog. After following this process, Pavlov eventually rang the bell but did not provide meat to the dog; despite this, the dog still salivated in response to hearing the bell. The dog was conditioned to associate the bell with food (Pavlov, 1927). This became known as the classical conditioning model. Skinner—unquestionably the best known behaviorist—built on this early body of research by developing what is known as operant conditioning. By watching pigeons and rats, Skinner observed that the increase in the frequency of a behavior was more likely to occur if followed immediately by a reinforcer (i.e., a reward) (Skinner, 1978). These concepts provided important insights that have helped provide understanding of the mind and how people think.

THE COGNITIVIST PERSPECTIVE Psychologists in the years following World War II began to move away from behaviorism toward a different perspective of the mind and how people think. This perspective was distinguished as cognitivism. With this perspective, internal mental processes were considered important and capable of being identified and studied (Brandt & Perkins, 2000; Ormond, 2009). From a cognitivist perspective, the human mind is considered to be highly complex. A metaphor typically used by cognitivists to describe the mind is a computer. Like a computer, the mind processes information through a series of different processes that work together as a complete system.

Several individuals have had tremendous influence on the cognitive perspective. The foundations of **cognitivism** were built on the work of Vygotsky (1896–1934), Dewey, Piaget (1896–1990), and Bruner (1915–).

Two More Recent Perspectives

Although behaviorist and cognitivist perspectives have dominated the way in which thinking has been perceived, two more recent perspectives have influenced instructional designers' views on how people think. These perspectives are **constructivism** and postmodernism.

CONSTRUCTIVISM Constructivism—a variant of cognitivism—is centered around the principle that an individual constructs his own understanding of the world he lives in by reflecting on his experiences. An individual generates his own mental models, which he uses to make sense of his experiences. Brandt and Perkins (2000) write: "Both a philosophical and psychological stance, constructivism argues that the human mind does not simply take in the world but makes it up in an active way. Brooks (1993) describes the underlying principle of constructivism in more detail:

> Each of us makes sense of our world by synthesizing new experiences into what we have previously come to understand. Often, we encounter an object, an idea, a relationship, or a phenomenon that doesn't quite make sense to us. When confronted with such initially discrepant data or perceptions, we either interpret what we see to conform to our present set of rules for explaining and ordering our work, or we generate a new set of rules that better accounts for what we perceive to be occurring. Either way, our perceptions and rules are constantly engaged in a grand dance that shapes our understandings. (p. 4)

The creative role of the mind is obvious in contexts such as scientific inquiry and artistic endeavor, but constructivists believe that the constructive process also figures prominently even in such seemingly routine mental operations as perception and memory" (p. 167). The work of Gardner (1943–), Sternberg (1949–), and Jonassen (1947–) have had tremendous influence on the development of constructivism.

POSTMODERNISM In the late twentieth century and into the early twenty-first century, an approach called "postmodernism" has provided a different perspective on how humans think. "Postmodernism is largely a reaction to the assumed certainty of scientific, or objective, efforts to explain reality. In essence, it stems from a recognition that reality is not simply mirrored in human understanding of it, but rather, is constructed as the mind tries to understand its own particular and personal reality." In addition, "in the postmodern understanding, interpretation is everything; reality only comes into being through our interpretations of what the world means to us individually. Postmodernism relies on concrete experience over abstract principles, knowing always that the outcome of one's own experience will necessarily be fallible and relative, rather than certain and universal" (PBS, 2003). As mentioned previously, postmodern philosophy questions (and often rejects) the idealized view of truth and of knowing inherited from past philosophical traditions. To the postmodernist, thinking is a dynamic, ever-changing function that depends on an individual's interpretation of the world the individual lives in (Butler, 2003; Goodman, 2009).

AN INSTRUCTIONAL DESIGNER'S VIEW ON THINKING

It is important to recognize that a person's perspective on thinking largely depends on a combination of that person's education, training, philosophical beliefs, and profession. The perspective of instructional designers is no different. An instructional designer's perspective on thinking—and, in turn, learning—is highly influenced by training and by the nature of the profession.

Instructional designers tend to look at thinking from a pragmatic point of view, asking themselves, "What do we need to know about thinking and the studies done on thinking that will help develop efficient and effective instructional interventions?" It is no surprise that the majority of instructional designers are considered to be **eclectic**—borrowing from different perspectives and using what works for a given situation to produce desired results. Instructional designers tend to take a systems theory approach when it comes to looking at thinking (and learning) by exploring it from several different perspectives rather than focusing narrowly on one aspect of what thinking is or is not. Instructional designers perceive thinking as a complex process that includes various interconnected elements and therefore cannot be encapsulated in one neat and tidy description or theory. This view has been shaped by centuries of thought and study conducted by philosophers and psychologists on thinking and how the mind works.

WHAT IS LEARNING?

As is the case with thinking, learning can be conceptualized in a variety of ways. Most often, learning is defined as being a relatively permanent change in either behavior or in mental representations or associations brought about by experience (Ormrod, 2009). The change that takes place will last for some time, but it may or may not last forever. These changes may be readily observable—such as when a child learns to tie his or her shoes—while other changes may be more subtle—such as when an individual gains a better appreciation for classical music (Ormrod, 2009). Additionally, these changes that occur may be deliberate or unintentional, correct or incorrect, and conscious or unconscious (Hill, 2002).

It is important to understand that change occurs as a result of experience. These experiences are events—planned or not—that occur in a learner's life. Thus, change occurs as an individual interacts with his or her environment. It is important to note, however, that not all changes that take place are learned and therefore cannot be attributed to learning. These types of change are based on maturation or on temporary body states (e.g., fatigue, hunger, intoxication); they are not based on experiences (thus, they are not considered learned).

In examining the definition of learning, we propose two very different types of changes can take place when learning occurs. The first is a change in behavior; the other is a change in mental representations or associations. It is important to note this difference because it reflects the divergent viewpoints of two psychological perspectives: behaviorism and cognitivism.

TWO MAJOR (AND VERY DIFFERENT) APPROACHES TO HOW PEOPLE LEARN

There unquestionably exist more than two perspectives that describe how humans learn. Arguably, however, two of the most influential and popular perspectives that have had the greatest impact on instructional design are behaviorism and cognitivism. Throughout much of the first half of the twentieth century, behaviorism dominated how instructional designers approached their work; it wasn't until after World War II that cognitivism began to supplant behaviorism by providing an alternative viewpoint. Both perspectives—along with their various branches—continue to have great influence on instructional design activities in the twenty-first century. The purpose of this section is to provide a brief overview on how each perspective approaches how people learn.

A Behavioral Approach to Learning

From a behaviorist perspective, learning is defined as a change in behavior due to experience that can be measured (Ormrod, 2009; Driscoll, 2004; Burton, Moore & Magliaro, 2004). Woolfolk (2004) writes, "Behaviorism attempts to explain learning by focusing on external events as the cause of changes in observable behaviors" (p. 198). Brandt and Jenkins (2000) add that behaviorists believe "organisms learn through classical and operant conditioning. Complex behaviors are built up through 'shaping,' starting with parts of or rough approximations of the target behavior and providing reinforcement in ways that gradually shape the pattern of behavior in the intended direction. Much learning in natural circumstances occurs because the environment shapes behavior in this way. Not only direct rewards like food but also indirect 'tokens' of reward shape behavior through learned associations" (pp. 161–162).

Classical and operant conditioning models provide explanations for how learning specifically takes place within the behaviorist perspective. The **classical conditioning model** (developed by Pavlov) describes a type of associative learning. Classical conditioning occurs when two stimuli are presented at approximately the same time. One of the

Step	Stimulus	Response
1	Neutral (bell)	None
2	Neutral (bell) plus Unconditioned (meat)	Unconditioned (dog salivates)
3	Conditioned (bell)	Conditioned (dog salivates)

FIGURE 2.1 Classical Conditioning Analysis—Pavlov's Experiment on Dogs

stimuli is an unconditioned stimulus (i.e., it has been shown to elicit an unconditioned response). The other stimulus (neutral stimulus)—through its association with the unconditioned stimulus—also begins to bring on a response; it becomes a conditioned stimulus that brings about a conditioned response. Figure 2.1 depicts an example of classical conditioning based on Pavlov's experiment with dogs.

The **operant conditioning model** was developed by Skinner. Skinner believed there were two types of learning: classical conditioning and operant conditioning. Operant conditioning results when a response is followed by a reinforcing stimulus. The response produced is a voluntary one. The individual (or other organism) producing the response has complete control over whether the response occurs. "Skinner's term operant reflects the fact that the organism voluntarily *operates* on, and thereby has some effect on, the environment" (Ormrod, 2004, p. 54). Figure 2.2 is a comparison of operant and classical conditioning.

Despite the variants of behaviorists, Ormrod (2004) writes that historically, behaviorists have shared certain basic assumptions:

- Principles of learning should apply equally to different behaviors and to different species of animals.
- Learning processes can be studied most objectively when the focus of study is on stimuli and responses.
- Internal processes are largely excluded from scientific study.
- Learning involves a behavior change.

	Classical Conditioning	Operant Conditioning
Occurs when	Two stimuli (UCS and CS) are paired	A response (R) is followed by a reinforcing stimulus (S_{Rf})
Nature of response	Involuntary: elicited by a stimulus	Voluntary: emitted by the organism
Association required	CS → CR	R → S_{Rf}

FIGURE 2.2 Differences between classical and operant conditioning (Ormrod, 2004, p. 55)

UCS = unconditioned stimulus; CS = conditioned stimulus; CR = conditioned response.

Source: From *Human Learning* (p. 55), by J. E. Ormrod, 2004, Upper Saddle River, NJ: Merrill/Prentice Hall.

- Organisms are born was blank slates.
- Learning is largely the result of environmental events.
- The most useful theories tend to be parsimonious ones. (pp. 30–31)

THE ROLE OF THE LEARNER Skinner (1968) stated that a learner "does not passively absorb knowledge from the world around him but must play an active role" (p. 5). Therefore, learners learn by doing, experiencing, and engaging in repeated trial and error. Burton, Moore, and Magliaro (2004) write that "The emphasis is on the active responding of the learner—the learner must be engaged in the behavior in order to learn and to validate that learning has occurred" (p. 9).

A Cognitivist Approach to Learning

From a cognitivist perspective, learning is a change in mental representations and associations brought about by experiences. Greeno, Collins, and Resnick (1996) write that cognitivists view learning as "transforming significant understanding we already have, rather than simple acquisitions written on blank states" (p. 18). This follows the standard cognitivist view of learning that assumes that mental processes exist and can be studied scientifically. Brandt and Perkins (2000) noted that early research in cognitivism "focused primarily on information processing, especially pattern recognition, memory, and problem solving. The mind was considered a rule-governed computational device. A scientist's task was to identify the specific rules by which the mind manipulates symbols to arrive at results" (p. 165). This view reflects a common metaphor used by many cognitivists that the mind works in the same way as a computer; therefore, learning takes place by applying set-in-place algorithms. Brandt and Perkins go on to write that, "over time, cognitive scientists gradually expanded their attention to include a remarkable array of human activities: the formation of judgments, decision making, creativity, critical thinking, and even the emotions" (p. 165).

THE ROLE OF THE LEARNER Cognitivists believe that learners are not passively influenced by environmental events; rather, they are active participants in their own cognition (Ashcraft, 2002). As individuals engage in the learning process, they "actively choose, practice, pay attention, ignore, reflect, and make many other decisions as they pursue goals" (Woolfolk, 2004, p. 236).

WHAT IS LEARNED? The behavioral and cognitive perspectives differ in their assumptions regarding what is learned. From the cognitive perspective, knowledge is learned. It is the increase of knowledge that makes it possible for changes in behavior to occur. According to the behavioral perspective, the new behaviors themselves are learned (Shuell, 1986).

A Constructivist Approach to Learning

In addition to the two major approaches to how people learn that we discussed previously, the **constructivist** approach has emerged over the past three decades and has had tremendous impact on learning. Constructivism has its roots in both psychology and philosophy. Constructivism goes beyond the traditional view of cognitivism that "people represent information in their minds as single or aggregated sets of symbols, and that cognitive activity consists of operating on these symbols by applying to them learn plans, or algorithms" (Winn, 2004, p. 79).

Marzano (2000) writes, "Constructivism refers to the general principle that learners use their prior knowledge to construct a personally meaningful understanding of new content that is the focus of learning" (p. 81). Driscoll (2004) adds that constructivism "rests on the assumption that knowledge is constructed by learners as they attempt to make sense of their experiences. Learners, therefore, are not empty vessels waiting to be filled, but rather active organisms seeking meaning" (p. 376).

Driscoll summarizes the conditions necessary for learning in a constructivist environment:

- Embed learning in complex, realistic, and relevant environments.
- Provide for social negotiation as an integral part of learning.
- Support multiple perspectives and the use of multiple modes of representation.
- Encourage ownership in learning.
- Nurture self-awareness of the knowledge construction process. (pp. 382–383)

Using Various Approaches to Learning

The different approaches to learning can provide very useful perspectives on how people learn. It is generally not advisable to strictly follow one approach when carrying out instructional design activities because every instructional context is different and brings with it different variables that need to be accounted for, such as the context, the learners, and the type of learning that needs to occur. No single approach is able to completely account for all these variables. For successful instructional design to occur, it is critical that instructional designers are able to borrow from the different approaches to develop instructional interventions that take into consideration all these variables.

TYPES OF LEARNING

As mentioned, one variable that is part of every instructional context is the type of learning that needs to take place. Instructional designers must have the ability to identify different types of learning in order to design efficient and effective instructional interventions. Probably the most well-known and used distinctions made regarding types of learning are that of learning domains. There are three commonly used learning domains that refer to specific types of learning: cognitive, affective, and psychomotor. The major idea behind the learning domains is that learning can be organized and measured along a continuum from low level to higher level knowledge, attitudes, or skills.

Benjamin Bloom (1913–1999) and colleagues are typically credited with developing the original idea and work behind the three learning domains in the mid-twentieth century (Eisner, 2000). The result of Bloom's work originated out of his efforts to improve university examinations (Ormrod, 2004; Eisner 2000). The result of this work was three taxonomies of educational objectives corresponding to three learning domains. In recent years, other researchers (e.g., Anderson & Krathwohl, 2001; Marzano, 2000; Cangelosi, 1990;) have published revisions to Bloom's original work. Despite this, the major premise behind Bloom's original work still remains intact.

One of the most useful ways that the learning domains can be used is to consider them when learning objectives are being developed for instruction. Learning objectives are descriptions of what an individual should know or be able to do once he or she has completed an instructional intervention. In addition to the development of learning objectives, the domains can be useful in planning assessments.

Cognitive Domain

The cognitive domain is formally referred to as Bloom's Taxonomy of the Cognitive Domain. This taxonomy describes six levels: knowledge, comprehension, application, analysis, synthesis, and evaluation (Bloom, Englehart, Frost, Hill & Krathwohl, 1956). It is common to consider these levels as a hierarchy—each level building on the ones below. This is not entirely accurate for every subject or discipline (Seddon, 1978); some subjects or disciplines—such as mathematics—do not fit this structure extremely well (Gronlund, 2000). At the bottom level of the domain (knowledge), individuals are able to remember basic information without necessarily understanding, using, or manipulating it. With evaluation—the highest level—individuals are capable of making judgments about complex ideas, materials, and processes as they are applied in various contexts.

Bloom, Engelhart, Frost, Hill, and Krathwohl's (1956) Cognitive Domain

Term	Definition
Evaluation	Ability to judge the value or worth of material for a given purpose
Synthesis	Ability to create something new from various parts
Analysis	Ability to break down material into its various components in order to understand the organizational structure of the material
Application	Ability to apply learned material in new and concrete contexts
Comprehension	Understanding of new material
Knowledge	Remembering previously learned material

Affective Domain

The affective domain deals with emotional responses. The levels range from least committed to most committed (Krathwohl, Bloom & Masia, 1964). The levels are: receiving, responding, valuing, organizing, and valuing. At the basic level of this domain (receiving), an individual is able to pay attention to a certain idea (e.g., listening to music at a concert) but does not show any concerted interest. With valuing—the highest level—an individual is capable of adopting a new idea or value and acting consistently with it (e.g., openly demonstrating an appreciation for classical music).

Krathwohl, Bloom, and Masia's (1964) Affective Domain

Term	Definition
Characterizing value	Acting openly and consistently with a new value; internalizing a new value
Organizing	Integrating a new value into a general set of values; giving the value some ranking among an individual's general priorities
Valuing	Exhibiting some explicit involvement or commitment; showing interest or motivation
Responding	Actively participating; exhibiting a new behavior as a result of experience
Receiving	Paying attention to something in the environment

Psychomotor Domain

The psychomotor domain deals with physical abilities and skills. There are several taxonomies (Harrow, 1972; Simpson, 1972; Cangelosi, 1990) that depict this domain that typically describe levels that move from basic physical actions to more skilled and creative movements. Simpson (1972) outlines a domain with seven levels: perception, set, guided response, mechanism, complex overt response, adaptation, and origination. Cangelosi (1990) looks at the psychomotor domain by stating that it is useful to look at it as either voluntary muscle capabilities (e.g., flexibility, agility, or speed) or the ability to perform a specific skill (e.g., tying shoes).

Simpson's (1972) Psychomotor Domain

Term	Definition
Perception	Ability to recognize sensory cues to guide physical activity
Set	Willingness to act; ability to show knowledge and awareness of the behaviors needed to perform a skill
Guided response	Ability to perform a complex skill: beginning stage
Mechanism	Ability to perform a complex skill: intermediate stage
Complex overt response	Ability to perform a complex skill correctly and without hesitation: advanced stage
Adaptation	Ability to modify and adjust a skill in a new context
Origination	Ability to create something original or to modify an existing skill with a new skill

Summary

Attempts to understand and describe the human mind and how it works can be noted throughout history. Consideration of the topic began in ancient times with the writings of the Greek and Roman philosophers and has continued into modern times with the research conducted in psychology, cognitive science, and neuroscience. As the understanding of the human mind and how it works continues to grow, instructional designers need to be able to continue to determine how this information can be used to positively impact their work. Successful instructional designers know that understanding different and often very divergent perspectives on how people think will provide insights into how people learn. This understanding is important because understanding how people learn is a key element in designing successful instructional interventions.

An instructional designer who has a solid understanding of how people learn can articulate the basics of various psychological perspectives that describe different approaches on how people learn. This ability allows him or her to use this knowledge to create instructional interventions that meet the goals of their clients.

As described in this chapter, behaviorism and cognitivism (and their various branches) are two major psychological perspectives that have dominated how learning has been viewed throughout the twentieth century and now into the twenty-first century. These two divergent perspectives provide unique approaches on how learning takes place. Behaviorism stresses that learning is a result of a change in behavior as a result of experience, while cognitivism stresses that learning is a change in mental representations and associations resulting from experience. It is important to understand that neither approach should be used exclusively.

Connecting Process to Practice

1. Why is it important for instructional designers to understand different perspectives on how people think?
2. You are having a discussion with a client. Your client says he recently read an article about behaviorism and cognitivism, but he is not certain whether he clearly understands how each views human thinking. He asks you if you could help him clear up any misconceptions he might have by describing the two perspectives. How would you describe the two perspectives to your client?
3. You have been asked to give a brief talk about how perspectives on how humans think and learn have changed over time. What would you include as major topics to discuss?
4. What might a simple training session to teach someone how to properly change a flat tire look like if you took a behaviorist approach in design the training? How about if you took a cognitivist approach or a constructivism approach?

Recommended Reading

Aquinas, T. (1998). *A summary of philosophy*. Indianapolis, IN: Hackett Publishing.

Bigge, M. L. & Shermis, S. S. (2004). *Learning theories for teachers*. Boston: Allyn & Bacon.

Brown, J. S., Collins, A. & Duguid, S. (1989). Situated cognition and the culture of learning. *Educational Researcher, 18*(1), 32–42.

Bruner, J. (1992). *Acts of meaning*. Cambridge, MA: Harvard University Press.

Dewey, J. (1997). *Experience and education*. New York: Free Press Publishing.

Heshusias, L. & Ballard, K. (1996). *From positivism to interpretivism and beyond: Tales of transformation in educational and social research (the mind-body connection)*. New York: Teacher's College Press.

James, W. (1955). *Principles of psychology*. Toronto, Canada: Dover Publishing.

James, W. (2002). *The meaning of truth*. Toronto, Canada: Dover Publishing.

Kant, I. A. (1999). *Critique of pure reason*. Cambridge, England: Cambridge University Press.

Kearsley, G. (2009). *Theory into practice (TIP)*. Retrieved on January 7, 2010, from http://tip.psychology.org.

McDonald, M. (2008). *Your brain: the missing manual: How to get the most from your mind*. Sebastopol, CA: O'Reilly Media.

Medina, J. (2008). *Brain rules: 12 principles for surviving and thriving at work, home, and school*. Seattle, WA: Pear Press.

References

Almog, J. (2002). *What am I?: Descartes and the mind-body problem*. London: Oxford University Press.

Anderson, L. M. & Krathwohl, D. R. (Eds.) (2001). *A taxonomy for learning, teaching, and assessing: A revision of Bloom's taxonomy of educational objectives*. New York: Longman.

Ashcraft, M. H. (2002). *Cognition, 3rd edition*. Upper Saddle River, NJ: Prentice-Hall.

Berliner, D. (1993). *In exploring applied psychology origins and analysis: Master lectures in psychology*. T. K. Fagan & G. R. VandenBos (Eds.) Washington DC: American Psychology Association.

Blackburn, S. (1996). *The oxford dictionary of philosophy*. London: Oxford University Press.

Bleiberg, J. (2001). *The road to rehabilitation: Guideposts to recognition—cognition, memory, and brain injury*. McLean, VA: Brain Injury Association of American. Retrieved January 7, 2010, from http://www.biausa.org/word.files.to.pdf/good.pdfs/roadToRehab3.pdf.

Bloom, B. S., Engelhart, M. D., Frost, E. J., Hill, W. H. & Krathwohl, D. R. (1956). *Taxonomy of educational objectives. Handbook I: Cognitive domain*. New York: David McKay.

Brandt, R. S. & Perkins, D. N. (2000). The evolving science of learning. In R. S. Brandt (Ed.), *Education in a New Era* (pp. 159–183). Alexandria, VA: Association for Supervision and Curriculum Development.

Burton, Moore & Magliaro (2004). Behaviorism and instructional technology. In D. Jonassen (Ed.), *Handbook of Research on Educational Communications and Technology* (pp. 3–36). Mahway, NJ: Lawrence Erlbaum Associates, Publishers.

Butler, C. (2003). *Postmodernism: A very short introduction*. London: Oxford University Press.

Cangelosi, J. (1990). *Designing tests for student achievement*. New York: Longman.

Collison, D. (1978). *Fifty major philosophers: A reference guide*. Routledge: New York.

Dewey, J. (1910). *How we think*. Amherst, NY: Prometheus Books.

Driscoll, M. P. (2000). *Psychology of learning for instruction, 2nd edition*. Boston: Allyn & Bacon.

Driscoll, M. P. (2004). *Psychology of learning for instruction, 3rd edition*. Boston: Allyn & Bacon.

Eisner, E. W. (2000). Benjamin Bloom 1913-99. *Prospects: the quarterly review of comparative education, XXX*(3). Retrieved from http://www.ibe.unesco.org/International/Publications/Thinkers/ThinkersPdf/bloome.pdf

Fieser, J. & Fowder, B., Eds. (2004). *The internet encyclopedia of philosophy*. Accessed January 7, 2010, from http://www.iep.utm.edu.

Flavell, J. H. (1979). Metacognition and cognitive monitoring: A new area of cognitive-developmental inquiry. *American Psychologist, 34*, 906–911.

Goodman, G. S. (2008). *Educational psychology: An application of critical constructivism*. New York: Peter Lang Publishing.

Greeno, J. G., Collins, A. M. & Resnick, L. B. (1996). Cognition and learning. In D. Berliner & R. Calfee (Eds.), *Handbook of educational psychology* (pp. 15–46). New York: Macmillan.

Gronlund, N. E. (2000). *How to write and use instructional objectives, 6th edition*. Columbus, OH: Merrill.

Harrow, A. J. (1972). *A taxonomy of the psychomotor domain: A guide for developing behavior objectives*. New York: David McKay.

Hill, W. F. (2002). *Learning: A survey of psychological interpretations, 7th edition*. Boston: Allyn and Bacon.

James, W. (1995). *Pragmatism*. Toronto: Dover Publishing.

Krathwohl, D. R., Bloom, B. S. & Masia, B. B. (1964). *Taxonomy of educational objectives. Handbook II: Affective domain*. New York: David McKay.

Kreitzer, A. E. & Madaus, G. F. (1994). Empirical investigations of the hierarchical structure of the taxonomy. In L. W. Anderson & L. A. Sosniak (Eds.), *Bloom's taxonomy: A forty-year retrospective*. Ninety-third yearbook for the National Society for the Study of Education: Part II (pp. 64–81). Chicago: University of Chicago Press.

Locke, J. & Winkler, K. (Eds.) (1996). *Essay concerning human understanding*. Indianapolis, IN: Hackett Publishing. (Original publication 1690).

Mager, R. (1962). *Preparing instructional objectives*.

Marzano, R. J. (2000). *Designing a new taxonomy of educational objectives*. Thousand Oaks, CA: Corwin Press.

Marzano, R. J. (2000). The 20th century advances in instruction. In R. S. Brandt (Ed.), *Education in a New Era* (pp. 67–95). Alexandria, VA: Association for Supervision and Curriculum Development.

Nichols, A. (2003). *Discovering Aquinas: An introduction to his life, work, and influence*. Grand Rapids, MI: William B. Eerdmans Publishing Company.

Ormrod, J. E. (2004). *Human learning*. Upper Saddle, NJ: Merrill Prentice-Hall.

Ormrod, J. E. (2009). *Educational psychology*. Upper Saddle, NJ: Merrill Prentice-Hall.

Pavlov, I. (1927). *Conditioned reflexes* (G.V. Anrep, Trans.). London: Oxford University Press.

Phillips, D. C. (1995). The good, the bad, and the ugly: The many faces of constructivism. *Educational Researcher, 24*(7), 16–25.

Public Broadcasting System. Document retrieved January 7, 2010, from http://www.pbs.org/faithandreason/gengloss/postm-body.html.

Saettler, P. (1990). *The evolution of American educational technology*. Englewood, CO: Libraries Unlimited.

Schwandt, T. (1998). Constructivist, interpretivist approaches to human inquiry. In N. Denzin & Y. Lincoln (Eds.), *The Landscape of Qualitative Research: Theories and Issues* (pp. 221–259). Thousand Oaks, CA: Sage Publications.

Seddon, G. M. (1978). The properties of Bloom's taxonomy of educational objectives for the cognitive domain. *Review of Educational Research, 48*, 303–323.

Shuell, T. J. (1986). Cognitive conceptions of learning. *Review of Educational Research, 56*, 411–436.

Simpson, E. (1972). *The classification of educational objectives in the psychomotor domain: The psychomotor domain* (Vol. 3). Washington, DC: Gryphon House.

Skinner, B. F. (1978). *About behaviorism*. New York: Random House Trade Books.

Sorell, T. (2001). *Descartes: A very short introduction.* London: Oxford University Press.

Sternberg, R. J. (1986). *Intelligence applied.* New York: Harcourt Brace Jovanovich, Publishers.

Winn, W. (2004). Cognitive perspectives in psychology. In D. Jonassen (Ed.), *Handbook of Research on Educational Communications and Technology* (pp. 79–112). Mahway, NJ: Lawrence Erlbaum Associates, Publishers.

Woolfolk, A. (2004). *Educational psychology*. Boston: Allyn & Bacon.

Part II

EXAMINING THE SITUATION: NEEDS, TASK, AND LEARNER ANALYSES

According to the principles of instructional design, before you can begin to create an instructional intervention for any group of learners, you need to first thoroughly analyze the situation in order to determine the best course of action. Chapters 3, 4, and 5 describe the instructional design processes that help to answer the question "What type of intervention is needed?"

Chapter 3 introduces the principles, processes, and practices of **needs analysis**, which helps determine what kind of change the instruction should help to bring about. Chapter 4 introduces **task analysis**, which is a way of understanding the content and/or tasks that will form the basis for the instruction being developed. Chapter 5 explains **learner analysis**, which is a way of getting to know the people the instruction is for.

These analysis activities are essential elements of instructional design. They help the instructional designer decide on the goals and objectives of the instructional event and help him or her select and organize the best possible activities for instruction.

Chapter 3

Needs Analysis

"Why is it that our teacher candidates' passing rate for the Teacher Performance Assessment is lower than the state average? Why are 25% not passing?" Hannah asked herself these questions after reading the summary data provided by the State Department of Education. Although the answers to these questions were not clear, one thing was clear: As department chair for elementary education, Hannah knew she must address the problem. A teacher candidate who did not pass the assessment was not eligible for a teaching credential.

At a nonprofit organization, Terrence has been told by his supervisor that the number of complaints about the call center volunteers had significantly increased over the past three months. Terrence was given the tasks of exploring why the sudden increase had occurred and what possible solutions could be implemented to lower the number of complaints.

Both Hannah and Terrence should conduct a needs analysis to gather information that will allow each to fully understand the problem they face. In doing so, each will be able to clearly indentify the particular needs that must be met in order to solve the problem each is up against.

GUIDING QUESTIONS

- What is a needs analysis?
- Why is it important to conduct a needs analysis?
- What do experts in instructional design recommend about conducting a needs analysis?
- What steps should an instructional designer follow to conduct a successful needs analysis?
- What is the final outcome of a needs analysis?
- How can an instructional designer evaluate the effectiveness of a needs analysis?

KEY TERMS

goal analysis *47*
needs analysis *41*
needs assessment *46*
performance analysis *44*

CHAPTER OVERVIEW

Instructional design is conducted for a purpose. That purpose is to help produce a desired change. The change could be many things, such as an improvement in attitudes of employees toward a particular job task, an increase in knowledge of students taking a high school history course, or an upgrade of the skill level of consumers using a new word processor. Therefore, an early step—if not the first step—in the instructional design process is to identify the change that is requested and the different variables surrounding this change. These variables include identifying the desired change that needs to occur, who wants the change to occur, and in what environment this change should occur. This process constitutes a **needs analysis**. The information gathered during a needs analysis will help the instructional designer to be clear about what instruction needs to be developed or if instruction is even necessary to help bring about the desired change.

As with all phases of the instructional design process, there are various perspectives for how a needs analysis might be approached and carried out. In this chapter, we will explore a variety of perspectives held by instructional design experts regarding needs analysis. Additionally, we will discuss how to conduct a thorough needs analysis to help ensure that proper data is collected that will accurately inform how the instructional designer should proceed through the instructional design process. Finally, a number of different methods for evaluating whether the needs analysis conducted was successful are described.

NEEDS ANALYSIS: AN OVERVIEW

As mentioned in the previous section, instructional design is carried out for a purpose: to bring about a particular change. Typically, the change is a need to improve performance of some kind. Attitudes, knowledge, and skills are all areas in which improvement might be needed. Therefore, the need to improve performance can take on different forms, such as increasing a student's knowledge of a particular content area, increasing the productivity of a factory worker, and increasing consumer ease in using a new product.

It is generally the job of an instructional designer to help determine exactly what the change is that needs to occur. The instructional designer comes into an environment and determines what needs to take place based on what is going on in the environment. On other occasions, however, an instructional designer may be told upfront what change is needed. Although this may be the case, the instructional designer is wise to confirm that need by getting others' perspectives on the situation. With either scenario, the instructional designer is being asked to solve a problem by identifying the problem and coming up with a solution to help solve it.

Instructional designers use a needs analysis process to get at the source of the problem. In order to do this, specific information is needed. This information is gathered by the instructional designer through various means, such as interviews, observations, and reviews of available artifacts. The information gathered is then used to inform how the rest of the instructional design process will be carried out.

Needs Analysis Questions

A typical needs analysis attempts to provide information that will help answer the following questions:

- What is the change being requested (including who is being asked to change and what is currently taking place)?
- Who is requesting this change?
- Where will this change need to take place?
- Is instruction the most appropriate means for bringing about the desired change?

It is the job of the instructional designer to find answers to these questions in order to help design, develop, and implement an elegant solution—one that is both efficient and effective in providing the appropriate change.

Formal and Informal Needs Analysis

A needs analysis plays a critical role at the beginning of the instructional design process because it helps an instructional designer identify the problem that needs to be solved. A needs analysis provides information that allows an instructional designer to get to the

Professionals in Practice

I work for a software company that creates telephony software. All instructional design—whether for classroom or distance learning—starts with a formal needs analysis built around one central question: Is this a concept the student needs? From there, we drill down more: What tasks need to be performed? What tasks are not being performed correctly? What is the gap between required performance and actual performance? Is there a single behavior or class of behaviors that will indicate the presence of the required performance, about which there is general agreement?

The method and instrument we use most frequently is the SME [subject matter expert] interview and/or questionnaire. The biggest challenge we face as instructional designers in a technology company is that our learning content is driven by the technology, not necessarily the learners. It's a classic "if we build it, they will come" situation. Our biggest challenge is in creating learner-centered content for a highly technical system.

—Erik Novak
distance learning course developer
at Interactive Intelligence, Inc.
Indianapolis, Indiana

core of the problem. If little or nothing is known about the problem, then a full-scale needs analysis is necessary. There are situations, however, where an instructional designer does not carry out a full-scale needs analysis because he or she is brought into the instructional design process at a stage where the client has already clearly determined what the problem is and has possibly even identified why it may be occurring. If this is the case, the instructional designer does not need to conduct a formal needs analysis because information that would be gained from doing so most likely currently exists and would be a waste of resources. This does not mean that the instructional designer will not require additional information. It only indicates that a formal needs analysis is unnecessary.

It is not clear to Hannah the approach she should take. Her instincts are telling her that training is needed for the instructors in her department who are working with the teacher candidates on the teaching performance assessments. However, what the specific training needs may be are not clear. She needs to have a clearer understanding of what is taking place in the core courses in the credential programs to lead to the teacher candidates failing the assessment.

Terrence contemplates the problem his organization is having with call center volunteers. He wonders whether instruction is necessary or whether it is a change in policy that is needed. Terrence is not quite sure. Determining exactly what is taking place with the volunteers will determine whether instruction or a change in policy is needed.

POPULAR APPROACHES TO NEEDS ANALYSIS

There are a variety of approaches that an instructional designer can utilize for carrying out a needs analysis. This section will discuss several of these approaches, which have been developed by respected instructional design scholars. These approaches are worth examining as you begin to develop your own understanding of and approach to the needs analysis process. As you read the different approaches, it is important to note that each approach uses varying terminology to refer to the needs analysis process. Despite the varying terminology used, the outcome of the approaches still remains the same.

Robert F. Mager is an author of instructional design texts that have been popular for decades. His approach to needs analysis is a good place to start. Mager (1988) describes a process for determining "the proper course of action in those instances where people aren't doing what they should be doing" (p. 24). Mager calls this process **performance analysis.** Performance analysis allows an instructional designer to determine what individuals are now doing and what they should be doing. If a difference exists, then it is the job of the instructional designer to determine why the difference exists. Differences could exist because an individual does not know how to do something; if so, then instruction is necessary. If the individual already knows how to do something and is not doing it, then another remedy other than instruction is needed.

Mager (1988) recommends the following steps when conducting a performance analysis (see Figure 3.1):

1. Describe the person or people whose performance is being questioned.
2. Describe as specifically as possible what it is they are doing that causes someone to say there is a problem.
3. Describe specifically what it is they should be doing.
4. Determine the cost of the discrepancy by estimating what it is costing in such things as aggravation, frustration, turnover, scrap, insurance rates, time lost, money lost, equipment damage, customers lost or good will damage, accidents, and so on.
5. If the estimated cost of the discrepancy is small, stop. In other words, if it is only a problem because you say it is and it is not having any impact on the rest of the world, stop.
6. If the cost is great enough to warrant going on, determine whether the target people know how to do what is expected of them. Answer the question, "Could they do it if their very lives depended on it?"
7. If they could, then they already know how. Now determine why they are not doing what they already know how to do. This is done by determining the consequences and obstacles of performing:
   i. What happens to the performers if they do it right?
   ii. What happens to them if they do it wrong?
   iii. What are the obstacles to performing as desired?
8. If they could not do it, answer these questions:
   i. Can the task be simplified to the point where they could do it?
   ii. Did they ever know how to do it? (If so, they only need practice.)
   iii. Is the skill used often? (If they do it often and still do not do it right, they need feedback. If they do not do if often and they used to know how, they need a job aid, such as a checklist or a piece of sheet music (job aids are described in Chapter 9.)
   iv. Do they have the potential to learn to do it? (If not, they should be transferred or terminated.)
9. The answer to these questions leads to the drafting of potential solutions. These solutions must address the problems exposed during the analysis. For example, if it is discovered that people are not performing because they do not have the authority to perform as desired, then one part of the solution must propose a way to remove that obstacle.

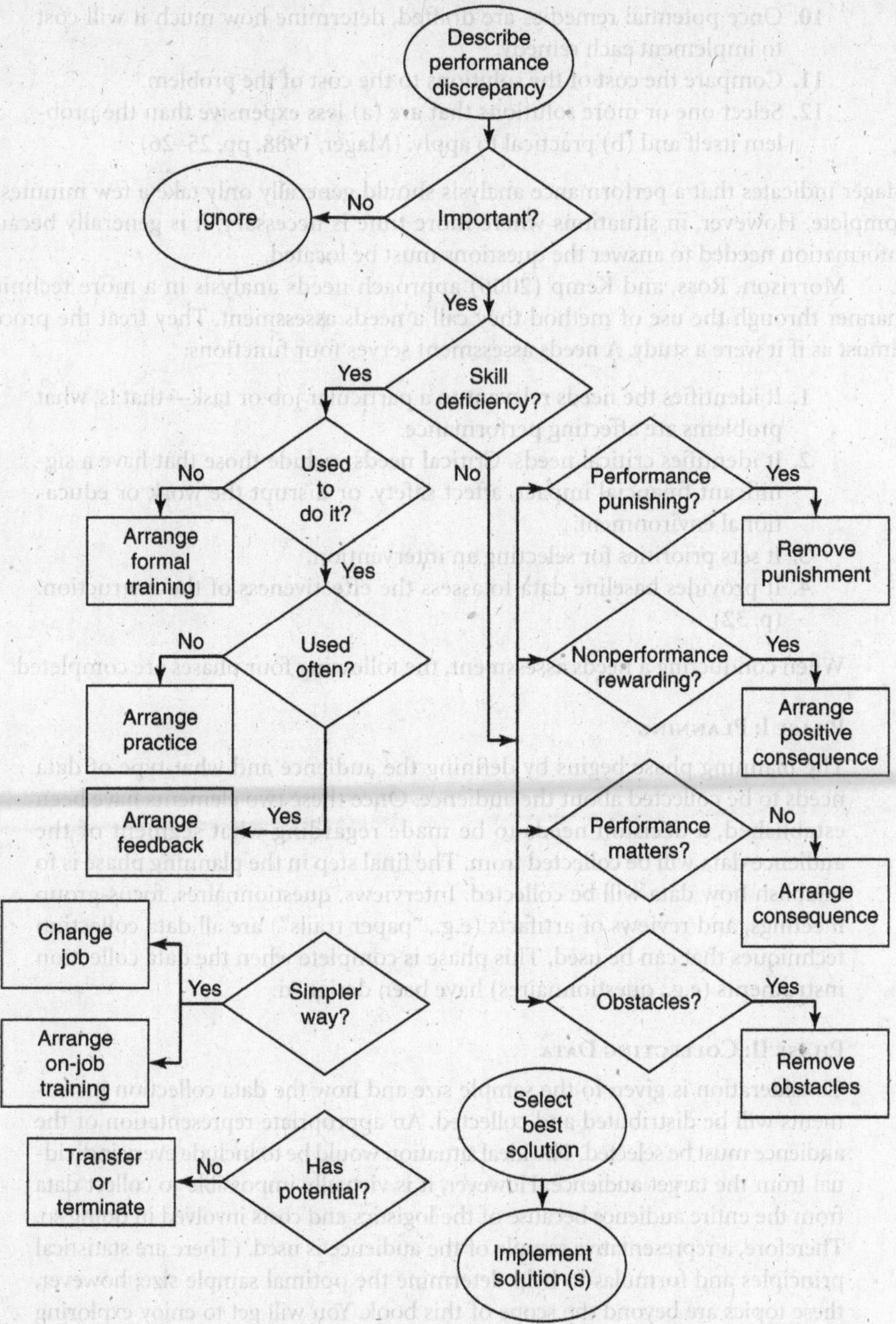

FIGURE 3.1 Mager's Performance Analysis Process: Flowchart Format

10. Once potential remedies are drafted, determine how much it will cost to implement each remedy.
11. Compare the cost of the solutions to the cost of the problem.
12. Select one or more solutions that are (a) less expensive than the problem itself and (b) practical to apply. (Mager, 1988, pp. 25–26)

Mager indicates that a performance analysis should generally only take a few minutes to complete. However, in situations where more time is necessary, it is generally because information needed to answer the questions must be located.

Morrison, Ross, and Kemp (2006) approach needs analysis in a more technical manner through the use of method they call a needs assessment. They treat the process almost as if it were a study. A needs assessment serves four functions:

1. It identifies the needs relevant to a particular job or task—that is, what problems are affecting performance.
2. It identifies critical needs. Critical needs include those that have a significant financial impact, affect safety, or disrupt the work or educational environment.
3. It sets priorities for selecting an intervention.
4. It provides baseline data to assess the effectiveness of the instruction. (p. 32)

When conducting a needs assessment, the following four phases are completed:

Phase I: Planning

The planning phase begins by defining the audience and what type of data needs to be collected about the audience. Once these two elements have been established, a decision needs to be made regarding what segment of the audience data will be collected from. The final step in the planning phase is to establish how data will be collected. Interviews, questionnaires, focus-group meetings, and reviews of artifacts (e.g., "paper trails") are all data collection techniques that can be used. This phase is complete when the data collection instruments (e.g., questionnaires) have been designed.

Phase II: Collecting Data

Consideration is given to the sample size and how the data collection instruments will be distributed and collected. An appropriate representation of the audience must be selected. The ideal situation would be to include every individual from the target audience. However, it is virtually impossible to collect data from the entire audience because of the logistics and costs involved in doing so. Therefore, a representative sample of the audience is used. (There are statistical principles and formulas to help determine the optimal sample size; however, these topics are beyond the scope of this book. You will get to enjoy exploring these topics—if you have not done so already—in an advanced statistics course.)

Phase III: Analyzing the Data

Morrison, Ross, and Kemp indicate that the output of the data analysis is an identification of needs (of which there are six different types: normative,

> comparative, felt, expressed, anticipated, and critical incident) and a prioritization of these needs. They state that needs can be prioritized in various ways, such as the relative cost to value for a company, the number of people impacted, a ranking scale, or the frequency that the need is identified (2006). Morrison, Ross, and Kemp suggest using the Delphi Method to prioritize needs. The Delphi Method is a structured process for collecting and analyzing knowledge gathered from a group of experts through the use of a series of questionnaires intermixed with controlled opinion feedback.
>
> **Phase IV: Compiling a Final Report**
>
> Preparing a final report on the findings is the concluding phase. Four sections should be included in a final report: 1) summary of the purpose; 2) summary of the process, including how it was carried out and who was involved; 3) summary of the results in both quantitative (e.g., charts, graphs) and qualitative formats (e.g., a brief narrative) if appropriate; and 4) recommendation(s) based on the data. The recommendation(s) given should be appropriate to the identified problem. As mentioned, the recommendation(s) may or may not be instruction. (pp. 36–39)

In addition to the needs assessment method, Morrison, Ross, and Kemp describe two other needs analysis methods: **goal analysis** and performance assessment (which is similar to Mager's performance analysis). They write: "Goal analysis takes less time than a needs assessment and its focus is typically much narrower. The goal analysis starts with a problem someone has identified, and then it focuses on a solution" (p. 43). This is the type of situation that instructional designers are generally involved in (instructional goals and goal analysis are covered in detail in Chapter 6).

A key element to keep in mind with goal analysis is that the instructional designer is not being asked to identify the problem (as is the case with a needs assessment). The job of the instructional designer is to focus primarily on determining an appropriate intervention. Another key element is that instruction may not always be the appropriate intervention needed to a problem that exists. "Problems that on the surface seem to require an instructional intervention can often be solved with a change in policy, coaching, or the environment" (Morrison, Ross & Kemp, 2006, p. 31).

Before the instructional goal(s) can be developed, the need or problem that is to be addressed must be identified through the use of needs assessment and analysis processes. "After the problem is identified, the designer attempts to identify the causes of the problem, and then identifies an array of solutions that could be implemented to solve the problem. Seldom is instruction the single answer to the problem. Usually a combination of changes is required to solve the problem effectively" (p. 18).

Allison Rossett (1995) writes that instructional designers engage in needs analysis when they are responding to a request for assistance. A needs assessment allows an instructional designer to gather information that will allow him or her to make "data-driven and responsive recommendations" (p. 184) about how to solve a problem, which is typically the need to improve some type of performance. She states that the needs assessment drives the entire instructional design process by eventually shaping the decisions made about design, development, implementation, and evaluation.

Rossett (1995) believes that when a needs analysis is conducted, it allows an instructional designer to gather information about the following factors:

- ***Optimal Performance*** What does an individual who is performing at an optimal level know or do that allows him or her to perform at this level? Instructional designers consult a variety of sources—such as experts, documentation, standards, practices, texts, and tests—to answer this question.
- ***Actual Performance*** How is an individual currently performing? What is happening to cause a particular event to take place? Why is a change being requested? An instructional designer can use employee performance records, observation, and interviews to help gather data to provide answers to these questions.
- ***Feelings*** Instructional designers want to know how individuals feel about the topic, training about the topic, the topic as a priority, and their confidence surrounding the topic.
- ***Cause(s)*** Rossett identifies four kinds of causes for why individuals may not be performing as they should: 1) They lack the skill or knowledge; 2) the environment is in the way; 3) there are no, few, or improper incentives; and 4) the employees are unmotivated.
- ***Solutions*** What solutions are possible?

Rossett outlines a five-step process for conducting a needs analysis:

STEP ONE: DETERMINE PURPOSES BASED ON INITIATORS

There are three types of initiating situations that may be taking place: performance problems, "new stuff", and mandates. The instructional designer must determine what type of situation initiated the problem. The instructional designer must then determine what purpose(s) need to be addressed in order to develop a solution for the existing problem. Figure 3.2 presents the relationship between the three types of initiators and the needs assessment purposes.

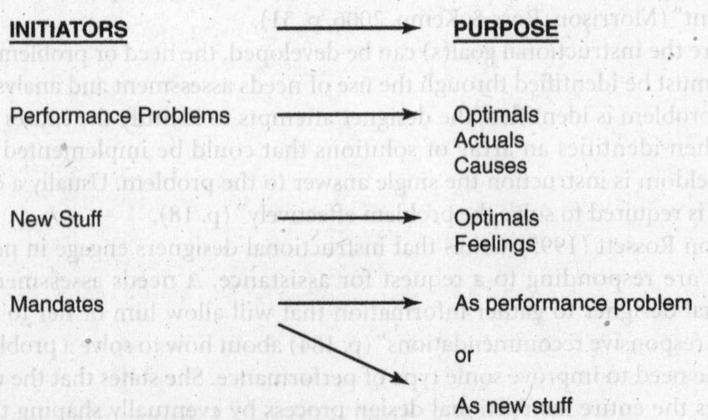

FIGURE 3.2 Initiators and Purposes (Rossett, 1995, p. 190)

Step Two: Identify Sources

The next step is to identify who has the information that is needed and where it is located. What constraints are there to gaining access to this information? What individuals need to know that you are involved in developing a solution to the existing problem?

Step Three: Select Tools

Gathering various types of data require different tools. Careful planning needs to take place in order to select the proper tool that will allow useful data to be effectively gathered. Interviews, observing employee performance, examining records and outcomes, group meetings, and questionnaires are tools that can be used.

Step Four: Conduct the Needs Assessment in Stages

Once you have identified the purpose (Step One), established the sources where data will be collected (Step Two), and determined the tools that will be used to collect the data (Step Three), you are ready to conduct the needs assessment. Most needs assessments are done in stages; that is, data is collected and analyzed and then a determination is made as to whether additional information is needed. The need for additional information from the identified sources may be gathered if it is determined that the data collected is not adequate. Inadequate collection of data may be a result of improper sources or data collection tools. If so, an instructional designer may need to revisit Steps Two and Three of this process before conducting another stage of needs assessment.

Step Five: Use Findings for Decision-Making

The information gathered during the needs assessment is used to develop a solution that is appropriate.

Smith and Ragan (2004) believe that instructional designers must learn to be "clever investigators" who are capable of clearly analyzing the learning context. They state that the analysis of the learning context includes two steps: (1) "the substantiation of a need for instruction to help learners reach learning goals" and (2) "a description of the learning environment in which the instruction will be used" (p. 31). They believe that a needs assessment helps determine whether the need exists for new instruction to be developed.

Smith and Ragan outline three needs assessment models: Discrepancy-Based Needs Assessment, Problem-Finding, Problem-Solving Model, and Innovation Model. Instructional designers use the Discrepancy-Based Needs Assessment model when learning goals are already identified and instruction is being offered that is related to these goals. Five phases are carried out when using this approach:

1. List the goals of the instructional system.
2. Determine how well the identified goals are already being achieved.
3. Determine the gaps between "what is" and "what should be."

4. Prioritize gaps according to agreed-upon criteria.
5. Determine which gaps are instructional needs and which are most appropriate for design and development of instruction. (pp. 32–35)

The Problem-Finding, Problem-Solving Model is used when "someone in management or administration; some member of the constituency, such as parents, clients, or community leaders; or some employees or students have identified that a problem exists in the organization's achieving its mission" (p. 35). There are four steps to this model: 1) Determine whether there really is a problem; 2) determine whether the cause of the problem is related to employees' performance in training environments or to learners' achievement in educational environments; 3) determine whether the solution to the achievement/performance problem is learning; and 4) determine whether instruction for these learning goals is currently offered (pp. 35–36).

The Innovation Model is used to examine "changes or innovations in the educational system or organization" to determine if adding new learning goals is necessary to account for the changes or innovations. Four steps make up this model: 1) Determine the nature of the innovation or change; 2) determine the learning goals that accompany this innovation; 3) if there is a choice, determine whether these goals are appropriate and high priority in the learning system; and 4) begin learning environment analysis design activities (that is, start the next phase of the instructional design process). With this model, it is extremely important to include the stakeholders (e.g., teachers/trainers, managers/ administrators) because an outcome could be the addition of or the change in goals for the organization (p. 36).

NEEDS ANALYSIS PROCEDURE

Although the needs analysis approaches described in the previous section employ different tactics, they each share a common outcome: to provide useful data that can be used by an instructional designer to create the best possible solution, which helps solve a problem that exists, meets a given need, or brings about a desired change. To gather the appropriate data, a thorough needs analysis must be conducted. A needs analysis is conducted by using various data-gathering tools to help answer fundamental questions.

Determining the Desired Change

The first step in a needs analysis is to determine what change is being requested. As mentioned early in this chapter, the desired change could be in behavior, skill, or attitude. You will want to find out information that can help you answer the following questions:

- What problem exists or what change is being requested?
- Who is being asked to change?
- What is currently taking place in this environment with this individual or individuals?

Typically, the client who hired you will be able to provide you with the necessary information or access to the information needed to answer these questions. In most cases, your client will specifically tell you what change is desired and the individuals who are being asked to change. This information can be gathered through an interview process. Additionally, through an interview, the client will be able to provide insights into what is currently taking place in the environment where the individual or individuals are being asked to change. However, it is good practice for an instructional designer to observe the environment personally rather than solely relying on the client's description. Your client will have a biased opinion on what is taking place and therefore may not provide you with a completely accurate picture of what is taking place.

It is important to note that not all instructional design projects are this straightforward. On occasion, you may be asked to come in to an organization to observe what is taking place and determine the type of change that needs to take place. This type of activity is often associated with the field of Human Performance Technology (HPT). According to the International Society for Performance Improvement (ISPI), HPT focuses on analyzing outcomes to identify the causes for why a gap in desired levels of performance exists (ISPI, 2004). Once the causes are identified, an intervention is developed to bridge the performance gap. The focus of HPT is on human performance—typically related to activities that take place in industry and business settings.

The Request for the Desired Change

After developing a clear understanding of the existing problem or the change being requested, it is important to understand who is asking for the change to occur. This is an extremely important element to understand because it will help you determine the type of intervention that may need to take place, the emotional and political climate of the situation, and the level of support that is present and that will most likely be needed for a change to take place. To come to an understanding of these elements, you will need to answer the following question: Who identified the problem or is requesting this change?

This information is generally easy to obtain. It is often the desire of client who hired you to have the change occur. It is important to keep in mind that there may be additional stakeholders who might be interested in having the change occur. However, talking to additional stakeholders to clarify how they feel about the problem or the change being requested may be difficult.

Implementation Location of the Desired Change

Finding out where the desired change will take place is another important element to consider. This will help you to better understand the context of where an intervention will need to take place. Where will the solution or change need to take place? Again, the client is the best source of information to answer this question. In most cases, it will be extremely obvious where the change will need to take place (e.g., a school, the workplace). It can be very helpful to visit the location where the change is to take place to help you gain a solid understanding of the environment. However, this may not always be possible. If not, it is important to do your research about the environment.

The Intervention

Once you have the appropriate data that allows you to understand the entire context—the desired change, who is requesting the change, who is being asked to change, and where the change needs to take place—it is time to determine if instruction is the most appropriate intervention. You will need to answer the following question: Is instruction the most appropriate means for solving the problem or bringing about the desired change?

The client will be relying on your expertise to determine this. There are no steadfast rules on whether instruction is the most appropriate intervention because each instructional design situation is different. However, instruction is most appropriate when a change in skill or knowledge is desired. Based on the information you have gathered through your needs analysis, you will need to determine an appropriate intervention. It is important to keep in mind that you may want to offer more than one type of intervention to your client. Allow your client to be part of the decision making process, but as previously mentioned, know that your client will be relying on your expertise to make the final decision.

A properly conducted needs analysis contributes significantly to how successful the entire instructional design process will be carried out. A thorough identification of the problem that needs to be addressed will lead to an effective and efficient solution being developed.

EVALUATING THE SUCCESS OF A NEEDS ANALYSIS

How do you know when you have successfully conducted a needs analysis? How do you know that the data gathered accurately describes the problem or the change that needs to take place (thus helping you to develop an appropriate solution)? One method used to evaluate the success of a needs analysis is to determine if the solution developed and implemented helped bring about the desired change. In other words, did performance improve? Although extremely important, this summative evaluation activity poses serious problems if it is the only method used to evaluate the success of a needs analysis. The most serious problem is that it is conducted well after the needs analysis has been carried out and consequently does not provide you with corrective feedback. It is an "all or nothing" method. It helps to determine whether you have succeeded or you have failed. Therefore, it is good practice to use formative evaluation activities throughout the needs analysis process in addition to this summative activity.

An important formative evaluation activity to use is sustained communication between you and the client during the entire needs analysis process. Data gathered should be periodically shared with the client during this process. This formative evaluation activity helps ensure that you are gathering accurate data by presenting the client with opportunities to provide feedback. How often should the communication take place is based on the nature of the project and the availability of the client. There is no typical answer; however, it is good practice to communicate at least once a week with your client. It is important to realize that it can be difficult to communicate with some clients on a consistent basis.

Another formative evaluation activity that can be conducted is to share data and interpretations of the data with a member of the target audience who the change is designed for (or with someone who has had a similar experience, although this situation is not as ideal). This can help determine if what you have found matches with what the individual perceives is taking place. If the data and interpretations seem familiar and appropriate to these individuals, it suggests that the needs analysis was successful. This process is referred to as a member check. A member check is a comparison method of evaluation that comes from a qualitative research paradigm.

Hannah has decided to gather information about the problem at a faculty meeting. She realizes that there are multiple issues that might be going on that could be contributing to the low passing rate. Hannah uses an approach that is similar to Rossett's approach in which information is gathered on various levels about the problem. With this approach, optimal performance, actual performance, feelings, and causes are explored. Hannah will investigate these areas with the faculty in her department in hopes of clearly identifying the need that must be met in order to increase the pass rate of the teacher candidates in her department. From this exploration, the department can identify a solution that Hannah can help the faculty carry out.

Terrence has decided to use Mager's performance analysis process. Using the performance analysis process will allow Terrence to determine if a difference exists between what the volunteers should be doing and what they are doing when they answering the phones and talking to clients. If Terrence determines there is a difference, then he will be able to identify what needs to be done fix this problem. It might be that the volunteers are not familiar with what is expected of them; thus, training may need to occur. The problem could also be that the volunteers know how to do what they are supposed to be doing but are just not doing it; if this is the case, then another solution other than instruction will be needed. As Terrence conducts the performance analysis, he finds out that many of the volunteers have not been through any training on how to handle certain problems they may encounter while talking on the phone to a particular segment of clients the nonprofit serves. Thus, Terrence suggests to his supervisor that training should be developed and provided to the call center volunteers.

NEEDS ANALYSIS AND THE INSTRUCTIONAL DESIGN PROCESS

A needs analysis is critical in helping the instructional designer determine what instruction needs to be developed or if instruction is even necessary to help bring about a desired change. No matter what approach you take, completing a needs analysis should help you answer the following questions:

- What problem exists or what change is being requested?
- Who is being asked to change?
- What is currently taking place with the individual or individuals being asked to change?
- Who identified the problem or is requesting this change?
- Where will the solution or change need to take place?
- Is instruction the most appropriate means for solving the problem or bringing about the desired change?
- What is the solution to be developed and implemented?

Summary

Numerous needs analysis methods exist that can be used by instructional designers. Popular approaches to needs analysis include those outlined by Mager; Morrison, Ross, and Kemp; Dick, Carey, and Carey; Rossett; and Smith and Ragan. Although these methods vary in how they are carried out, each shares the common goal of providing an instructional designer with the appropriate data that helps inform and influence the design and development of an effective and efficient solution. This solution is one that helps solve a problem or bring about some type of change—typically, an improvement in performance. This improvement can be to knowledge, skills, and/or attitudes.

A needs analysis is conducted using various data gathering tools to help answer fundamental questions. Evaluating the success of a needs analysis is accomplished by using a combination of formative and summative evaluation techniques to determine if an instructional designer created the best possible solution, which helped solve a problem that exists, meet a given need, or brought about a desired change. A properly conducted needs analysis contributes significantly to how successfully the entire instructional design process will be carried out.

Connecting Process to Practice

1. You are the lead instructional designer recently hired for a large-scale project. Your client has asked you to describe why a needs analysis is important to the success of the project. What do you tell your client? Do not assume your client even knows what a needs analysis is.
2. Several perspectives on needs analysis were discussed in the chapter. What key elements for conducting a needs analysis do these perspectives have in common? How do these perspectives differ?
3. When examining the approaches taken by Hannah and Terrence, do you believe each took the appropriate needs analysis approach? Explain why you believe the approach each took is appropriate or what you might do differently if you were in their positions.
4. What do you believe are the most important data that Hannah must gather in order to complete a successful needs analysis? Do you foresee any potential issues with Hannah's being able to gather the data she needs? Answer the same questions from Terrence's perspective.
5. Describe an instructional design scenario where you believe a formal needs analysis would not need to be conducted.
6. You have been hired by a client to work on an instructional design project. The client is a company that owns several nursing home facilities located throughout California. Your client has indicated to you that incidents of complaints from those living at the company's nursing homes have steadily risen during the past six months. The client wants the residents of their nursing homes to have comfortable living experiences. Therefore, a solution that will help reduce the number of complaints is needed. However, tour client is not sure what needs to be done. It could be a variety of issues that could be contributing to why the complaints have increased. Your task is to conduct a needs analysis to determine what type of solution(s) may be necessary. Describe how you would conduct a needs analysis in this situation. Include the steps you would take, data you would gather, how you would analyze the information, and how you would report the findings back to your client, which would include what you feel needs to be done.
7. Is it appropriate to conduct a needs analysis when preparing instruction in a K–12 setting? How might one go about conducting a needs analysis for instruction to be delivered in a third-grade classroom?

Recommended Readings

Dick, W., Carey, L. & Carey, J. O. (2009). *The systematic design of instruction, 7th edition.* Columbus, OH: Allyn & Bacon.

Gagne, R. M., Wager, W. W., Golas, K. C. & Keller, J. M. (2004). *Principles of instructional design, 5th edition.* Belmont, CA: Wadsworth/Thomson Learning.

Kaufman, R., Rojas, A. M. & Mayer, H. (1993). *Needs assessment: A user's guide.* Englewood Cliffs, NJ: Educational Technology Publications.

Mager, R. F. & Pipe, P. (1996). *Analyzing performance problems.* Belmont, CA: Pitman.

Mager, R. F. (1989). *Making instruction work.* Belmont, CA: Lake Publishing Company.

Morrison, G. R., Ross, S. M. & Kemp, J. E. (2006). *Designing effective instruction, 5th edition.* New York: John Wiley & Sons.

Rossett, A. (1999). Analysis for human performance technology. In H. D. Stolovitch & E. J. Keeps (Eds.), *Handbook of performance technology: Improving individual and organizational performance worldwide* (pp. 139–162). San Francisco, CA: Jossey-Bass.

Rossett, A. (1995). Needs assessment. In G. Anglin (Ed.), *Instructional technology: Past, present, and future, 2nd edition* (pp. 183–196). Englewood, CO: Libraries Unlimited.

Seels, B. & Glasgow, Z. (1998). *Making instructional design decisions, 2nd edition.* Upper Saddle River, NJ: Prentice-Hall.

Smith, P. L. & Ragan, T. J. (2004). *Instructional design, 3rd edition.* New York: John Wiley & Sons.

References

Dick, W., Carey, L. & Carey, J. O. (2009). *The systematic design of instruction, 7th edition.* Columbus, OH: Allyn & Bacon.

Gagne, R. M., Wager, W. W., Golas, K. C. & Keller, J. M. (2004). *Principles of instructional design, 5th edition.* Belmont, CA: Wadsworth/Thomson Learning.

Mager, R. F. (1989). *Making instruction work.* Belmont, CA: Lake Publishing Company.

Morrison, G. R., Ross, S. M. & Kemp, J. E. (2006). *Designing effective instruction, 5th edition.* New York: John Wiley & Sons.

Rossett, A. (1995). Needs assessment. In G. Anglin (Ed.), *Instructional technology: Past, present, and future, 2nd edition* (pp. 183–196). Englewood, CO: Libraries Unlimited.

Seels, B. & Glasgow, Z. (1998). *Making instructional design decisions, 2nd edition.* Upper Saddle River, NJ: Prentice-Hall.

Smith, P. L. & Ragan, T. J. (2004). *Instructional design, 3rd edition.* New York: John Wiley & Sons.

Chapter 4

Task Analysis

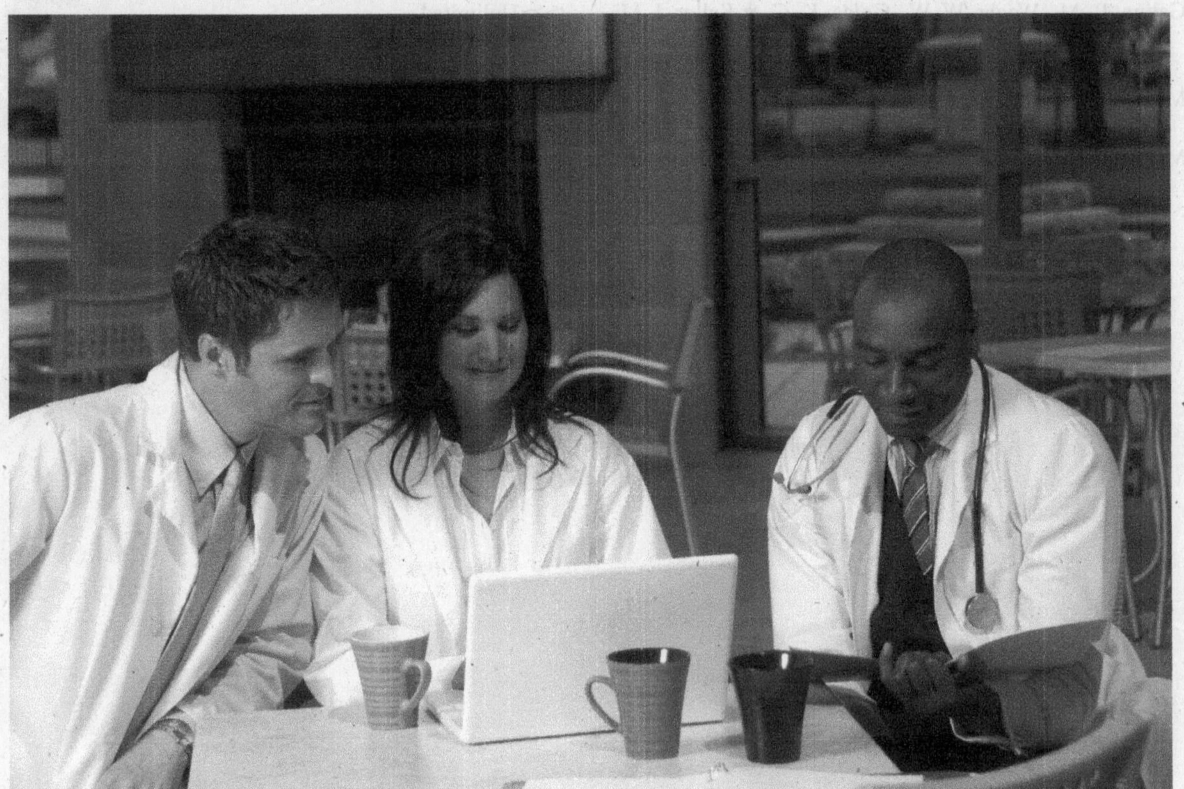

Jody is the head nurse in a hospital maternity ward at a large teaching hospital. She is in charge of ensuring that the nurses she manages are following the most current procedures for patient care. She provides ongoing training to her nurses to help them stay current. There have been several recent incidents where nurses have not followed proper procedures for admitting new patients. Jody explored the problem and determined that a group of new hires were responsible for the majority of the occurrences. These nurses lacked some knowledge and skill and thus need to be trained on the proper procedures.

Ben teaches an advanced qualitative research course for doctoral students in a college of education at a large university. A major goal of Ben's course is for students to be able to determine which qualitative approach to take when given various research scenarios. Ben is not happy with the amount of depth in which his students are able to defend the choices. He wonders if the instruction he has provided his students is missing key information.

Both Jody and Ben have identified a problem that needs to be solved. Although the problems are different, each problem stems from a lack of skill and knowledge on the part of those Jody and Ben teach. A task analysis needs to be completed by both to determine the instructional content that will help the students most.

GUIDING QUESTIONS

- What is task analysis?
- What important information is gathered as a result of conducting a task analysis?
- What do experts in instructional design recommend about conducting a task analysis?
- What is the final outcome of a task analysis?
- How can an instructional designer evaluate the effectiveness of a task analysis?

KEY TERMS

Content Analysis *58*
Learning Task Analysis *58*
Subject Matter Analysis *58*
Subject Matter Expert (SME) *58*
Task Analysis *57*

CHAPTER OVERVIEW

After a needs analysis has been conducted to determine if instruction should occur, who is requesting the instruction, and in what environment this instruction needs to take place, it is common practice to conduct a **task analysis**. Task analysis is a critical component in the instructional design process because it provides important information about the content and/or tasks that will form the basis for the instruction being developed. According to many instructional design experts (Jonassen, Hannum & Tessmer, 1998; Richey, Klein & Nelson, 2004; Morrison, Ross & Kemp, 2006), task analysis is often considered to be the most important part of the instructional design process.

This chapter describes various methods for gathering information about the content and/or activities that need to be included in the instruction. Various task analysis approaches taken by instructional design experts will be introduced and explained. This chapter also suggests how an instructional designer can evaluate the effectiveness of a task analysis.

WHAT IS TASK ANALYSIS?

Careful consideration must be taken to ensure that there is a clear understanding of what learners are to know or are able to accomplish by participating in instruction. Coming to this understanding requires the identification of the type of content that will make up the instruction and in what sequence this content should be provided. The systematic process used by instructional designers to accomplish this is typically called task analysis. It is important to note that you may find that instructional designers refer to task analysis as a **content analysis, subject matter analysis**, or **learning task analysis.** Despite their different names, each refers to the task analysis process, and the goal remains the same: to gather information about the content and/or tasks that need to be part of the instruction being developed.

Morrison, Ross, and Kemp (2006) write that a task analysis solves three problems for an instructional designer:

1. It defines the content required to solve the performance problem or alleviate a performance need. This step is crucial because most designers work with unfamiliar content.
2. Because the process forces the **subject matter expert** to work through each individual step, subtle steps are more easily identified.
3. During this process, the designer has the opportunity to view the content from the learner's perspective. Using this perspective, the designer can often gain insight into appropriate teaching strategies. (p. 78)

Jonassen, Hannum, and Tessmer (1999) provide a slightly expanded view of what instructional designers are trying to determine when a task analysis is carried out. They write that a task analysis helps determine:

1. The goals and objectives of learning
2. The operational components of jobs, skills, learning goals or objectives—that is, to describe what task performers do, how they perform a task or apply a skill, and how they think before, during, and after learning
3. What knowledge states (declarative, structural, and procedural knowledge) characterize a job or task
4. Which tasks, skills, or goals should be taught—that is, how to select learning outcomes that are appropriate for instructional development
5. Which tasks are most important—which have priority for a commitment of training resources
6. The sequence in which tasks are performed and should be learned and taught
7. How to select or design instructional activities, strategies, and techniques to foster learning
8. How to select appropriate media and learning environments
9. How to construct performance assessments and evaluation. (p. 3)

Gagne et al. (2004) state that task analysis includes a number of various procedures that are conducted by an instructional designer to obtain information that is needed to plan instruction. Two such approaches are information-processing analysis and learning-task analysis. These types of analyses focus on lesson or course target objectives (Gagne et al., 2004).

Jody knows that she needs to conduct a task analysis to determine the various elements of the procedures her nurses need to complete. She must determine if the current training is leaving out certain steps or if the new hires are simply not retaining what they are being taught.

Ben has determined that he needs to break down the process of choosing and defending a qualitative research approach. This will help him determine if he is leaving out important information for his students. He needs to look at the content and the skills that experts use in choosing a qualitative research approach.

POPULAR APPROACHES TO TASK ANALYSIS

Numerous approaches to task analysis exist that have been developed by instructional design scholars and practitioners. The approaches vary based on the context surrounding the instruction that needs to be developed. Most approaches have similar elements, although their procedures may be slightly different. They all share the same goal: determining the type of content and/or skills that need to be included in the instruction. The various approaches to task analysis are important to understand as you develop your own understanding of how this process is accomplished.

According to Jonassen, Hannum & Tessmer (1998), task analysis is a "process of analyzing and articulating the kind of learning that you expect the learners to know how to perform" (p. 3). They assert that the task analysis process consists of five discrete functions: a) inventorying tasks; b) describing tasks; c) selecting tasks; d) sequencing tasks and task components; and e) analyzing tasks and content level. These functions consist of the following activities:

- ***Inventorying Tasks*** Identifying tasks that need to be developed for instruction
- ***Describing Tasks*** The process of elaborating the tasks identified in the inventory
- ***Selecting Tasks*** Prioritizing tasks and choosing those that are more feasible and appropriate if there is an large quantity of tasks
- ***Sequencing Tasks and Task Components*** Defining the sequence in which instruction should occur in order to successfully facilitate learning
- ***Analyzing Tasks and Content Level*** Describing the type of cognitive behavior, physical performance, or affective response required by the tasks

Morrison, Ross, and Kemp (2006) state that the content required for instruction is influenced by the goals derived during a needs analysis and the information gathered during the learner analysis. The needs analysis provides instructional designers with a focus and the overall breadth of the instruction that needs to be developed. The learner analysis provides an understanding of the learner's knowledge and background related to the content. The combination of the needs and learner analyses provides a starting point for the instructional designer to determine the scope and sequence of the content to be included in instruction. The result of a task analysis is used to provide input for developing instructional objectives.

Three different techniques for analyzing content and tasks are provided by Morrison, Ross, and Kemp (2006): topic analysis, procedural analysis, and the critical incident method. Topic analysis is designed to help analyze cognitive or declarative knowledge. A topic analysis provides two types of information: 1) the content that will make up the instruction and 2) the structure of the content components. The content components can be facts, concepts, principles and rules, procedures, interpersonal skills, or attitudes. Conducting a topic analysis is much like creating an outline where you start with the major topic and work your way down to subordinate information that is associated with the major topic.

Procedural analysis is utilized to analyze tasks by identifying the steps that are required to complete them. In conducting a procedural analysis, the instructional designer typically walks through the steps with an SME. This is preferably done in the environment (or as close as possible to the actual environment) where the task will be performed. The result of a procedural analysis is typically a flowchart that identifies the different substeps that need to take place in order for the learner to accomplish the task.

The major element of a critical incident method is an interview. The interview allows the instructional designer to gather important information about the conditions in which an individual successfully and unsuccessfully accomplished a task. This method was developed during World War II by Flanagan (1954) to help determine why military pilots were not learning how to fly correctly. Pilots were interviewed to determine the conditions that were present when successful and unsuccessful missions were performed. The pilots were asked three types of questions:

1. What were the conditions before, during, and after the incident?
   a. Where did the incident occur?
   b. When did it occur?
   c. Who was involved?
   d. What equipment was used, and what was its condition?
2. What did you do?
   a. What did you do physically (e.g., grabbed the rudder)?
   b. What did you say and to whom?
   c. What were you thinking?
3. How did this incident help you reach or prevent you from reaching your goal? (Flanagan, 1954, as cited in Morrison, Ross, and Kemp, 2006, pp. 91–92)

The interview process in the critical incident method allows the instructional designer to identify knowledge and skills that an individual (the SME) uses to accomplish a task. The information identified during the interview can be combined with a topic and/or procedural analysis in order to gather additional information about the content or tasks that are to be part of the instruction (Morrison, Ross & Kemp, 2006).

Dick, Carey, and Carey (2009) write that the process of identifying the skills and knowledge that should be included in instruction is a complex process. They call this process instructional analysis. "Instructional analysis is a set of procedures that, when applied to an instructional goal, results in the identification of the relevant steps for performing a goal and the subordinate skills required for a student to achieve the goal" (p. 38). They separate this process into two parts. The first part involves the instructional designer determining the major components of the instructional goal through the use of goal analysis. The second part involves how each step of the instructional goal can be further analyzed to identify subordinate skills learners must have in order to meet the instructional goal.

The instructional analysis process can begin once the instructional goal has been identified. Dick, Carey, and Carey (2001) write that the instructional designer should start the instructional analysis process by asking, "What exactly would learners be doing if they were demonstrating that they already could perform the goal?" (p. 37). This question keeps the focus on what learners should be able to accomplish by participating in instruction rather than just on the content of the instruction. This focus is called a goal analysis procedure. The result of a goal analysis includes two items: 1) the classification of the kind of learning that will occur and 2) a visual representation (e.g., a flowchart) that displays the specific steps (and substeps) a learner should do when performing an instructional goal. There are a variety of goal analysis procedures an instructional designer can use.

The second part of the instructional analysis process is referred to as the subordinate skills analysis. The purpose of this analysis is to identify the appropriate set of subordinate skills that a learner will need in order to perform a specific step that helps the learner meet an instructional goal. Several techniques for conducting a subordinate skills analysis have been identified by Dick, Carey, and Carey; the hierarchical approach and cluster analysis are two examples. A particular technique is selected for use by an instructional designer based on the type of knowledge that is needed in order to meet the instructional goal.

Smith and Ragan (2004) refer to task analysis as "analysis of the learning task." They state: "The process of task analysis transforms goal statements into a form that can be used to guide subsequent design. Designers expend a great deal of effort in obtaining as clear a description and as thorough an analysis as possible of the learning task" (p. 63). They list five steps that are performed during the learning task analysis:

1. Write a learning goal.
2. Determine the types of learning of the goal.
3. Conduct an information-processing analysis of the goal.
4. Conduct a prerequisite analysis and determine the type of learning of the prerequisites.
5. Write learning objectives for the learning goal and each of the prerequisites. (p. 63)

The result of a learning task analysis is a listing of the goals that describe what learners should know or be able to accomplish as a result of the instruction. Included in the list are the prerequisite skills and knowledge learners will need to achieve these goals.

A key element of this approach is the information-processing analysis of the goal (step 3). This allows the instructional designer to determine the content that is needed for the instruction. Smith and Ragan state that when instructional designers conduct an information-processing analysis, they are attempting to identify the mental and/or physical steps an individual needs to go through to complete the learning task. They state that although the information-processing analysis is not the only approach to examining and dissecting the task, "it seems to be the easiest, most straightforward approach to take" (p. 69).

Professionals in Practice

I often do a task analysis when creating self-paced training. To facilitate this, I go into the factory with a technician and my notepad. I also have an associate go with us to shoot video of the tasks to be performed. I observe the technician performing the tasks that are required for the training and take judicious notes throughout the training. While I take notes, my colleague will shoot video of the tech performing the tasks. This video is a great tool to document the procedures and helps me later ensure I've captured everything, as I can go back through the procedure repeatedly.

This video also helps when I have questions. I can show the particular piece I have questions about to the technician and get further details about the task. Once I have completed observing and have double-checked the process and procedure using the video, I validate the procedures with the technician and the tool owner. I begin categorizing the tasks from simple knowledge tasks to complex performance tasks. Once this is completed, I begin looking at the tasks independently and bundling them together into like tasks by subject. For example, if there are several tasks related to safety, I'll put them together. I continue looking for common themes until all tasks are categorized. Using this process helps later when defining the goals and objectives.

— Jona Titus
senior training specialist
for Intel Corporation
Beaverton, Oregon

TASK ANALYSIS PROCEDURES

The different approaches described in the previous section share the common goal of gathering information about the content and/or tasks that will make up the instruction that needs to be developed. Each approach has its own specific set of techniques that help to accomplish this goal. It is beyond the scope of this book to describe the techniques of each approach in great detail; you will most likely be able to study these approaches and their techniques in depth during more advanced instructional design

Professionals in Practice

When I was the director of distance education, I managed a team that worked with various faculty members to develop online courses. The typical context that my team worked in was one in which a faculty member had taught a course face-to-face numerous times and for various reasons needed to transition the course into an online format. Because the course had been previously taught, the content had been developed and approved by university committees. Formal task analyses were typically not conducted. The instructional designer working with the faculty member did, however, conduct a modified task analysis by taking a look at the content with the faculty member in order to get a thorough understanding of the content involved in the course. The result was an outline of the content and skills that students needed in order to be successful in the course.

— Tim Green
former director of distance education
California State University–Fullerton

courses you will take, specifically one on task analysis (however, if you are too anxious to wait until then, you can start with some of the recommended readings listed at the end of this chapter).

Involving a Subject Matter Expert

An additional element that all the approaches emphasize is the need for a subject matter expert (referred to as an SME; pronounced *SMEE or S-M-E*) to be part of the task analysis process. The job of the SME is to help the instructional designer gather the necessary information about the content and/or tasks that will be used to develop the instruction. In some instances, the instructional designer may work as the subject matter expert because of his or her expertise in the content. In most task analysis procedures, instructional designers work with a subject matter expert. An SME is an individual who is an expert in the content area that will make up the instruction being developed. Subject matter experts play a critical role in the task analysis process by providing insights into what makes up the content and how it should be sequenced.

Task Analysis Documents

With all task analysis procedures, the result is a document created by the instructional designer that depicts the content and/or tasks. This document can take on several forms. The two most common are outlines of the content or flowcharts that depict the different tasks and subtasks that the learner will need to accomplish (see Figures 4.1 and 4.2).

Influencing Factors

The task analysis approach that an instructional designer will use depends on the context that surrounds the instruction that needs to be developed. A major influencing factor in the approach that is selected is the goal of the instruction. The goals of the instruction will relate to the type of content and/or task that will make up the instruction. For example, if the goal of instruction is for learners to know how to change a flat

Important

Professionals in Practice

Our task analysis is based on the skills a person must have to successfully install, implement, and modify our software in their business setting. Setting up a computer-based telephone system is an unforgiving assignment. Our task analysis starts at the bottom (installation and configuration) and works upward toward the ultimate goal ([a] dial tone or a working automatic call distribution system, for example). Typically, we rely on flowcharting to map out the expected output of each task and the dependencies of subsequent tasks. Failure to complete a task or incorrect execution of a task becomes apparent very quickly.

— Erik Novak
distance learning course developer
at Interactive Intelligence, Inc.
Indianapolis, Indiana

Teaching a dog to touch his or her nose to the end of a stick is a skill that can lead to many other tricks, such as closing an open door.

Please keep in mind that this example is provided to illustrate a relatively simple task that most people can identify with. In providing this example, we do not intend to minimize the role of instructional designer to that of someone who solely creates training that deals with dogs. We recognize that most tasks you will analyze will not be as simplistic and follow such a strictly behavioristic approach. As an instructional designer, you will be involved in analyzing many complex behaviors, such as the performance of a cardiac catheterization by a doctor.

1. **Obtain the necessary supplies.**
    a. Training clicker
    b. Dog treats
    c. Yardstick
    d. Plastic lid from a yogurt container (or a similar-size, round, flat object)
    e. Adhesive to attach lid to the end of the yardstick
2. **Get ready to train your dog.**
    a. Break the treats into small pieces.
    b. Place the treats in your pocket or in an easily accessible place.
    c. Put the clicker in your dominant hand.
    d. Find a comfortable area where you and your dog will not be distracted.
3. **Train your dog to respond to the clicker.**
    a. Have your dog in front of you.
    b. Click the clicker one time.
    c. Immediately give your dog a treat.
    d. Repeat steps b and c several times until your dog recognizes that he or she will receive a treat each time he or she hears the clicker.
        i. An attentive dog means the dog recognized that a click will be followed by a treat.
    e. Stop the activity for at least 15 minutes.
    f. Repeat steps a through c.
4. Train your dog to "touch."
    a. After you think your dog recognizes that he or she will receive a treat each time he or she hears a click, a new step can be added.
        i. Typically, you will not attempt this step until at least 1 day has passed.
    b. Make sure you have plenty of small pieces of dog treats.
    c. Put your clicker in your hand.
    d. Have your dog in front of you.
    e. Touch the palm of your hand to your dog's nose and at the same time click the clicker and say, "Touch."
    f. Immediately give your dog a treat.
    g. Repeat this process several times.
    h. Touch the palm of your hand to your dog's nose and say, "Touch" at the same time.
    i. Do not use the clicker.

FIGURE 4.1 Result of a Task Analysis: Outline Format

i. Immediately give your dog a treat.
j. Repeat this process several times.
k. Move back at least 1 foot from your dog.
l. Hold out your hand to the side with your palm open.
    i. Your hand should be at the level of your dog's height.
m. Say, "Touch."
    i. Your dog should move and touch his or her nose to your palm.
        (1) Immediately give your dog a treat and praise.
        (2) If your dog does not touch his or her nose to your palm, you may need to move your hand closer to his or her nose and attempt the process again or go back to step e if moving your palm closer to his or her nose does not work.
    ii. Repeat steps l and m several times.

5. Train your dog to touch a round lid on the end of a yardstick.
a. Attach the round lid to the end of the yardstick.
b. Make sure you have plenty of small pieces of dog treats.
c. Put your clicker in your hand.
d. Have your dog in front of you.
e. Hold out the yardstick with the lid on the end of it.
f. Touch the lid to your dog's nose and say, "Touch" at the same time.
g. Immediately give your dog a treat.
h. Repeat this process several times.
i. Move back at least 1 foot from your dog.
j. Hold out the stick with the lid on the end.
k. Say, "Touch."
    i. Your dog should move and touch the lid with his or her nose.
    ii. If your dog does not do this, repeat steps e through h.
l. Immediately give your dog a treat and praise.
m. Repeat this process several times.
n. Move back several feet and hold out either your palm or the yardstick and give the command "Touch."
    i. Immediately give a treat and praise when the dog touches your palm or the stick.
    ii. Eventually move the target higher and lower to challenge the dog.

FIGURE 4.1 *Continued*

tire, the task analysis approach that should be used will be one that is best-suited for analyzing procedural tasks. An important thing to remember regarding task analysis is that no single approach works for every situation. Successful instructional designers are able to select the appropriate approach based on the context and the instruction that needs to be developed and then modify the approach to meet their particular needs.

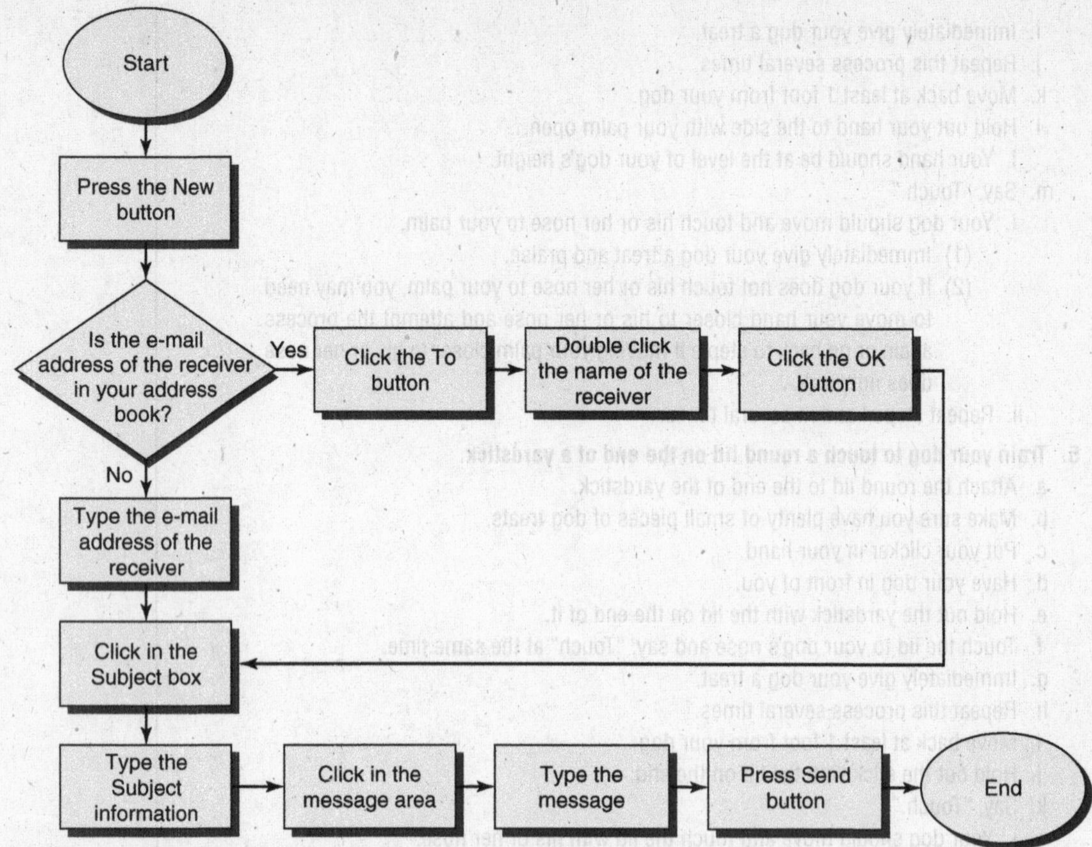

FIGURE 4.2 Result of a Task Analysis: Flowchart Format

This flowchart depicts the process of sending an e-mail in Microsoft Outlook.

EVALUATING THE SUCCESS OF A TASK ANALYSIS

How do you know that you have conducted a successful task analysis? How do you know that you correctly analyzed the content and/or tasks that will be part of the instruction that needs to be developed? Probably one of the most effective methods for determining the success of your task analysis during the design and development of instruction is to ask a subject matter expert who was not part of the task analysis to look over what you created and evaluate it for accuracy and thoroughness. This formative evaluation activity will provide a valuable perspective that you can use to compare to the data you gathered during your task analysis.

Another method to evaluate the effectiveness of your task analysis is to compare it to the other available information that has been gathered during the instructional design process, such as the needs analysis and learner analysis. Do the results of the task analysis match what is known about the goal of the instruction being developed? Have you gathered the necessary information about the content and/or tasks that will help learners meet the instructional goal? Additionally, what is known about the learners? Have the correct prerequisite content and/or skills that need to be included in instruction been correctly identified? Taking a step back from the task analysis results and comparing them to other information you have available will allow you to evaluate—to some degree—the initial effectiveness of your task analysis.

Finally, an obvious summative evaluation activity that can be conducted once the instruction has been implemented is to take a look at the success of the instruction. Were the learners able to accomplish the instructional goal? If the learners were successful, more than likely your task analysis was effectively conducted.

TASK ANALYSIS AND THE INSTRUCTIONAL DESIGN PROCESS

A task analysis is vital in helping an instructional designer to identify the task or tasks that guide the instruction being developed. A task analysis should help you answer the following questions, regardless of the approach taken:

1. What is the task that individuals need to be able to accomplish or perform?
2. What are the key components of this task (that is, the skills and knowledge an individual needs in order to successfully complete or perform the task)?
3. What is the sequence in which a task is accomplished or performed and should be learned and taught?
4. How can you determine whether an individual is able to complete the task?

Jody followed the procedural analysis approach. With this approach, she analyzed the task of admitting new patients by identifying the various steps required to successfully complete the task. In conducting the procedural analysis, Jody went through the steps with a veteran nurse and a hospital admissions expert. Once they had the steps listed, the group performed the process with an actual patient being admitted on the maternity ward. This helped Jody identify if there were any missing steps. The result of the procedural analysis was a flowchart that identified the different substeps that needed to take place in order for a nurse to successfully admit a new patient. The flowchart was compared to the information used in the current training. Jody determined that the current training left out important steps and that new training needed to be developed.

Ben's task analysis focused on the content he was teaching. He created an inventory (a list) of the steps he taught his students to go through—along with the content associated with the steps. Ben took this inventory and shared it with several colleagues who are experts in qualitative research design to determine if he was leaving something out. His colleagues agreed that the inventory was thorough and that Ben was including the proper content and skills in his instruction. Ben was happy and puzzled with the results—happy because his colleagues helped him determine he was not leaving anything out but puzzled because his students were not doing well. This led Ben to suspect that the organization, presentation, and management of his instruction may be causing the problem.

Summary

Task analysis is often considered to be the most critical component of instructional design. For effective instruction to be developed, instructional designers need to be able to determine the content and/or the tasks that will make up the instruction. A properly conducted task analysis will help an instructional designer to accomplish this. Numerous task analysis procedures exist that can be used by instructional designers depending on the context that surrounds the instruction that needs to be developed. Popular approaches to task analysis include those outlined by Jonassen, Hannum, and Tessmer; Morrison, Ross, and Kemp; Dick, Carey, and Carey; and Smith and Ragan. Most task analysis procedures include the use of a subject matter expert (SME), who assists the instructional designer by providing guidance on the scope and sequence of the content and tasks that need to be included in the instruction (which in most cases is based on the needs analysis and learner analysis). The result of a task analysis is a scope and sequence of the content and/or tasks that will make up the instruction. Typically, this will take the form of an outline or a graphical representation, such as a flowchart. Evaluating the effectiveness of a task analysis is often done during the design and development of the instruction by having an SME not involved in the initial task analysis critique the results of the task analysis or by comparing the results to other information gathered during instructional design (e.g., needs analysis or learner analysis). Once the results have been evaluated and modified (if necessary), they are used to develop specific learning goals and objectives that learners will be expected to meet during instruction.

Connecting Process and Practice

1. A variety of approaches to task analysis were outlined in the chapter. What key elements for conducting a task analysis do these approaches have in common? How do these approaches differ?
2. Examine the approaches taken by Ben and Jody. Do you believe each took the appropriate task analysis approach? Explain why you believe the approach each took is appropriate or what you might do differently if you were in their positions.
3. Consider Ben's approach. Does his approach follow one that was discussed in the chapter? Explain your answer.
4. Describe an instructional design scenario where you believe a task analysis would be difficult to carry out?
5. Select a common activity that you regularly do. Conduct a task analysis on this activity.
6. You have been hired by a client to work on an instructional design project. The client is an international phone company. The client has indicated that over 100 operators need to be trained on how to provide customers who call a toll-free number with information about the company's different products and services. The operators need to be trained on how to access this information through the company's electronic knowledge base and provide this information to the customers in a timely and accurate manner.
7. How might a high school teacher go about conducting a task analysis when preparing instruction on the causes of World War II that will be delivered in his or her Advanced Placement History class?

Recommended Reading

Chipman, S. F., Schraagen, J. M. & Shalin, V. L. (2000). An introduction to cognitive task analysis. In J.M. Schraagen, S. F. Chipman & V.L. Shalin (Eds.), *Cognitive task analysis* (pp. 3–23). Mahwah, NJ: Lawrence Erlbaum Associates.

Jonassen, D. & Hannum, W. (1995). Analysis of task analysis procedures. In G. J. Anglin, (Ed.), *Instructional technology: Past, present, and future*. Englewood, CO: Libraries Unlimited.

Jonassen, D., Hannum, W. & Tessmer, M. (1989). *Handbook of task analysis procedures.* New York: Praeger.

Jonassen, D., Hannum, W. & Tessmer, M. (1999). *Task analysis methods for instructional design.* Mahwah, NJ: Lawrence Erlbaum Associates.

Mager, R. & Pipe, P. (1984). *Analyzing performance problems: Or you really oughta wanna.* Belmont, CA: Lake Publishing Company.

Morrison, G. R., Ross, S. M. & Kemp, J. E. (2006) *Designing effective instruction, 4th edition.* Hoboken, NJ: John Wiley & Sons.

References

Dick, W., Carey, L. & Carey, J. O. (2009). *The systematic design of instruction, 7th edition.* Columbus, OH: Allyn & Bacon.

Gagne, R., Wagner, W., Golas, K. & Keller, J. (2004). *Principle of instructional design, 5th edition.* Florence, KY: Wadsworth Publishing.

Heinich, R., Molenda, M., Russell, J. & Smaldino, S. (2002). *Instructional media and technologies for learning, 7th edition.* Boston: Merrill Prentice Hall.

Jonassen, D. S., Hannum, W. H. & Tessmer, M. (1989). *Handbook of task analysis procedures.* New York: Praeger.

Jonassen, D. S., Tessmer, M. & Hannum, W. H. (1999). *Task analysis methods for instructional design*, New Jersey: Lawrence Erlbaum Associates.

Mager, R. & Pipe, P. (1984). *Analyzing performance problems: Or you really oughta wanna.* Belmont, CA: Lake Publishing Company.

Morrison, G. R., Ross, S. M. & Kemp, J. E. (2006) *Designing effective instruction, 4th edition.* Hoboken, NJ: John Wiley & Sons.

Smith, P. L. & Ragan, T. J. (2004). *Instructional design, 2nd edition.* Hoboken, NJ: John Wiley & Sons.

Chapter 5

Learner Analysis

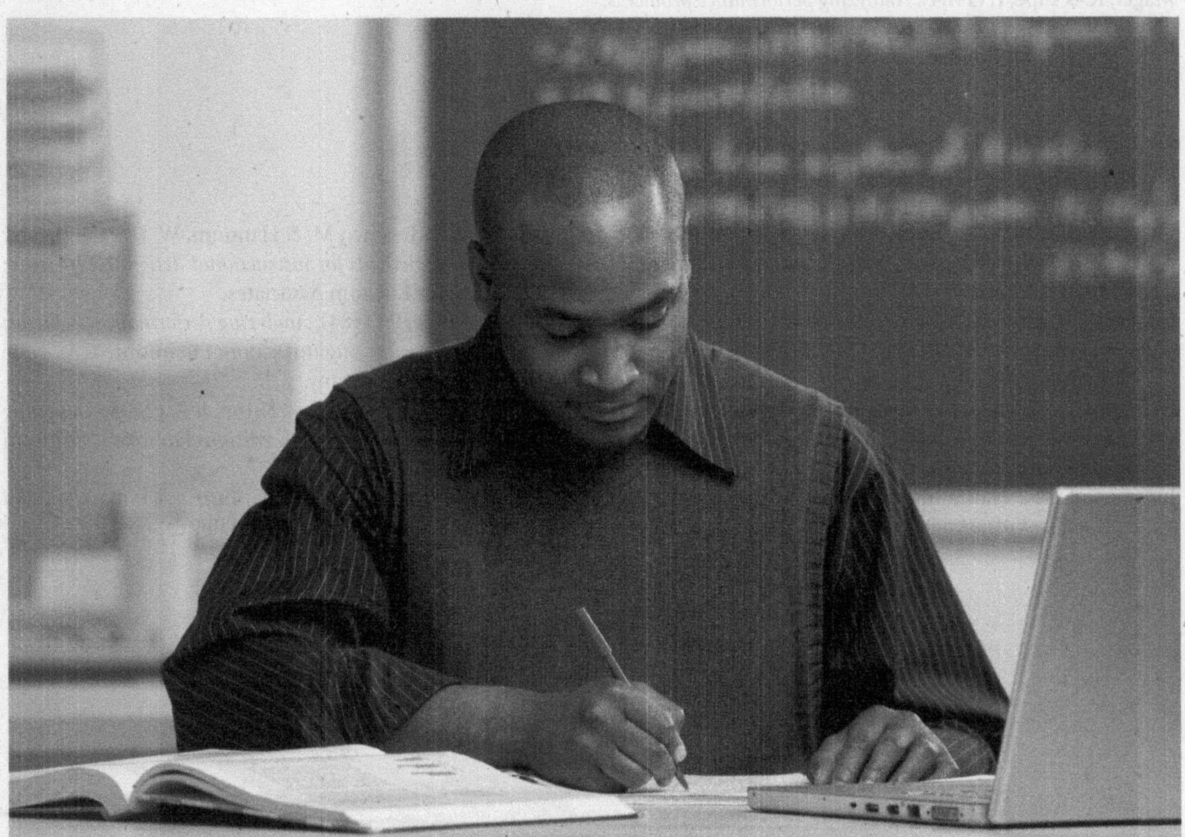

"I don't know how I'm going to make this work!" exclaimed Alice after receiving an assignment to create a Web-based course on dealing with harassment in the workplace. "Everyone in the company—from senior executives to new hires in the mailroom—is supposed to take this course. How am I supposed to design something that is appropriate for everyone?"

Alice is aware of the company's need for the instruction, and she knows the tasks necessary to complete the instruction. What she is having trouble with is finding a way to design the instruction that is appropriate for her audience—an audience that consists of a great many people, all of whom have different levels of skill and experience.

Meanwhile, across town at Washington Middle School, David is developing a set of lessons for the upcoming school year's oceanography unit. David will have over 70 middle school students in his classes, and although he knows they are all similar in age and educational background, David recognizes they are each unique individuals. David asks himself, "How do I present lessons that everyone will consider interesting and engaging?"

Alice and David both need to conduct a learner analysis, and each one needs to decide on the best learner analysis approach for his or her situation.

GUIDING QUESTIONS

- What does an instructional designer need to know about the learners for whom he or she is creating instruction?
- How does one determine the common attributes of a group of learners?
- What common attributes among a group of learners are most important to determine for purposes of designing instruction?
- How does one organize the data collected about the learners into a format that is useful?
- How can one determine if a learner analysis is accurate?

KEY TERMS

Changing Differences *80*
Changing Similarities *80*
Diagnostic Teaching *72*
Entry Competencies *78*
Learner Characteristics *81*
Learner-centered Environments *72*
Learning Styles *78*
Member Check *83*
Motivation *74*
Stable Differences *80*
Stable Similarities *79*
Universal Design for Education *80*

CHAPTER OVERVIEW

A corollary activity to task analysis is learner analysis. Determining the learners' approach to the instruction—including prerequisite knowledge, skills and attitude toward the task—is an important part of effective design and development. This chapter describes various methods of determining and articulating learner predispositions, knowledge, and skills. Approaches taken by a variety of instructional design experts are presented and explained. This chapter also offers suggestions for formatting the data gathered in order to make it useful during the design and development of the instruction and recommends methods of evaluating the effectiveness of a learner analysis.

ANALYZING LEARNERS

There is not much point to creating an instructional intervention that the intended audience cannot or will not use. Understanding the target audience of learners and determining in advance what they can and will do is an essential element of any instructional plan. In order to gain understanding of the target audience, one must conduct some form of preliminary evaluation of that group. Learner analysis is considered a critically important component of the instructional design process.

There was a time when the majority of educators perceived the learner as an "empty vessel." The learner was without knowledge, and teaching was considered the act of "filling up" students with facts, procedures, and concepts. This approach has long since fallen into disfavor; most educators now perceive learners as individuals who come to each instructional situation with a variety of background experiences that affect the new experience. To appropriately prepare instruction requires consideration of the learners' prior knowledge, abilities, point of view, and perceived needs.

Bransford, Brown, and Cocking (2000) describe the importance of "**learner-centered environments**" where careful attention is given to the skills, knowledge, beliefs, and attitudes that learners bring to an instructional situation. This fits well with the concept of "**diagnostic teaching**" (Bell, O'Brien & Shiu, 1980), which approaches instructional problems through the development of a thorough understanding of the conceptual and cultural knowledge students bring with them to the educational environment.

Just about everyone would agree that instructional design requires some understanding of the learner, but actually gaining that understanding through a trustworthy, reliable process can be a challenge. There is no single, correct method of learner analysis that every instructional designer uses. However, the goal of every type of learner analysis is the same: to understand and interpret learner characteristics in a way that helps in the design of effective instruction.

Gagne, Wager, Golas, and Keller (2005) explain goals of learner analysis as a rational approach to reducing the vast number of individual learner characteristics to a single set of general characteristics that make instructional planning feasible through the identification of common learner characteristics that have a direct impact on the instructional design and the range of learners' experiences and abilities that will affect the learning results. In other words, a learner analysis identifies the critically important general traits of a group as well as identifying the range of skills and talents within that group that are relevant to the instructional situation.

Some aspects of learner analysis are easily quantifiable, and gathering this data is a relatively simple matter. For example, it is not difficult to accurately determine physical characteristics such as age or gender. However, cultural and psychological information can be far more difficult to define accurately.

While it is important to carefully consider the cultural and psychological aspects of the target audience, the number of variables involved in determining in advance precisely what will be "culturally appropriate" or "psychologically optimal" instruction are beyond our current control. The most thorough learner analysis is still a matter of taking a "best guess" at how the instruction should be designed to work efficiently and effectively for the target audience.

There are a number of theoretical constructs and recommended practices that can help an instructional designer conduct the best possible learner analysis. Approaching the task by making use of these constructs and practices can significantly improve the chances of determining what type of instruction will work for the target audience.

Human Needs

Before looking at the intended audience as a group of learners, it is a good idea to recognize them as a group of *human beings.* Basic human wants and needs must be addressed before any instructional intervention is attempted. While it is not the instructional designer's role to provide for each of these needs, it is in everyone's best interest to be at least familiar with how to gauge an individual or group's instructional readiness at this most essential level.

One of the most popular theoretical constructions to address the issue of human needs is Maslow's *Hierarchy of Needs* (Maslow, 1968). Maslow's theory assumes that at any given time, a person's behavior is determined by his or her needs. The Hierarchy of Needs is typically depicted as a pyramid that has at its base the general physiological comforts, such as hunger and thirst. Once these bodily comforts are met, one may address the more abstract needs of knowledge, aesthetics, and self-fulfillment. At its pinnacle, Maslow's hierarchy (see Figure 5.1) places the ability to help others find self-fulfillment (transcendence) (Orlich, Harder, Callahan, Trevisan & Brown, 2007).

An example of addressing the needs of the learner according to Maslow's hierarchy would be ensuring that learners are not particularly hungry when they participate in instruction (in schools, this may be addressed through a free lunch or breakfast program; in a corporate setting, this may be addressed by providing snacks or a meal as part of the instructional event). Once it has been established that the intended audience's needs are met to a point where they are ready to receive instruction, the designer must determine

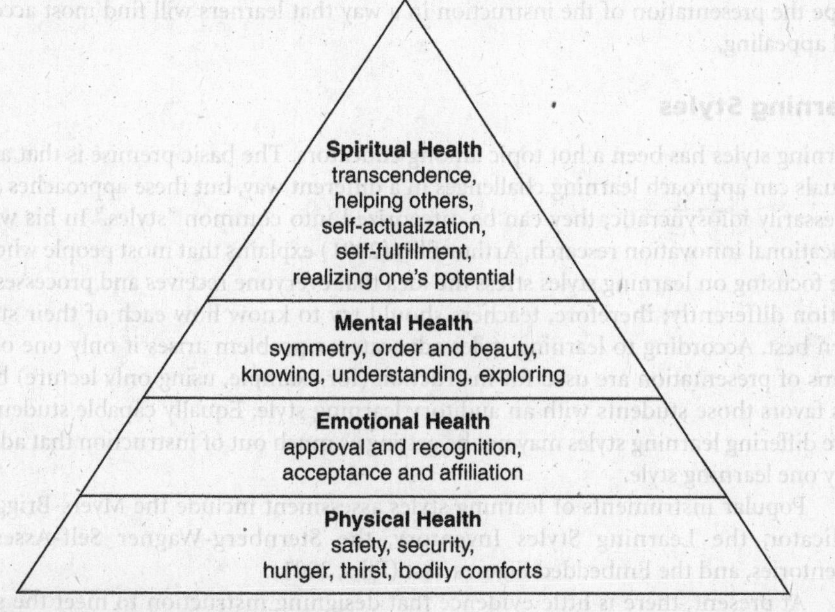

FIGURE 5.1 Maslow's Hierarchy of Needs

what content the learners are prepared for and how best to deliver that content to keep all participants active and interested.

Captive Audience or Willing Volunteers?

For any instructional activity, participants can be divided into two categories: "captive audiences" or "willing volunteers." Captive audiences are those people who receive a mandate to receive the instruction developed (for example, in the United States, children are required to attend school; they are a captive audience). Willing volunteers participate in the instructional activity because they are motivated to do so without a mandate: taking courses for pleasure or pursuing an advanced degree are most often instructional activities in which individuals choose to participate. It is important to distinguish between captive audiences and willing volunteers because the two groups can behave very differently toward the instruction presented. One almost never hears an adult who has chosen to take a course in painting at a local community college ask, "Why are we doing this?" while grade-school pupils in a state-mandated mathematics class ask that question quite often. Determining the learners' motivations to participate in the developed instruction can greatly improve its effectiveness.

Motivation is a complicated subject that deserves continued study; here, we will discuss only its basic elements. Motivation can be essentially divided into two classes: intrinsic and extrinsic. If learners enjoy the instruction for its own sake and take pleasure in the activity, the motivation is said to be intrinsic. If learners participate in the instruction because they anticipate some reward beyond the instruction itself (for example, they are paid or completing the instruction allows them to do something they truly enjoy), the motivation is said to be extrinsic (Malone and Lepper, 1987). The question that must be answered while conducting a learner analysis is, "What motivates the target audience to participate in this instruction?" Determining what makes the students participate can help shape the presentation of the instruction in a way that learners will find most acceptable and appealing.

Learning Styles

Learning styles has been a hot topic among educators. The basic premise is that all individuals can approach learning challenges in a different way, but these approaches are not necessarily idiosyncratic; they can be categorized into common "styles." In his work on educational innovation research, Arthur Ellis (2001) explains that most people who advocate focusing on learning styles stress the idea that everyone receives and processes information differently; therefore, teachers should try to know how each of their students learn best. According to learning styles advocates, a problem arises if only one or a few forms of presentation are used for instruction (for example, using only lecture) because this favors those students with an auditory learning style. Equally capable students who have differing learning styles may not be getting as much out of instruction that addresses only one learning style.

Popular instruments of learning styles assessment include the Myers-Briggs Type Indicator, the Learning Styles Inventory, the Sternberg-Wagner Self-Assessment Inventories, and the Embedded Figures Test (Ellis, 2001).

At present, there is little evidence that designing instruction to meet the specific learning styles of individuals increases academic achievement (Ellis, 2001). However, awareness that learners comprehend information differently should remind anyone responsible for designing instruction to provide a number of activities that stimulate learners' thinking in a variety of different ways.

Universal Design for Education

Universal design for education or universal design for learning is an outgrowth of the universal design movements in architecture (Howard, 2003; Curry, 2003). Federal legislation, including the Architectural Barriers Act of 1968 and the Americans with Disabilities Act of 1990, support a universal design approach that makes all situations accessible to the widest possible variety of learners. Taking into consideration that physical and intellectual ability, cultural and ethnic background, and socioeconomic status can affect how people perceive and process information, the universal design for education movement seeks to create environments and instructional contexts that provide equal access to the resources necessary for academic success (Curry, 2003).

> "When schools introduce universal design, student diversity becomes a powerful component of the education environment. But implementing the universal design framework goes beyond accommodating individual learners. Because it makes education environments seamlessly and inherently functional for almost all students, universal design minimizes the need for individual accommodations."
>
> (Curry, pp. 56–57)

It is important to keep in mind that universal design for education is not only about accommodating learners who are mentally or physically disabled, but it is also about providing appropriate activities and challenges for gifted and talented students. Universal design for education strives to provide appropriate instructional opportunities for all learners in a way that goes beyond attaching "add-on" activities after the instructional design is completed (Howard, 2003). Instructional designers must be aware of the needs of diverse learners and plan activities that welcome meaningful participation by all members of the target audience. Following the principles of universal design for education can help make the planning process easier and the final product more efficient and effective for all participants.

User-Centered Design

Specialists in Human Computer Interaction (HCI) often discuss the need for a user-centered design approach. The essential premise of user-centered design is that learner (or user) analysis should be an ongoing activity throughout the process of designing and developing software. Consideration for the characteristics of the end user must be a part of the designer's thinking from beginning to end, "gathering, analyzing and specifying user personas, their tasks, their work environment, and usability and [user interface] requirements," (Seffah, 2003). An essential part of user-centered design is usability testing. Put simply, usability testing is an analysis method whereby observers watch individuals or groups use the product to complete a set of prescribed tasks. The problems the subjects encounter in completing the tasks indicate where product revision needs to occur.

Baek, Cagiltay, Boling, and Frick (2008) point out that user-centered design can be viewed as either product-oriented or process-oriented. With a product-oriented approach, the designer may view his or her task as that of creating a specific, fixed product others will use as is once it is released. With a process-oriented approach, the designer may view his or her task "in the context of human learning, work, and communication," (Baek et al.); the development of the product is then the result of a series of revisions based on end-user feedback.

> *"I remember watching a group of graduate students design an interactive kiosk display. In the prototype, a little bell sound accompanied the "next" button that took one to a new screen. During usability testing, it became obvious the bell sound was not helpful; the team observed that many of the end-users assumed the bell indicated some problem and they stopped using the software as soon as they heard the bell. Fixing this problem made the final product far more "usable" and effective."*
>
> *— Abbie Brown*
> *former teacher at George Washington Middle School*
> *Ridgewood, New Jersey*

User-centered design is intended as a way of looking at the entire software development process in terms of the end user instead of in terms of the programmer or the machine. Keeping the end user in mind is the key to learner analysis. A user-centered design approach is often useful for designing instruction in general and learner analysis in particular.

Alice ponders how best to approach her learner analysis. She does not have to worry about her learners' basic needs because the instruction is online and learners will engage with it at their convenience. However, the group is radically disparate in terms of age, education, and experience. Alice is determined to find a learner analysis approach that will help her create instruction that everyone finds effective and appealing.

David continues to consider how best to present instruction to his middle school students. They are all similar in age and education, they all have to work together during a specific class time, and they all need to feel safe and secure within the school setting. However, David recognizes his students are also unique and different from each other. Determining how these differences affect his instructional design is critically important to him.

POPULAR APPROACHES TO ANALYZING LEARNERS

A number of respected instructional design scholars have addressed the issue of learner analysis. The elements that are common to and unique among these approaches are worth examining as you begin to develop your own learner analysis methodology.

Robert F. Mager is an author of instructional design texts that have been popular for decades. His approach to learner analysis is a good place to start. Mager (1988) recommends the following procedure:

1. Begin with the realization that a learner analysis is a working document that will not be published or seen by anyone other than yourself and perhaps other members of the instructional design team. It is not necessary to organize the content into specific categories.

2. Write down everything you think you know about the target audience. If it seems challenging to get started, begin with trigger questions, such as: Why are they taking this course? Do they want to be in this course? What training and experience do they have in relation to the subject matter?
3. Describe the range of characteristics whenever possible.

A few critically important things to do when conducting a learner analysis include: Take care to describe the learners as they are, not as you would like them to be; describe people, not institutions or policies; describe the differences among the learners as well as the similarities; remember that you are creating a working document that can be amended during the development process (Mager, 1988).

Mager recommends analyzing and articulating the following about the target audience:

1. Age range
2. Sex distribution
3. Nature and range of educational background
4. Reason(s) for attending the course
5. Attitude(s) about course attendance
6. Biases, prejudices, and beliefs
7. Typical hobbies and other spare time activities
8. Interests in life other than hobbies
9. Need-gratifiers (rewards that would work)
10. Physical characteristics
11. Reading ability
12. Terminology or topics to be avoided
13. Organizational membership
14. Specific prerequisite and entry-level skills already learned (Mager, p. 60).

A common approach to the problem of learner analysis is to "ask the students themselves" by generating and distributing a survey or questionnaire. However, Mager asserts that questionnaires are *not* a useful source of information about the target audience:

> "Questionnaires are not a useful source of information about your students. Why izzat, you may wonder? It's because it takes a great deal of skill and time to prepare a questionnaire that will elicit the type of information you may want. Items have to be drafted, and they absolutely must be tested and then revised, and maybe tested again, before one can have any assurance at all that the questionnaire will work. And people with this specialized skill are rare. If they are skilled in questionnaire development, they are not likely to be working in a training department."
>
> (Mager, p. 59)

Mager's statement about questionnaires is open to debate. Powerful arguments can be developed for and against the use of questionnaires. It is important for instructional designers to consider the potential problems and benefits of this popular strategy.

Professionals in Practice

Learner analysis is difficult [at] the company I work for. We have a diverse group of people with varied education levels and performance abilities. For this reason, when considering implementing a new training project or program, it may not always be possible to complete a learner analysis for all those that may be using the training. I try to identify the key users of the new training material and the skill sets they should have. One method I use is surveying. Once the tasks have been identified, I will ask a random sample of technicians if they know how to complete the task or know the answer to the knowledge questions. I clarify with the technicians that this is just to get an understanding of the general knowledge of those that will be required to complete the tasks. This also helps in identifying if additional training information may be required, such as job aids, 1:1 training, etc.

— Jona Titus
senior training specialist
for Intel Corporation
Beaverton, Oregon

Smaldino, Lowther, and Russell (2008) take a different approach. They suggest that the learner analysis should focus on three aspects of the target audience: general characteristics, specific **entry competencies,** and **learning styles.**

- ***General Characteristics*** Demographic information, such as the learners' ages, physical abilities, or socioeconomic status; the learner's cultural identification or shared values; and the amount of previous experience with the content to be covered can all help the designer make informed decisions about how to prepare and deliver the instruction.
- ***Specific Entry Competencies*** Prior knowledge that is necessary for learners to succeed with the instruction is critically important to the success of any instructional design project (for example, there is not much point to creating instruction on how to conduct research on the Web if the target audience does not know how to use a mouse).
- ***Learning Styles*** The psychological predilections of individuals affect what they find to be attractive and effective instruction. Gardner's (1993) aspects of intelligence (verbal/linguistic; logical/mathematical; visual/spatial; musical/rhythmic; bodily/kinesthetic; interpersonal; naturalist and existentialist) and Gregorc's "mind styles" (Butler, 1986) (concrete-sequential, concrete-random, abstract-sequential, and abstract-random) are examples of explanations of how people prefer to approach and deal with problem-solving and instruction. Knowledge of these preferences may help the designer create instruction that is easily understood and accepted by the target audience.

Dick, Carey, and Carey (2009) list the following as useful information for instructional designers about the target population:

- Entry skills (similar to Heinich, Molenda, Russell, and Smaldino's entry competencies)
- Prior knowledge of topic area
- Attitudes toward content and potential delivery system
- Academic motivation

Professionals in Practice

We don't usually have the luxury of doing a formal learner analysis. For live classes, we have a list of prerequisites that a person should possess before attending. If someone attends without the prerequisites, they may be in for a rough ride. We are very specific about prerequisites. Here are several examples:

- Have experience with graphical user administration tools on a data or voice network.
- Have installed Windows NT or Windows 2000 and service packs.
- Be able to establish a Windows 2000 LAN connection.
- Have a current working knowledge of a fourth-generation programming language or event-driven language (e.g., Visual Basic, C, C++, PowerBuilder, Delphi, Basic, or another procedural language) and have built an application using tools associated with that language.

If we are building an online class, the same criteria apply.

— Erik Novak
distance learning course developer
at Interactive Intelligence, Inc.
Indianapolis, Indiana

- Educational and ability levels
- General learning preferences
- Attitudes toward the training organization
- Group characteristics

Two items from this list—*attitudes toward content and potential delivery system and attitudes toward the training organization*—are important reminders to take into consideration the impressions and prejudices that the learners may have about the instructional content, the method of instruction, and the group providing the instruction. These impressions can have a tremendous impact on the effectiveness of the instruction. Furthermore, it is possible to improve the learners' receptiveness to the instruction by recognizing and addressing the learners' pre-existing attitudes either by capitalizing on positive impressions or addressing early on the concerns raised by negative impressions.

Smith and Ragan (2005) approach learner analysis by suggesting that the designer categorize learners by their stable and changing similarities and differences:

- ***Stable Similarities*** Learners are generally "configured" similarly (the eyes and ears are located in the same location—as are legs and arms—and the vast majority of learners convert oxygen to carbon dioxide through respiration). Perhaps more important to an instructional designer is knowledge of the perceptual similarities among human beings. For example, human beings can only see what is in their field of vision, and the eyes come with a mechanism for blocking out visual stimuli altogether (the eyelid); however, human hearing is not something that needs to be directed (there is no "field of hearing"; we hear everything around us whether or not we direct our attention toward the noise) nor can humans block hearing (there is no "ear-lid"). As another example, healthy human vision systems can read static text (this is called "scanning"), and they can follow movement within their field of vision (this is called "tracking"), but they cannot do both at the same time (although the vision system can switch between these two tasks in microseconds, which coincidentally causes considerable fatigue). The way human vision works is something anyone designing instructional multimedia should take into consideration.

- ***Stable Differences*** Any group of learners can be divided into subgroups that are inherently different from the larger group. These differences may be physical (such as gender or age), psychological (including differing learning styles and levels of intelligence), or psychosocial (Smith and Ragan describe these as personality traits that affect one's performance in a learning environment).
- ***Changing Similarities*** Certain types of human development have been studied extensively, and the observations made by researchers indicate that processes such as physical, intellectual, and language development are by and large the same for all people. For example, children develop physical dexterity more slowly than they do intellectual and language skills. Indeed, a typical six-year-old can describe the activity of creating a toy parachute and can discuss why the parachute slows the descent of the object to which it is attached, but the child will probably not have the dexterity necessary to assemble the parachute. An instructional designer can use knowledge of human development to prepare lessons and activities that are most appropriate for the learner.
- ***Changing Differences*** Knowledge, values, skills, beliefs, and motivations change over time, and they combine uniquely for each individual. These changing differences may be the most difficult thing for an instructional designer to effectively prepare for. Nonetheless, it is important to recognize that a number of changing differences come into play when considering a group of learners.

Morrison, Ross, and Kemp (2007) approach learner analysis in a manner similar to Smaldino, Lowther, and Russell (2008) by examining the learners' general characteristics, entry competencies, and learning styles.

Morrison, Ross, and Kemp recommend special attention be paid to the needs of culturally diverse learners as well as learners with disabilities. Designing with diverse learners in mind has become a popular topic in recent years. An approach that is gaining popularity is **universal design for education**, which plans for instruction by planning for the active participation of culturally and physically diverse learners.

Professionals in Practice

When I taught 8th-grade English, I would meet with the 7th-grade teachers each summer to learn about the students who would be entering my class in the fall. It was important to hear about individuals and the group as a whole in order to prepare coursework and activities. However, I knew the vast physical and emotional changes that many of the students would go through over the summer would alter both individuals themselves as well as the group dynamic. I used the information the 7th-grade teachers provided while keeping in mind that the students I would meet in the fall would be three months older and would have summer experiences that might change their values and perceptions.

— *Abbie Brown*
former teacher at George Washington Middle School
Ridgewood, New Jersey

LEARNER ANALYSIS PROCEDURES

All the approaches described previously have one thing in common: They stress the need to gather information about the target audience in order to create instruction that is effective, efficient, and appealing for that specific group. All the approaches point out that some types of data are more useful than others in determining appropriate instruction and recognize that even the most careful analysis is going to result in taking a "best guess" at the learners' skills and needs. Another element common to most learner analysis approaches is the recognition that members of any group are going to range in ability and interest. Keeping all this in mind, the instructional designer must create a useful working document that describes the target audience. There are numerous possibilities for creating such a document; two of these possibilities are:

1. A chart of **learner characteristics** data
2. A fictitious profile of the average member of the target audience

Charting Learner Characteristics Data

This activity involves deciding what data to gather and creating a chart that illustrates the range of the learners' abilities (see Figure 5.2). Typically, instructional designers define the range by describing the *average* learner, the *challenged* learner, and the *gifted and talented* learner. An average learner can be defined as the typical participant—the person who is most similar to the largest portion of the target audience. The challenged learner can be defined as an individual who does not have all the entry competencies as the average learner; the challenged learner may also have some differing physical abilities or learning characteristics. The gifted and talented learner can be defined as an individual with exceptional skills or abilities in all or part of the instructional content; this person may have had more training in the area or may excel naturally.

Learner Ability Chart

	Learners		
Data Type[a]	**Challenged**	**Average**	**Gifted and Talented**
Reading ability			
Maturity level			
Mechanical dexterity			

[a] The abilities listed were chosen from those described in Mager's (1997) and Morrison, Ross, and Kemp's (2004) approaches to learner analysis for illustration purposes only. The actual abilities chosen for a specific chart depend on the goal of and the context for the instruction.

FIGURE 5.2 A Learner Ability Chart

Creating a Fictitious Profile of the Typical Learner

Another method of compiling the data gathered about the target audience is to create a fictitious profile of the "typical" member of the group. This requires a little creativity; the learner has to be created from the data provided plus some fictional elements (such as a name).

To fully develop a profile of the typical learner, consider what the learner might say about him or herself, what other people might say about him or her, and what performance evidence is available about the target audience (e.g., grades in previous courses or projects completed in other instructional settings). Comparing the perceptions and reports of different sources about the same subject is sometimes referred to as "triangulation" by those who conduct research in the social sciences. Triangulation is a very good way to develop a complete profile (see Figure 5.3).

Both charting and the creation of fictitious profiles have strengths and weaknesses. A chart is a handy reference that provides information at a glance, but charts tend to be a bit clinical and can lead to a less humanistic approach to designing instruction. Also, charts tend to imply that the information is perfectly reliable even though learner analysis is not an exact science.

On the other hand, profiles are far less clinical, creating a target human being to design for. However, the information is less readily accessible than a chart, and the creative embellishments may prove more distracting than productive. The job of the instructional designer is to find the right balance between clinical data and creative interpretation that works for the context of the assignment.

EVALUATING THE SUCCESS OF A LEARNER ANALYSIS

After conducting a learner analysis, how do you know that the results of the analysis are accurate? How do you know that the data gathered has helped to create the best possible instruction? The only sure way to know is to compare the learner analysis results with information on the students who participate in the instruction and listen to what students have to say about the instruction after they have completed it. This is an important summative evaluation activity that will help in determining the best course of action for subsequent learner analyses.

Learner Profile

This profile describes characteristics similar to those listed in Table 7.1, but some embellishments were added to give the example personal characteristics that a designer can relate to on a human level. Separate profiles can be created to describe challenged learners and gifted and talented learners.

Shirley is 24 years old with a bachelor's degree in liberal arts from a local university. She is married and has a toddler son. She is concerned about spending too much time at work, away from her family. Shirley reads at a ninth-grade level (above average nationally, average for college graduates). She is a competent computer user and types about 60 words per minute.

FIGURE 5.3 A Learner Profile

One way to evaluate the learner analysis during the design and development of the instruction (part of a formative evaluation) is to conduct a **member check.** A member check is a comparison method of evaluation; the interpretations drawn from the data gathered are shared with a peer who has similar experiences with developing instruction for a similar population. If the data and interpretations seem familiar and appropriate to the person with similar experiences, it suggests that the learner analysis was successful.

A member check can also be conducted with someone from the target audience. Asking a member of the target audience if the profile developed seems appropriate (essentially asking, "Is this you?") can be very helpful in determining the success of the analysis.

Alice comes to a decision regarding her learner analysis approach. She knows that everyone in the company must complete the training, and the company employs people who vary widely in age, work experience, and education. She also recognizes that her learners are a "captive" audience (they are required to complete the harassment training), and the vast majority will be motivated extrinsically (they must complete the training to continue working for the company). Alice decides to take a universal design for education approach: She will identify members of the company who represent the range of learners and conduct regular member checks, asking the representatives to respond to draft versions of the instruction periodically as she develops the instruction. Alice also decides to use Smaldino, Lowther, and Russell's suggestion to focus on her learners' general characteristics—entry competencies and learning styles to create instruction that can be used successfully by everyone in the company.

David has also come to a design decision. David knows his learners are a homogeneous group in terms of age and education, but they will vary in terms of ability. David recognizes that his learners are motivated both extrinsically and intrinsically (they are interested in learning, but grades are also a motivating factor). David understands that his learners are a "captive audience" because they are required to be in school, but many of them may see themselves as "willing volunteers" because school is an enjoyable and interesting activity. Because ability level is what varies most within his target audience, David has decided to chart learner characteristics data to determine how best to present lessons for average, challenged, and gifted and talented learners.

LEARNER ANALYSIS AND THE INSTRUCTIONAL DESIGN PROCESS

Conducting a learner analysis is a critically important part of the instructional design process. Regardless of the approach you take, completing a learner analysis should help you answer the following questions:

- Who is the intended audience for the instruction?
- What common traits do members of the learning group possess?
- What are the differences among learners within the group?
- What is the range of ability among the learners?
- What is the motivation for participating in the instructional event?
- Do the learners' have noninstructional needs (e.g., rest, food, safety) that must be met so that they may focus on the instructional activity?
- What will make the instruction effective, efficient, and appealing for the target audience of learners?

- How has the instructional designer or design team planned for the accommodation of culturally and physically diverse learners?
- What evaluation strategies will the instructional designer or design team use to determine the success of the learner analysis and how to refine future analyses for the instructional event?

Summary

Careful consideration of the target audience helps to ensure that the instructional design is effective and efficient for that audience. Learner analysis is a critically important component of any instructional design project. Although many educators once considered students to be "empty vessels" to fill with knowledge, the current perception is that students come to each instructional episode with their own skills, knowledge, and attitudes. There is no single, correct method of learner analysis. Some learner data is easily quantifiable (e.g., age); some data is difficult to quantify (e.g., cultural perspective). Even the most thorough learner analysis is a matter of taking a "best guess" about the target audience. It is not possible to know precisely how the learners will react to new instruction. However, a number of theoretical constructs exist to help the instructional designer conduct an effective learner analysis. At the most basic level, the instructional designer can determine in advance if the learners' human needs are being met. The designer can also determine whether the learners are choosing to participate in the instruction or if they are under some obligation to do so. Popular approaches to learner analysis include those outlined by Mager; Smaldino, Lowther, and Russell; Dick, Carey, and Carey; Smith and Ragan; and Morrison, Ross, and Kemp. Most experts agree that it is important to consider the entire range of the target audience when conducting a learner analysis; the high achieving and the challenged learners must be considered as well as the "average" learners. Two possible procedures for organizing learner analysis data are to create a chart of the data or to use the data to create a fictitious learner profile. Determining the accuracy and effectiveness of the learner analysis is an important evaluation activity in its own right. Comparing data and conclusions drawn with other educators who work with the same or similar populations is part of a formative evaluation. Gathering data about student reactions to the instruction (and interpreting that data) is an important summative evaluation activity.

Connecting Process to Practice

1. After reading about Alice's and David's instructional design challenges, do you think each of them made the right decision in how to approach a learner analysis for their respective projects? Explain why you think their approaches are appropriate or what you might do differently if you were in their positions.
2. You are an instructional designer for a large corporation. How would you go about conducting a learner analysis for a new course on maintaining good customer relations that every sales representative will be required to take?
3. You are the instructional designer for a university library and have been assigned the task of creating computer-based instruction on how to find and retrieve journal articles from an electronic database that will be delivered via the World Wide Web. What learner analysis processes will you use before you begin to design the instruction?
4. Try conducting a small learner analysis on your own family or a group of friends. Assuming the entire group is going to learn how to prepare the pasta dish fettuccini alfredo, what are the similarities and differences among the group that must be accounted for in order to make the instruction effective, efficient, and appealing?
5. You have been asked to design instruction on the history of jazz music for a local senior citizens center. What information about the learners would be most helpful to have before developing this instruction?
6. What general characteristics, entry competencies, and learning styles would you want to know about your learners before designing instruction on the proper method for taking a person's blood pressure?

Recommended Reading

Bransford, J. D., Brown, A. L. & Cocking, R. R. (Eds). (2000). *How people learn: Brain, mind, experience, and school.* Washington, DC: National Academy Press.

Mager, R. F. (1988). *Making instruction work.* Belmont, CA: Lake Publishing Company.

Norman, D. A. (1988). *The design of everyday things.* New York: Currency Doubleday.

References

Baek, E., Cagiltay, K., Boling, E. & Frick, T. (2008). User-centered design and development. In Spector, J. M., Merrill, M. D., Merrienboer, J. & Driscoll, M. P. (Eds.), *Handbook of research on educational communications and technology, 3rd edition.* New York: Lawrence Earlbaum Associates.

Bell, A. W., O'Brien, D. & Shiu, C. (1980). Designing teaching in the light of research on understanding. *Proceedings of the Fourth International Conference for the Psychology of Mathematics Education.* Berkeley, CA: The International Group for the Psychology of Mathematics.

Bransford, J. D., Brown, A. L. & Cocking, R. R. (Eds). (2000). *How people learn: Brain, mind, experience, and school.* Washington, DC: National Academy Press.

Butler, K. A. (1986). *Learning and teaching style: In theory and in practice, 2nd edition.* Columbia, CT: Learner's Dimension.

Curry, C. (2003). Universal design accessibility for all learners. *Educational Leadership, 61*(2), 55–60.

Dick, W., Carey, L. & Carey, J. O. (2009). *The systematic design of instruction, 7th edition.* Columbus, OH: Allyn & Bacon.

Ellis, A. K. (2001). *Research on educational innovations, 3rd edition.* Poughkeepsie, NY: Eye on Education.

Gardner, H. (1993). *Multiple intelligences: The theory in practice.* New York: Basic Books.

Gagne, R. M., Wager, W. W., Golas, K. C. & Keller, J. M. *Principles of instructional design, 5th edition.* Belmont, CA: Wadsworth/Thomson Learning.

Howard, J. (2003). Universal design for learning: An essential concept for teacher education. *Journal of Computing in Teacher Education, 19*(4), 113–118.

Mager, R. F. (1988). *Making instruction work.* Belmont, CA: Lake Publishing Company.

Malone, T. W. & Lepper, M. R. (1987). Making learning fun: A taxonomy of intrinsic motivations for learning. In R. E. Snow & M. J. Farr (Eds), *Aptitude, learning, and instruction III: Cognitive and affective process analysis.* Hillsdale, NJ: Lawrence Earlbaum Associates.

Maslow, A. H. (1968). *Motivation and personality.* New York: D. Van Nostrand.

Morrison, G. R., Ross, S. M. & Kemp, J. E. (2007). *Designing effective instruction, 5th edition.* New York: John Wiley & Sons.

Orlich, D. C., Harder, R. J., Callahan, R. C., Trevisan, M. S. & Brown, A. H. (2007). *Teaching strategies: A guide to effective instruction, 8th edition.* Houghton Mifflin Company.

Seffah, A. (2003). Human-centered design skills and patterns for software engineers' education. *Interactions: New Visions of Human-Computer Interaction, X*(5), 36–45.

Smaldino, S., Lowther, D. L. & Russell, J. D. (2008). *Instructional technology and media for learning, 9th edition.* Merrill Prentice Hall.

Smith, P. L. & Ragan, T. J. (2005). *Instructional design, 3rd edition.* New York: John Wiley & Sons.

Part III

CREATING INSTRUCTION: PLANNING, DESIGNING, AND IMPLEMENTING THE INTERVENTION

The needs, task, and learner analyses described in the previous part help you determine what kind of instructional intervention is best for your learners. Now it is time to decide how to best organize the events that make up that instructional intervention. Chapters 6, 7, and 8 describe the principles, processes, and practices of setting instructional goals and objectives, organizing instruction and selecting appropriate instructional activities.

Chapter 6 explains how instructional designers create **instructional goals and objectives**, which determine what students will actually do during the instruction. Chapter 7 introduces the principles, processes, and practices of **organizing** instruction, which helps the designer determine the scope and sequence of the activities that the learner will engage in. Chapter 8 describes the variety of **learning environments and instructional activities** that may be incorporated into an instructional design.

These goals, objectives, sequences, and activities are the elements of the instructional design to which learners will be directly exposed.

Chapter 6

Instructional Goals and Objectives

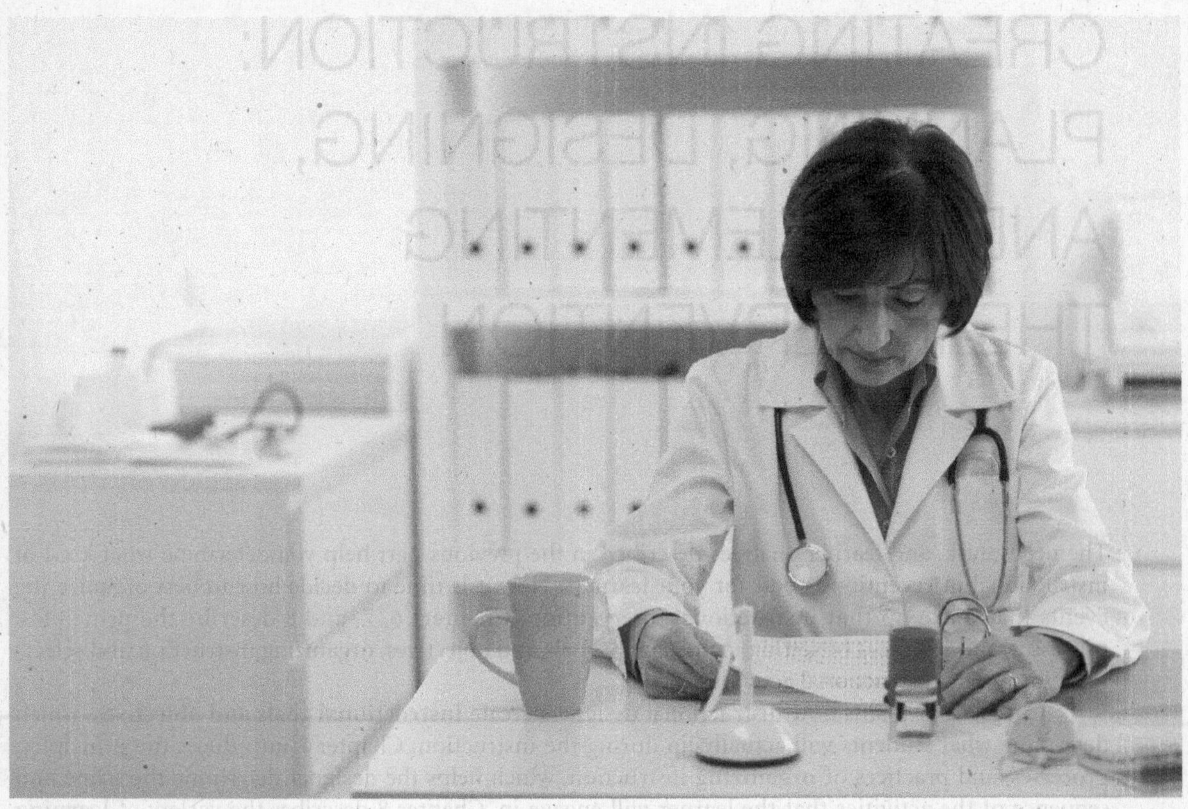

Susan is preparing instruction for hospital employees. Everyone at the hospital must follow the hand-washing procedure that hospital administration has identified as most effective. A need for instruction has been identified, and Susan knows the learners well. "What I need to do now," thinks Susan, "is determine exactly the goals and objectives for this instruction so we can determine the right activities and assessments to ensure a healthy and safe work environment."

At a northern university, Brian has been given the task of developing instruction on how to protect human subjects involved in research studies. The university president feels that the faculty need more information about how study participants are to be treated and the processes involved in getting the institution's approval of the research procedures. Like Susan, Brian understands the need for the instruction and is knowledgeable about the learners. Brian tells his instructional media production team: "The instruction needs to begin with an explanation its purpose. Faculty are going to want to know why they are doing this and what they are expected to accomplish."

GUIDING QUESTIONS

- What is an instructional goal?
- What is an instructional objective?
- How do instructional goals and objectives differ?
- How does one begin writing or identifying instructional goals?
- How does one create instructional objectives?

KEY TERMS

"ABCD" Approach *92*
Affective Knowledge *94*
Bloom's Taxonomy *93*
Cognitive, Affective, and Psychomotor Domains *90*
Declarative Knowledge *93*
Enabling Objective *90*
Functional Analysis System Technique (FAST) *91*
Gagne's Hierarchy of Intellectual Skills *93*
Performance Objectives *89*
Performance Technology Approach *89*
Procedural Knowledge *94*
Subject Matter Expert *89*
Subordinate Skills Analysis *90*
Terminal Objective *90*

CHAPTER OVERVIEW

Determining goals is an essential part of instructional design and development. Defining specific instructional objectives are also more often than not a critically important consideration. This chapter explains the differences between instructional goals and instructional objectives and examines a variety of approaches used to define and develop them. Approaches taken by a number of instructional design experts are presented and explained. Common methods of describing learning outcomes are presented, as are methods of evaluating the success of setting goals and objective specifications.

INSTRUCTIONAL GOALS AND OBJECTIVES

"My goal is simple: It is a complete understanding of the universe—why it is as it is and why it exists at all."

—*Stephen Hawking*

There is no point to creating any form of instruction without first setting goals for that instruction. The instructional intervention has to be designed to *do something*—to cause some change in the learner's knowledge, skill, or attitude. Otherwise, it is nothing more than a toy, a collection of artifacts, or an aimless discussion or presentation.

The Difference Between Goals and Objectives

Instructional goals and instructional objectives are different from each other. An instructional goal can be a general statement about the intention of the instruction. For example, "Students will become better writers" is an instructional goal. However, an instructional objective is usually much more specific about how and to what degree the instruction will affect the learners. Based on the goal "Students will become better writers," one instructional objective might be: "Upon completing the lesson, students will produce a traditional five-point essay with a recognizable introductory paragraph that includes a thesis statement, three paragraphs supporting the thesis statement, and a concluding paragraph that restates the thesis."

An instructional goal can be used as an organizing topic for subordinate instructional objectives. For example, the instructional goal "Students will recognize and value the behaviors of a healthy lifestyle" might serve as the organizing topic for a number of specific instructional objectives (see Figure 6.1).

The example goal and objectives used in Figure 6.1 all have one thing in common: They focus on what the learner will do upon completing the instruction. Keep in mind that this approach to designing instruction is a key component of instructional *systems* design. Other approaches to instructional design might not put as much emphasis on specific, observable learner outcomes and thus may not require objectives written in this manner.

Goal	Students will recognize and value the behaviors of a healthy lifestyle.
Objective 1	Students will *describe* the differences between complex and simple carbohydrates.
Objective 2	Students will *predict* the consequences of including too many simple carbohydrates in their diet.
Objective 3	Students will *create* an appropriate exercise plan for themselves on the basis of their personal requirements.
Objective 4	Students will *produce* a personal daily schedule that includes sufficient time for rest and recreation.

FIGURE 6.1 An Example of an Instructional Goal and Subordinate Objectives
Notice that all the objective statements include active verbs (*describe, predict, create, produce*).

Some designers feel that important outcomes of the instruction are difficult to define and measure (Morrison, Ross & Kemp, 2004); some would go as far as to say generating goals and objectives through traditional systems methods is not a useful pursuit. This would be in keeping with a postmodern philosophy that suggests that instruction should not necessarily be designed on the premise of a positivist worldview. The learner may deem the instruction successful because it accomplishes personal goals and objectives that the designer cannot determine in advance. We would argue that regardless of one's view, a design—by the very definition of the word—must have some goal defined at the outset, and instructional design is not an exception.

The development of instructional goals and objectives depends on the type and purpose of the instruction one is creating. Creating instructions on how to fly a fighter jet requires specific objectives that have demonstrable outcomes. However, creating instruction about the history of flight may not require objectives written according to a systems approach.

Susan considers how best to approach hand-washing instructions. The subject matter experts have provided her with a set of specific steps a person must follow to effectively wash one's hands. When she writes the goals and objectives for the instruction, Susan knows the objectives will have to describe how well the learners complete the steps involved in the hand-washing procedure because she will need to be able to point out specific actions taken by the learners that indicate they understand correct hand-washing methods.

Brian considers how best to explain the purpose of the instruction on treating human subjects. Because the instruction is a presentation of the reasoning behind creating safeguards for human subjects and the processes in place that protect people involved in research studies, he realizes that the goal will be relatively easy to state, but there will probably be few if any immediate and overt changes in the learners' behaviors as a result of this instruction.

POPULAR APPROACHES TO SETTING GOALS AND OBJECTIVES

The approach to developing learning objectives most often used by instructional designers was created by Robert Mager. Mager's approach is designed to generate **performance objectives** and is inextricably connected to behavioristic instructional design applications. Mager recommends using three components in writing learning objectives:

1. ***Action*** Identify the action the learner will take when he or she has achieved the objective.
2. ***Condition*** Describe the relevant conditions under which the learner will act.
3. ***Criterion*** Specify how well the learner must perform the action.

According to Mager, a learning objective is "a description of a performance you want learners to be able to exhibit before you consider them competent" (1984, p. 3). Dick, Carey, and Carey (2009) and Smaldino, Lowther, and Russell (2008) take similar approaches, focusing on the actions, conditions, and criteria.

Dick, Carey, and Carey suggest that goals and objectives are determined through one of two approaches. They are either prescribed by a **subject matter expert** (SME) or they are determined by a **performance technology approach**. SMEs may be called on to

Topic	Magnetic attraction
General purpose	To acquire knowledge and understanding of the properties of magnetic materials
Terminal objective	To describe the general properties of magnetic materials
Enabling objective	To discriminate between magnetic and nonmagnetic materials

FIGURE 6.2 An Example of Terminal and Enabling Objectives

work with the instructional designer to articulate the appropriate goals and objectives for an instructional design project. Instead of having an SME prescribe goals and objectives, a performance technology approach derives them from the data gathered during a needs analysis. According to Dick, Carey, and Carey, once the goals are established, a **subordinate skills analysis** should be conducted in order to determine the specific performance objectives for the instruction.

Smaldino, Lowther, and Russell (2008) describe the "**ABCDs**" of well-stated objectives. ABCD stands for Audience, Behavior, Conditions, and Degree:

- ***Audience*** Identify and describe the learners.
- ***Behavior*** Describe what is expected of the learner after receiving instruction.
- ***Conditions*** Describe the setting and circumstances in which the learners' performance will occur.
- ***Degree*** Explain the standard for acceptable performance.

Smaldino et al. also classify learning as belonging to one of four domains: cognitive, affective, motor skill (psychomotor), and interpersonal. It is the interpersonal domain classification that is unusual about this scheme. Skills that are people-centered, such as teamwork, administration, and salesmanship, are separated from the more traditional **cognitive, affective, and psychomotor domains** and are given a place of their own.

Morrison, Ross, and Kemp (2007) discuss the idea of terminal and **enabling objectives.** A **terminal objective** is the major objective for an instructional intervention. The terminal objective explains the overall learning outcome. The enabling objectives are supporting descriptions of observable behaviors or actions that indicate the terminal objective has been achieved (see Figure 6.2).

SETTING GOALS

Goals describe the intention of the instruction. According to Mager, "A goal is a statement describing a broad or abstract intent, state or condition," (1984, p. 33). In general, goals cannot be directly perceived. For example, the statement "Students will appreciate classical music" is a very reasonable instructional goal, but it does not have specific, observable features. The students may be listening, but how does one determine if they are appreciative?

Regardless of any lack of visible evidence, setting goals for instruction is a critically important part of the instructional design process. It is often relatively easy to write goals if one is starting with a "clean slate" situation—one in which no instructional interventions have been attempted and no past practices have been established.

Professionals in Practice

When I taught 8th-grade English, I traditionally ended the year by having my classes read Shakespeare's *As You Like It*. The goal was to build students' confidence with a difficult text (we did this through activities that included "translating" passages into modern language and acting out and illustrating scenes from the play). One year, I had a particularly difficult group of students; I decided not to read *As You Like It* with the group because I felt the goal of building their confidence would not be met—I felt that trying to do something this ambitious with this particular group might actually have the opposite effect.

When the students found out I was not planning to read Shakespeare with them in the spring, they expressed deep disappointment. I learned from them that reading a Shakespeare play in 8th grade was now considered a rite of passage by the students who had me as a teacher before. Regardless of the fact that I did not feel this activity was an appropriate way to address one of my goals for this particular group of students, I wound up doing it anyway because the students would have felt "cheated" if I had not. I realized that one goal for this activity was not something that I had created but that had grown out of the student community.

— Abbie Brown
former teacher at George Washington Middle School
Ridgewood, New Jersey

However, one is rarely offered a completely clean slate when designing instruction. Often, a number of established instructional interventions are in place, and people may have lost sight of the original goals for this instruction. Instructional designers almost always work within an organizational structure with its own idiosyncratic demands. More than likely, tradition, politics, and the predilections of decision-makers will be critical factors in determining the goals for any instructional design project (Dick, Carey & Carey, 2009).

In order to gain some sense of what the goals are for an instructional situation, one may have to begin by working backward by using the established practices as a foundation for articulating the larger goals. One method of determining instructional goals in this manner is to apply the **functional analysis system technique (FAST)** to create a FAST chart (Thornburg, 1998).

FAST charting was developed within the field of value engineering, where it is used to decrease costs, increase profits, and improve quality (for more on this, visit the Society of American Value Engineers website at http://www.value-eng.com or the SAVE International website at http://www.value-eng.org).

Using a FAST chart to determine the goals for instruction, one generates verb/noun pairs to describe the specific activities that apply directly to the outcome of the instruction (e.g., "write poem," "fix sink"). Increasing the abstraction of the verb/noun pairs with each successive description of the activity (putting the verb/noun pairs on sticky notes makes it particularly easy to rearrange things if and when the need arises). A simple example can be seen in Figure 6.3.

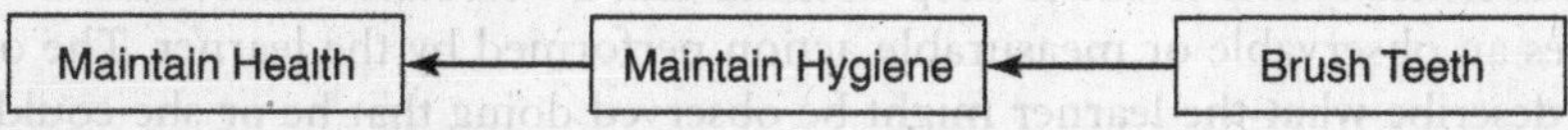

FIGURE 6.3 A Simple *FAST* Chart

Professionals in Practice

I begin setting the instructional goals and objectives when I am completing the front-end analysis. It is at this time that I can get a clear understanding of what the goals and objectives of the person requesting the training are. Because I've categorized the tasks required for the training into knowledge and performance activities, I can then verify these objectives once the task analysis is completed and include additional goals and objectives to the training. Often, I will have a large list of potential goals and objectives. Once I have my list, I work with the content expert and pare down the goals and objectives to a few key items, making sure to include a good balance of knowledge and performance objectives.

—Jona Titus
senior training specialist for Intel Corporation
Beaverton, Oregon

In the example FAST chart in Figure 6.3, "Maintain Health" would be the goal derived from the action of brushing one's teeth. To some, this may be obvious, but to many, the fact that children are taught to brush their teeth is so ingrained as a given activity that they lose sight of the fact that the larger goal is maintaining a healthy body. The FAST chart technique is particularly helpful when there is an established or expected set of instructional activities that are part of standard practice, where you as the instructional designer are trying to determine why those activities are important.

TRANSLATING GOALS INTO OBJECTIVES

Just as a goal is the intention of the instruction, an objective is the intended outcome of each instructional activity. The intended outcome can be described as what the learner will be able to do upon completing the instruction. Determining the intended outcome in advance is an important step in the design process if student success will ultimately be measured against some standard or specific evaluation criteria. Clearly stated instructional objectives also make it easier for a design team to produce instruction that meets with the approval of everyone involved. Smith and Ragan (2005) write:

> Objectives are valuable to all members of the learning system. They aid the designer since they provide a focus of the instruction, guiding the designer in making decisions about what content should be included, what strategy should be used, and how students should be evaluated. The specification of clear objectives is especially critical when a number of individuals—such as designers, content experts, graphic artists, and programmers—are working together to produce instruction. In these situations, learning objectives serve as a concrete focus of communication. (p. 97)

It is critically important to keep in mind that a well-stated instructional objective describes an observable or measurable action performed by the learner. The objective should describe what the learner might be observed doing that he or she could not do prior to the instruction. A typical "rookie mistake" is to write an objective that is actually a description of the instructional activity. "Students will view a 30-minute videotape on the basics of photography" is *not* a well-written instructional objective; a better objective would be: "At the end of viewing a 30-minute videotape on the basics of photography, students will demonstrate their ability to choose the correct f-stop setting for a variety of lighting conditions."

It would be difficult to discuss creating instructional objectives without making reference to **Bloom's taxonomy** (Bloom, Engelhart, Furst, Hill & Krathwohl, 1956). For fifty years, Bloom's taxonomy has been used by educators as a common point of reference for setting instructional objectives:

> Perhaps the taxonomy's greatest contribution has been in the development of a professional language. Teachers and administrators who describe and analyze instruction know that terms such as *knowledge level* and *higher levels of learning* will be understood by educators everywhere. (Orlich, Harder, Callihan, Trevison & Brown, 2010 p. 75).

Bloom's taxonomy is divided into three domains: cognitive, affective, and psychomotor (each of the domains is described in greater detail in Chapter 3). It is the cognitive domain (Figure 6.4) that is most often used by educators—no doubt because cognition is most often the focus of formal education.

The headings of Bloom's taxonomy can be used to write performance objectives. Objectives that begin with phrases such as "Students will *know* . . ."; "Students will *apply* . . ."; or "Students will *evaluate* . . ." are reasonably well-understood by educators because the taxonomy's description of the active verbs in these phrases creates a common understanding among those who are familiar with the taxonomy. The levels of the three domains are very good places to start when writing objectives. The headings for the levels of the cognitive and affective domains (words such as organize, value, respond, characterize, apply, know, evaluate, and analyze) are well-understood by most educators and make excellent verbs in written objectives.

Another theoretical construct that is popular among instructional designers and useful for determining instructional objectives is **Gagne's hierarchy of intellectual skills** (Gagne, 1985; Zook, 2001). Gagne takes an approach to the domains of instruction similar to that of Bloom's taxonomy, but there are important differences. Gagne divides what can be learned into three categories: **declarative knowledge** (verbal information),

Evaluating the value of material for a given purpose
Synthesizing something new from given material
Analyzing material by breaking it down into its components to understand its organizational structure
Applying learned material in new and concrete contexts
Comprehending new material
Knowing previously learned materia

FIGURE 6.4 Bloom's Taxonomy of Educational Objectives: Cognitive Domain

Problem solving. Students are asked to determine if the platypus is a mammal or a bird.

Rule or principle. The defined concepts are restated into general rules about how to decide if an animal is a mammal or a bird.

Defined concept. Students use their observations of mammals and birds to determine the differences between mammals and birds.

Discrimination. Students look at various mammals and birds.

FIGURE 6.5 Gagne's Hierarchy of Intellectual Skills.
In this hierarchy, you start at the bottom (discrimination) and work up to problem solving.

learning outcome: intellectual skill, cognitive strategy, verbal information, motor skill, and attitude. Gagne's hierarchy of intellectual skills (the skills most often addressed through instruction) states that there is a progression that can be followed to bring a student to the point of being able to solve problems on his or her own. The four steps in this progression are discrimination, defined concept, rule or principle, and problem-solving (see Figure 6.5).

Traditionally in instructional design, a goal is a general statement of the educator's intentions, and an objective is a specific instance of the goal in action. If the goal is "Students will develop social skills," specific objectives may include: "Students will say 'please' and 'thank you' at the appropriate times" or "Students will hold the door for each other as they enter and exit the building."

Articulating instructional goals is important; they are the written embodiment of the intention behind the instructional intervention. Using instructional goals to create instructional objectives can be equally important, particularly if the effectiveness of the instruction and the achievement of the learners will be tested by measuring them against a set of standards or a list of specific evaluation criteria. Well-stated objectives help everyone involved in creating and supporting the instructional event by providing focus for the instructional activities.

EVALUATING THE SUCCESS OF SETTING GOALS AND OBJECTIVE SPECIFICATIONS

The specified instructional goals and objectives should be supported by the data gathered during learner and task analysis. The question to answer about the goals and objectives is, "Do these goals and objectives direct us to create instruction that supports the identified population of learners in gaining skill with the tasks that have been identified?" In traditional instructional design, it is important to take some time to consider whether the goals and objectives developed have truly grown out of the learner and task analyses.

Another approach to evaluating the success of the specified goals and objectives is to compare them against each other. As the project takes shape, the designer continues to ask him or herself if the objectives support the goals to determine whether the objectives are appropriate. At the same time, the designer asks him or herself whether the goals realistically reflect the objectives to determine whether the instructional goals are appropriately articulated.

Professionals in Practice

I personally do not like setting strict instructional goals and objectives. Since each learner is different from others, we cannot make something that is "one size fits all." As Prensky (2001) stated, such an approach was the old paradigm. Since learning is an active process, it shows an adaptive nature. For me, setting strict objectives does not seem realistic. Instead, I like to define more general goals and objectives. Moreover, strict goals and objectives put learners in a passive mode. While talking about the instructional system–building process, Prensky (2001) stated, "The words 'objective,' 'learn,' and 'know how to' were banned, replaced with imperative action verbs like 'build,' 'get through,' 'repair,' and 'rescue.'" (p. 14). I can't be that radical, but I like this approach. Moreover, while defining them, the focus must not be put only on individuals—organizational structure and culture must also be considered. This is necessary because individuals live in this social setting, so the issues about individuals should not be isolated from their environments.

Based on my experience, I can say that the results of learner, task, and needs analyses almost always give the general goals and objectives of the instruction.

—Kursat Cagiltay
professor at Turkey's Middle East Technical University in Ankara
Department of Computer Education and Instructional Technology

After careful consideration, Susan uses the FAST approach to help articulate her instructional goal, which is, "Hospital employees will help maintain a healthy environment for patients and staff by keeping their hands clean." Susan takes the ABCD approach to writing a performance objective for the instruction: "After viewing a demonstration on the correct method for washing one's hands, hospital employees will perform the procedure correctly by washing for at least 20 seconds and using a separate paper towel to turn off the water faucet."

Brian decides his instruction on treating people humanely when conducting research does not have specific performance objectives. His goal statement is, "University faculty will increase their understanding of the need for institutional approval of research that includes people as part of the study." His instructional objectives include: "After completing the instruction, faculty will seek institutional approval for using human subjects as part of their research" and "After completing the instruction, faculty will know the reasons why institutions require approval for studies that include human subjects."

GOALS AND OBJECTIVES AND THE INSTRUCTIONAL DESIGN PROCESS

Setting goals and objectives is a critically important part of the instructional design process. No matter which approach you take, setting goals and objectives should help you answer the following questions:

- What is the overall purpose of the instructional activity?
- Is the intention of the instruction accurately reflected in the goals and objectives?

- Have the traditions, politics, and predilections of the organization been accounted for when developing the instructional goals? Do the goals and objectives match the instructional intent regardless of the organization's influence?
- Are there any specific, observable behaviors the learners should exhibit after they have completed the instruction?
- What evaluation strategies will be used to determine if the instructional goals and objectives are appropriate?

Summary

Goals and objectives define the intention of the instruction. An instructional goal is a general statement about the ultimate intention of the instruction. An instructional objective is a more specific statement about how and to what degree the instruction will affect the learners. The objective should describe an action taken by the learner at the conclusion of the instructional event that can be empirically measured by an observer.

Goals must be articulated in order to create instruction. However, objectives are subordinate to goals and may not be necessary to an instructional design. Objectives are critically important if the learners are to be evaluated based on standards or specific criteria. If learners will not be evaluated in this manner—for example, if the instruction is intended to foster creativity or critical thinking—then writing specific instructional objectives may actually be an inappropriate step for the instructional designer.

Popular approaches to writing goals and objectives include Mager's development of performance objectives (determining the action, condition, and criterion); Dick and Carey's dual approaches of determining goals and objectives by either consulting subject matter experts or taking a performance technology approach (deriving goals and objectives from the data gathered during needs and task analysis); Heinich, Molenda, Russell, and Smaldino's ABCD approach (audience, behavior, conditions, degree); and Morrison, Ross, and Kemp's terminal and enabling objectives.

It is important for novice instructional designers to realize that they will most often be creating instruction for organizations that have their own traditions and political necessities; instructional objectives may be well-articulated, while the instructional goals may not be written down. Missing or poorly articulated instructional goals may be determined by using a FAST chart, working from a specific instructional objective back to a general goal.

Writing instructional objectives can be facilitated through the use of hierarchies or taxonomies that define the types and levels of instructional outcomes. Bloom's taxonomy and Gagne's hierarchy of intellectual skills are reference tools popular among educators.

In evaluating the success in writing instructional goals and objectives, one critically important question to consider is whether the goals and objectives lead to the creation of instruction that is appropriate and effective for the learners. Constant comparison of the goals to the objectives (and vice versa) can help make the final instructional product one that is truly useful.

Connecting Process to Practice

1. After reading about Brian's instructional design challenge, do you think he did the right thing by creating objectives that are not performance objectives? Could Brian have written performance objectives for the instruction on human subjects?
2. You have been asked to create a six-week unit on writing poetry for a high school English class. How would you go about determining the appropriate goals and objectives for this?

3. Using the ABCD approach, write two performance objectives for this goal: "Students will understand the importance of making healthy snack choices."
4. You are the instructional designer in the Human Resources department of a mid-sized corporation. You have been assigned the task of creating instruction that addresses the appropriate use of corporate expense accounts. What factors may affect the goals you set for this instruction?
5. Your employer wants to be sure that everyone in the organization knows CPR. What goals might you derive for instruction that supports this?
6. You are teaching a group of ten-year-olds how to play soccer. You want them to improve their ball-passing skills. What goals and objectives might you set for your instruction?

Recommended Reading

Bloom, B. S., Engelhart, M. D., Furst, E. J., Hill, W. H. & Krathwohl, D. R. (1956). *Taxonomy of educational objectives: The classification of educational goals. Handbook I: Cognitive Domain.* New York: David McKay.

Gagne, R. (1985) *The conditions of learning, 4th edition.* Philadelphia: Holt, Rinehart and Winston.

References

Bloom, B. S., Engelhart, M. D., Furst, E. J., Hill, W. H. & Krathwohl, D. R. (1956). *Taxonomy of educational objectives: The classification of educational goals. Handbook I: Cognitive Domain.* New York: David McKay.

Dick, W., Carey, L. & Carey, J. O. (2009). *The systematic design of instruction, 7th edition.* Columbus, OH: Allyn & Bacon.

Gagne, R. (1985) *The conditions of learning, 4th edition.* Philadelphia: Holt, Rinehart and Winston.

Mager, R. (1984). *Goal analysis.* Belmont, CA: Lake Publishing Company.

Morrison, G. R., Ross, S. M. & Kemp, J. E. (2007). *Designing effective instruction, 5th edition.* New York: John Wiley & Sons.

Orlich, D. C., Harder, R. J., Callahan, R. C., Trevisan, M. S. & Brown, A. H. (2010). *Teaching strategies: A guide to effective instruction, 9th edition.* Wadsworth.

Prensky, M. (2001). *Digital game-based learning.* McGraw-Hill.

Smaldino, S., Lowther, D. L. & Russell, J. D. (2008). *Instructional technology and media for learning, 9th edition.* Merrill Prentice Hall.

Smith, P. L. & Ragan, T. J. (2005). *Instructional design, 3rd edition.* New York: John Wiley & Sons.

Thornburg, D. D. (1998). *Brainstorms and lightning bolts: Thinking skills for the 21st century.* San Carlos, CA: Thornburg Center.

Zook, K. (2001). *Instructional design for classroom teaching and learning.* Houghton Mifflin.

Chapter 7

Organizing Instruction

Steve is preparing an afterschool Fun with Science program for his elementary school. The program is intended to provide a variety of science-oriented experiences for students in the first through fifth grades. The school's principal and the school PTA have expressed a need for the program, and Steve has developed the program's instructional goals and objectives. Steve knows his learners well and is excited at the prospect of putting together a series of activities that are both educational and fun. However, he is having trouble deciding how to sort and arrange the lessons so that children of different ages engage in different activities.

Erin is an instructional designer for an international package delivery service. She has been given the task of creating a program that helps to ensure employee safety and wellness. She knows the instructional goals and objectives, and she has conducted a thorough task analysis to better understand the safety protocols and procedures employees need to learn. Erin now needs to decide what kinds of instruction will be offered.

GUIDING QUESTIONS

- How does organizing content and learning activities help an instructional designer?
- What is a curriculum?
- What are the events of instruction?
- What is the continuum of learning experiences?
- What are the various methods of instructional delivery?

KEY TERMS

Curriculum *102*
Dale's Cone of Experience *105*
Distance Education *102*
Enactive Experiences *105*
Events of Instruction *103*
Generative (Instructional Event) *104*
Iconic Experiences *105*
Job Aids *110*
Learning Management System (LMS) *109*
Lesson Plans *102*
Program of Study *102*
Programmed Instruction *107*
Scope and Sequence *102*
Supplantive (Instructional Event) *104*
Syllabus *102*
Symbolic Experiences *105*
Units (of Instruction) *102*

CHAPTER OVERVIEW

Designing the best instruction possible involves organizing instructional activities to create a satisfying and effective learning experience. This is particularly important when the content to be covered is sizable (e.g., yearlong training; multiple years of study for a degree; an entire K–12 curriculum). The activities of any one lesson often have to fit appropriately into a larger educational scheme. Understanding how these larger schemes work and how to develop such a scheme allows one to deliver better instruction.

Organizing content allows one to see the depth and breadth of the content to be covered, while organizing instructional activities allows one to see the range of methods used to communicate that content to the learner. A course of study organized by the content to be covered and the activities employed to cover them is called a **curriculum**. A curriculum for any course of study is described by its scope and sequence, the instructional events and learning experiences it encompasses, and the methods in which these events and experiences are delivered.

SCOPE AND SEQUENCE

There is a wide range of possibility when it comes to determining **scope and sequence** of instruction. Instruction can be designed to incorporate many activities over a long period of time (e.g., a **program of study** leading to a graduate degree), a single activity in a brief period of time (e.g., the instructions on the back of a packet of instant soup), or anything in between. The scope and sequence of the activities are determined by the instructional designer based on the goals and objectives he or she has developed through needs, task, and learner analyses.

In K–12 settings, people most often think in terms of curriculums, **units**, and **lesson plans**. The curriculum is the entire scope of what is to be learned from beginning (pre-K) to end (twelfth grade); therefore, a curriculum is most often measured in years. Units are measured in months or weeks; they are large sets of activities that relate to a specific theme (e.g., oceanography or Greek myths). Lesson plans contain the specific, day-to-day activities that comprise a unit. The activities articulated in lesson plans are measured in hours or minutes.

The word "curriculum" is Latin in origin. Its original meaning is related to racing and racecourses. Literally translated, a curriculum is a race, a lap in a race, or a racetrack. Today, the word curriculum is used to refer to the organization of a course of study. A curriculum can be thought of as the set of markers necessary to define a course. (Translation source: "Words" by William Whitaker.)

In college and university settings, people think in terms of programs of study, syllabi, and classes. A program of study is the entire set of courses that, once completed, leads to the conferring of a degree (e.g., Bachelor of Arts; Master of Science). A **syllabus** is the scope and sequence description for a single course (which is usually one semester in length), and classes are the individual meetings held regularly throughout the semester (classes are sometimes referred to as lessons in postsecondary education, particularly in the case of nonsynchronous **distance education**, when students and the instructor do not meet at a specific time on a specific day but instead complete assignments that include presentations as well as reading and responding within a given period of time, usually a week or a few days).

Nonacademic settings, such as business or government, may approach instruction in terms of competencies and certifications. These organizations may organize instructional activities in terms of courses or study guides that support individuals in improving work-related skills or achieving passing scores on professional certification examinations.

According to Orlich, Harder, Callahan, Trevisan, and Brown (2010), sequencing instruction serves two essential purposes: either to isolate a piece of knowledge (a concept or principle) to help students comprehend its unique characteristics or to relate that concept or principle to a larger organized body of knowledge. Determining the scope of instruction serves the essential purpose of placing some restriction on just how much of any topic is covered as part of the instruction.

For any instructional event, one must determine both the scope (the amount of information) and the sequence (the order in which the information will be presented). Regardless of how one organizes and divides up the instruction, some scope and sequence must be developed at the outset in order to determine what is to be taught and the order in which it will be presented.

Levels of Organization: Macro, Micro, Vertical, and Horizontal

Curriculum expert George Posner (2003) describes organizing instruction by "macro and micro levels" and by "vertical and horizontal dimensions." Macro and micro levels are relative terms when used in connection with instructional organization. According to Posner, the broadest macro level is that which refers to educational levels (e.g., the difference between elementary and secondary education). The micro level at its most specific refers to the relationships between concepts, facts, or skills within lessons. Posner's descriptions of horizontal and vertical dimensions of instruction help to clarify the difference between scope and sequence. If one thinks of a program of study laid out sequentially (like a timeline), the sequence of study is the vertical dimension (for example, first grade, second grade, third grade, etc.). The horizontal dimension describes the scope—that is, all the various concurrent and integrated activities. Posner refers to organizing curriculum content that is taught concurrently as the "horizontal organization." He refers to sequencing of content and activities (that is, deciding when content will be presented) as "vertical organization" (Posner, 2003).

Organizational Structures: Content and Media

Posner (2003) states there are only two basic methods of organizing a curriculum or program of study. Instruction can be organized by using either a content or a media structure. A content structure organizes the instruction by the concepts, skills, or attitudes students are to acquire (as described by the instructional objectives). A media structure organizes the instruction by the activities, methods, and materials used to teach the concepts, skills, or attitudes described by the instructional objectives.

THE EVENTS OF INSTRUCTION

Associated with Posner's micro level organization of instruction is determining the order of the activities within a given lesson, known commonly as the events of instruction. These events are discrete activities that work best in a specific order. The most elemental series of instructional events consists of an introduction, a body (a variety of activities related to the content), a conclusion, and an assessment (Smith & Ragan, 2005). As an example, consider a K–12 teacher's daily lesson plan (see Figure 7.1). The activities and evaluation sections have been labeled by using the four elemental events of instruction.

The eminent instructional designer and scholar Robert Gagne (1916–2002) theorized that there are nine **events of instruction** (1985):

1. Gain the learners' attention.
2. Inform learners of the objective.
3. Stimulate recall of prior learning.
4. Present the stimulus.

Background: A class of 24 second-grade students

Goal: To understand the concept "Air takes up space"

Objective: By the end of the lesson, students will be able to describe how a parachute works.

Activities:

Introduction

1. *Introductory discussion:* Remind students about making scientific observations and introduce the new concept.

Body

2. *Toy parachutes:* Using clothespins, string, and paper towels, students create their own parachutes.
3. *Sailboat submarines:* Using walnut shells, toothpicks, construction paper, and glue, students create small sailboats.

Conclusion

4. *Summative discussion* about air: Ask students to think of other demonstrations of the concept "Air takes up space."

Assessment

Evaluation: Students were asked to devise their own demonstrations for the concept "Air takes up space." Acceptable responses range from . . .

FIGURE 7.1 An Example of a K–12 Teacher's Daily Lesson Plan

5. Provide guidance for the learners.
6. Elicit learner performance.
7. Provide feedback.
8. Assess learner performance.
9. Enhance retention and transfer (varied practice and reviews).

To put this theory into practice, each of the events described requires at least one instructional activity. The order of the activities makes a difference in the effectiveness of the instruction. The careful consideration of instructional events is analogous to the consideration that goes into a well-planned meal: The order of dishes served affects the overall experience.

Although the events of instruction are most often described in terms that make it seem as if the teacher is the active participant while the learners passively receive instruction, this should not be the case. Both directed and open-ended learning environments have carefully planned instructional events. In both environments, students may take an active role in each of the instructional events. Smith and Ragan (2005) observe that each instructional event can be viewed as having two aspects: the **supplantive**—those supplied by the instruction itself—and the **generative**—those generated by the student. For example, during an introduction event, the instructor may present activities intended to gain the learner's attention, but the learner must activate his or her attention in order to participate effectively. During the body of a lesson, the instructor may present the activities, but the learner must actively participate by doing such things as focusing his/her attention, employing learning strategies, and offering and responding to feedback. The events of instruction should be considered a reciprocal process, with instructors and students making contributions that lead to an effective learning experience.

THE CONTINUUM OF LEARNING EXPERIENCES

All learning experiences can be placed within a continuum. At one end of this continuum are the experiences in which the learner picks up skills, concepts, and attitudes by participating in a concrete, real-world activity. As an example of an extreme version of this, a person may learn to swim by being thrown into deep water, and the only option available short of drowning is to figure out how to stay afloat and propel oneself. At the other end of this continuum are the experiences in which the learner is exposed to skills, concepts, and attitudes through completely contrived or abstract activity. An example of an extreme version of this would be learning to swim by having someone describe it without actually getting near water.

The vast majority of instructional activities fall somewhere between the two extremes of this concrete-abstract continuum. One of the most popular methods of categorizing learning activities within this continuum is Edgar **Dale's Cone of Experience** (Dale, 1969; Smaldino, Lowther & Russell, 2008). At the base of Dale's Cone are direct, purposeful experiences (real-world activities), simulations, and dramatizations. In the middle of Dale's Cone are film or video presentations, pictures and photographs, and audio recordings. At the top of the cone are visual and verbal symbols (text and speech).

The psychologist Jerome Bruner describes learning experiences as being one of three types: enactive, iconic, or symbolic (Bruner, 1966). **Enactive experiences** are those at the base of Dale's Cone. As Bruner puts it:

> We know many things for which we have no imagery and no words, and they are very hard to teach to anybody by the use of either words or diagrams or pictures. If you have tried to coach somebody at tennis or skiing or to teach a child to ride a bike, you will have been struck by the wordlessness and the diagrammatic impotence of the teaching process.

Iconic experiences are those that are placed within the middle of Dale's Cone. The iconic experience, " . . . depends upon visual or other sensory organization and upon the use of summarizing images." Iconic experiences offer explanations through symbols or representations.

Symbolic experiences are those that are placed at the top of Dale's Cone. A symbolic experience is one in which the entire communication is conducted by using sounds and signs that have no direct association with the actual event. For example, languages are symbolic communication systems; the words we speak or read may arbitrarily represent concepts and real things, but they do so by completely artificial means. Bruner points out that symbolic systems are capable of conveying a tremendous amount of information in a compact and efficient manner. For example, scientists and poets convey vast amounts of information through symbols and words. Consider Einstein's $E = mc^2$ or Frost's "Nature's first gold is green." Each are brief expressions that carry a tremendous amount

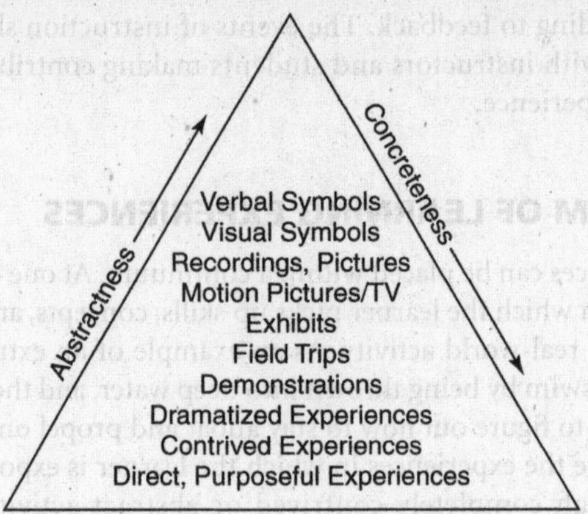

FIGURE 7.2 Dale's Cone of Experience

of information to individuals who know how to interpret the symbols in the case of Einstein's theorem and symbolism in the case of Frost's words. It would take quite a long time to enact the content of either expression.

Dale's Cone of Experience (see Figure 7.2) and Bruner's descriptions are used by instructional designers to analyze the characteristics of various activities in order to make informed decisions about their use within an instructional plan. It is generally considered a good idea to make use of a wide range of enactive, iconic, and symbolic activities in order to provide students with a variety of learning opportunities.

Enactive, iconic, and symbolic activities each have their own instructional strengths. For example, enactive activities generally give students greater opportunity to synthesize and apply what they are learning; however, these activities can be expensive to produce and time-consuming to participate in. Symbolic activities can be easily controlled to focus on the most important aspects of the instructional content and often make the best use of time when time is limited, but they often do not offer students an opportunity to explore the content details in a deeply meaningful manner.

Professionals in Practice

For a few years, I taught a judo class at The Bank Street School for Children. I had taught judo in a number of settings before that. There is a traditional method of teaching judo and an established curriculum for the sport. However, at Bank Street, I had to organize things a little differently to suit a special group of students. Judo is normally a highly physical activity and is generally taught in an enactive manner; students observe the instructor in action and[then] try out the movements by practicing with peers. My students at Bank Street were particularly verbal in their approach to learning, and it became obvious after the very first meeting that some portion of class time had to be devoted to more symbolic experience (in this case, discussion) in order to make the enactive experiences meaningful for this particular group.

—Abbie Brown
former teacher at The Bank Street School for Children
New York City

Understanding where learning experiences fall within the continuum between concrete and abstract helps answer questions such as:

- How does this activity help students apply the content to situations outside the learning environment?
- How quickly can students learn important content features from this experience?

Steve is going to use Posner's idea of vertical and horizontal curriculum organization to help him arrange his program's science activities by grade. He is going to consider each grade level as a step in the program's sequence, and he will gather together age-appropriate activities that support the program's instructional goals. Steve also wants the activities to be fun, and he knows his students like to do the experiments instead of watch them conducted by others or read about them. Steve will therefore be careful to provide as many appropriate enactive experiences as he can.

Erin's instructional design is going to focus on producing a number of iconic and symbolic media for employees to serve as visual reminders about safety procedures which which everyone is already familiar. Because Erin plans to use a variety of activities, methods, and materials to provide instruction on both safety and wellness, she is going to use a media structure to organize her instruction.

METHODS OF DELIVERY

Instructional events and learning experiences can be organized for a variety of delivery methods. The most popular of these include the traditional in-person approach (classroom teaching), distance education, **programmed instruction**, and instructional media.

Classroom Teaching

Most people are familiar with classroom teaching through personal experience. In the United States, the traditional approach to organized instruction consists of one teacher working with a group of students who are similar in age and/or experience with the subject matter to be taught. This is the basis of our K–12 system; the assumption is that most students in a given grade are similar in age and have similar experiences with school subjects (e.g., one assumes someone in third grade has satisfactorily completed the first and second grades). This approach extends to postsecondary settings, where groups of students take a class with one or a few instructors; students in that class must meet the prerequisites (i.e., completion of specific courses or status as an undergraduate or graduate student) for the class in order to participate. Other groups that employ classroom teaching, such as businesses and military organizations, also follow this approach, grouping students by experience and ability to work with one or a few instructors.

Current classroom teaching practice traces its roots to Joseph Lancaster (1778–1838), an English educator who created a unique set of manuals that detailed the organization and management of group instruction (Saettler, 1990). Although instructional methods have changed considerably, Lancaster's physical models for organization continue to heavily influence the classrooms of today.

The setup of a traditional classroom is a number of desks and chairs for students, generally organized to face a chalkboard, whiteboard, or projection screen. A teacher directs the instructional activities, offering and receiving feedback from students as the lesson progresses.

Professionals in Practice

I work in an ethnically diverse middle school and therefore have a great deal of second-language learners. My goals and objectives must meet state standards, but they must also meet the very different needs of all of my students. Therefore, I have to structure my lessons to fit the class. In social studies, I incorporate a variety of strategies, including G.L.A.D. (Guided Language Acquisition and Development) strategies, when introducing new cultures and concepts. Lessons always begin by activating background knowledge, getting students to make the connections between their world and the ancient world. Repetition is a key factor to success, and we do chants and sing songs to help remember what has been learned. Prior to a new lesson, we discuss the previous lesson and watch as each lesson builds upon the next in order to better grasp the ancient cultures that we study.

—Jody Peerless
sixth-grade teacher at Washington Middle School
La Habra, California

Programmed Instruction

Programmed instruction is the arrangement of content materials that allows a student working independently to form responses and receive feedback on those responses (receiving positive reinforcement for correct responses). The feedback and reinforcement come from the instructional media, not from a live instructor or facilitator. Although forms of programmed instruction have been part of teaching since the days of ancient Greece (Saettler, 1990), it became particularly popular in the 1960s based in large part on the work of the noted behavioral psychologist B. F. Skinner. Skinner described a need for the refinement of "teaching machines," which are automated methods of providing instruction that would allow a multitude of learners to work through content at each learner's own pace. With the advent of affordable computing systems and software that allows nonprogrammers to create software with relative ease (e.g., Adobe's Flash), programmed instruction has increased. A number of programmed instruction software titles, often referred to as "skill and drill" programs teaching everything from basic reading to preparation for the Graduate Record Examination, are currently available.

It is important to recognize that it is the instruction, not the technology used to deliver it, that is the focus of programmed instruction. Highly effective programmed instruction can be designed and delivered without the use of computing tools. The book *Bobby Fischer Teaches Chess* (Fischer, Margulies & Mosenfelder, 1972) is an example of excellent programmed instruction that makes sole use of the printed page.

Distance Education

At present, the most common perception of distance education is that of a traditional classroom experience (one teacher, many students) translated into a communications environment that allows students to participate without having to congregate in a specific geographic location. Distance education may be synchronous (everyone involved participating within a specified time period; using videoconferencing or online chat) or asynchronous (everyone involved participating at a time of his or her own choosing; sharing messages using an online discussion board, postal letters, or e-mail messages). Asynchronous distance education may also be delivered in the form of programmed instruction, allowing the student to review the material at an individualized pace without the need (or support) of a teacher or peer group.

With the ubiquity of inexpensive computing tools and telecommunications and the extensive networking of colleges and universities, Internet-based distance education has become a particularly popular topic among educators (Brown & Green, 2008, 2009).

In a distance education setting, all instructional activities are delivered through some communications medium that links geographically remote participants. One example is the use of a Web-based **learning management system (LMS)**, such as Blackboard or eCollege. A learning management system essentially provides a computer-based empty classroom that an instructor may fill with assignments and presentations; online message boards and chat areas are also a part of the courseware, facilitating communication among participants.

Distance education has a number of appealing features for education and training. Students do not have to travel to a classroom, and in asynchronous situations, they may participate at a time that works best for them. However, there is an interesting opposition of forces at work with distance education. At the same time that more students demand distance education options, most students say they do not really want to learn at a distance—that a live instructor and the presence of learning group peers is important to them (Simonson, Smaldino, Albright & Zvacek, 2008).

Two Categories of Instructional Delivery

The methods of delivery can be thought of as belonging to two categories: those that involve immediate feedback to both the student and the instructor or those that offer immediate feedback to the student alone.

- ***Providing Immediate Feedback to Both Students and the Instructor(s)*** In instructional settings such as a traditional classroom or distance education, the students and instructors communicate with each other in a way that allows them to adjust their activities according to feedback received. For example, the teacher in a traditional classroom may notice his or her students are looking drowsy and decide it is time for a short break or the instructor of an online course may receive a number of messages asking for clarification of a particular concept and decide that he or she needs to offer a mini-lesson covering that concept in greater detail.
- ***Providing Immediate Feedback to the Student Alone*** Education conducted through programmed instruction does not have an instructor making adjustments to the experience based on learner feedback. The instruction may be programmed to respond to a student's responses, but all possible responses are determined in advance of the student's participation.

There are strengths and weakness associated with all methods of delivery. One strength of methods that provide feedback to both the instructor and students is that it can make the experience a more personal one for each learner; however, this method requires a great deal of work on the part of the instructor and requires students to follow a specific schedule for participating in and completing activities. Methods that offer feedback to the student but not the instructor are less personalized but can be offered to a much larger number of learners, all of whom may participate at a time of their own choosing and for however long they would like. Therefore, choosing the delivery method is a critically important instructional design decision, and the method used affects the selection of activities for purposes of effectiveness and efficiency.

THE HIDDEN CURRICULUM

Although the content for a course of study can be described in terms of a curriculum, it is important to realize that there is often a *hidden* curriculum that accompanies the one described. The content and activities used to teach it combine to create a set of experiences for the learner that causes a change in how he or she relates to the world or at least that part of his or her world that the content focuses on. For example, young people do not just learn facts and figures while in school; they learn how to deal with others outside their home environment. This is referred to as "socialization" and is an important aspect of the school experience. People preparing to enter a profession also learn from the hidden curriculum. Participating in instructional activities with peers and other members of that professional community reveals the methods, expectations, and actual practices of that community.

INSTRUCTIONAL ACTIVITIES IN NON-EDUCATIONAL SITUATIONS

There are times when instructional activities can be used to improve performance without specifically striving to teach people new information, skills, or attitudes. The field of human performance technology (HPT) directly addresses these issues. According to the International Society for Performance Improvement (ISPI), human performance technology " . . . has been described as the systematic and systemic identification and removal of barriers to individual and organizational performance" (ISPI).

HPT makes use of a wide range of interventions drawn from many other disciplines, including behavioral psychology, instructional systems design, organizational development, and human resources management. HPT stresses the analysis of present and desired levels of performance, looks for causes of performance gaps, guides the process of eliminating or minimizing those gaps, and evaluates the results (ISPI).

If analysis of a human performance problem indicates the need for an instructional activity, the goal of that activity is to provide support that fills the performance gap. One type of activity that supports performance is commonly referred to as a job aid.

Job Aids

Job aids are devices that relieve an individual of the need to memorize a set of steps or procedures. Often presented in paper or electronic format, job aids do not teach; instead, they support performance. One typically finds job aids wherever esoteric procedures are necessary to complete a task. The task itself is understood by the individual, but the steps involved in completing the task may be difficult to remember. Examples of job aids can be found in public transportation settings where ticketing machines provide instructions for their use and in most business offices where the steps involved in using the copy or fax machines are posted.

USING ORGANIZATION TO IMPROVE INSTRUCTION

Understanding the organization, scope and sequence, instructional events, types of learning experiences, and methods of delivery gives one greater understanding of how to organize instructional activities and present them in the most effective way for a particular group of students. This facilitates creating an instructional situation that accommodates a range of learners, keeping in mind the ideas of universal design for education introduced in Chapter 5. Understanding the organization of instruction helps an instructional designer with the following tasks:

- Choosing activities that support remediation and extension by using scope and sequence organization to identify appropriate content for students who need either extra support or an extra challenge
- Choosing activities that support the needs of a variety of learning styles, selecting a variety of different types of enactive, iconic, and symbolic experiences, and using Dale's Cone as an organizer
- Selecting activities most appropriate to each instructional event in order to create an effective series of activities for a given lesson or instructional intervention
- Making available job aids that support the student and allow him or her to focus on the concepts to be learned instead of the steps involved in completing a specific task
- Choosing activities that are best-suited to the delivery method or choosing the best delivery method to meet an individual's or an organization's needs

The goal of every instructional designer is to create effective, efficient, and satisfying learning experiences for every student. Understanding the organization of instruction and making considerate use of a variety of instructional activities can help instructional designers meet this goal.

Steve has decided that the Fun with Science program will present a series of hands-on experiments that increase in complexity from first grade to fifth grade. The content will be unique for each grade level (for example, first grade will focus on biology, and second grade will focus on physical science). The experiments will be presented in a traditional classroom by using Gagne's nine events as the lesson structure.

Erin has decided to produce a series of computer-based tutorials and presentations, printed brochures, and job aids that help employees follow the company's safety protocols and procedures. The materials are not sequential and can be used in any order.

ORGANIZING INSTRUCTION AND THE INSTRUCTIONAL DESIGN PROCESS

Organizing content and activities is an important part of the instructional design process. No matter which approach you take, organizing instruction should help you answer the following questions:

- How much content will the instruction have?
- When will different parts of the content be introduced within the instructional design?

- What kind of enactive, iconic, and symbolic activities will be presented to the learners?
- What kind of support activities will be offered for students who need extra help?
- What kinds of activities will be offered for students who seek a greater challenge?

Summary

The content to be covered and the instructional activities used to convey that content can be organized into a curriculum. A curriculum defines and describes the content to be covered in terms of its scope (the amount of information) and sequence (the order in which the information is presented). Instructional content can be further organized at the macro level (for example, "elementary" versus "advanced" levels) or the micro level (the relationships between concepts, facts, and skills within any given lesson). Instructional content can also be described as having horizontal and vertical dimensions. The horizontal dimension is the range of content taught concurrently at any one time; the vertical dimension describes the sequence of the content taught over time. The organization of a curriculum can be based on either a content structure (the concepts, skills, or attitudes students are to acquire) or a media structure (the activities, methods, and materials used to teach the content).

The order in which activities are presented in a lesson is referred to as the events of instruction. Although instructional events may be described in much greater detail, the four basic events are introduction, body, conclusion, and assessment. Each instructional event has two aspects: the supplantive (that which is provided by the activity) and generative (that which is created by the student).

Learning experiences can be said to exist within a continuum that ranges from the concrete (real-world situations) to the abstract (symbolic representation). Jerome Bruner describes three types of learning experiences: enactive, iconic, and symbolic. These experiences are divided into more specific instances by using Edgar Dale's Cone of Experience.

The methods of delivering instructional experiences include traditional classroom teaching, programmed instruction (the arrangement of content that allows students to work independently while receiving feedback from the instructional presentation), and distance education (students and teachers working in geographically diverse locations). These methods can be described as providing either feedback to both instructor and students or providing feedback to the student alone.

Non-educational instructional events are a part of the discipline of human performance technology (HPT). A common example of an instructional design that is not intended to teach is the job aid. A job aid supports performance by relieving an individual of the need to memorize a set of steps or procedures.

Understanding the organization, scope, sequence, events, experiences, and delivery methods helps the instructional designer understand what is necessary to create instruction that is effective for a variety of learners—from the average student to those who require either more support or greater challenges.

Connecting Process to Practice

1. Could Steve have taken a different approach to organizing the Fun with Science program? Explain at least one other possibility for organizing and presenting the program.
2. What are some possible hidden curriculum issues that may be associated with Steve's and Erin's instructions?
3. If Erin's superiors had requested that the safety and wellness program include a certificate of completion, what would she have to do to alter the organization of her instruction?
4. A multinational corporation has hired you as a consultant. The corporation is considering ways to offer business management courses to its employees worldwide. Explain the options for course delivery methods to the organization's CEO.

5. You have been asked to develop a unit on ancient Egypt for fifth-grade students. What enactive, iconic, and symbolic experiences might you include in this unit?
6. You are the instructional designer for a nonprofit organization with a number of volunteer workers. The volunteers are often unfamiliar with the organization's phone system, making it difficult for them to transfer calls. What might you do to address this problem?
7. You are the instructional designer for a university. The vice president of the university has asked to meet with you to discuss the possibility of offering a distance-education program leading to a bachelor's degree in liberal arts. In order to make well-considered recommendations, what questions will you ask the vice president?

Recommended Reading

Dale, E. (1969). *Audio-visual methods in teaching, 3rd edition.* New York: Holt, Rinehart and Winston.

Posner, G.J. (2003). *Analyzing the curriculum, 3rd edition.* New York: McGraw Hill.

References

Brown, A. & Green, T. (2008). Issues and trends in instructional technology: Making the most of mobility and ubiquity. In Orey, M., McClendon, V. J. & Branch, R.M. (Eds.), *Educational Media and Technology Yearbook, 33*, 4–16.

Brown, A. & Green, T. (2009). Issues and trends in instructional technology: Web 2.0, Second Life, and STEM share the spotlight. In Orey, M., McClendon, V. J. & Branch, R.M. (Eds.), *Educational Media and Technology Yearbook, 34.*

Bruner, J. S. (1966). *Toward a theory of instruction.* Cambridge, MA: Harvard University Press.

Dale, E. (1969). *Audio-visual methods in teaching, 3rd edition.* New York: Holt, Rinehart and Winston.

Fischer, B., Margulies, S. and Mosenfelder, D. (1972). *Bobby Fischer teaches chess.* New York: Bantam Books.

Gagne, R. M. (1985). *The conditions of learning and theory of instruction.* New York: Holt, Rinehart and Winston.

International Society for Performance Improvement (ISPI). *What is HPT*? Retrieved from http://www.ispi.org/content.aspx?id=54&terms=What+is+human+performance+technology.

Orlich, D. C., Harder, R. J., Callahan, R. C., Trevisan, M. S. & Brown, A. H. (2010). *Teaching strategies: A guide to effective instruction, 9th edition.* Florence, KY: Wadsworth.

Posner, G. J. (2003). *Analyzing the curriculum, 3rd edition.* New York: McGraw Hill.

Saettler, P. (1990). *The evolution of American educational technology.* Englewood, CO: Libraries Unlimited.

Simonson, M., Smaldino, S., Albright, M. & Zvacek, S. (2008). *Teaching and learning at a distance: Foundations of distance education, 4th edition.* Upper Saddle River, NJ: Merrill Prentice Hall.

Smaldino, S., Lowther, D. L. & Russell, J. D. (2008). *Instructional technology and media for learning, 9th edition.* Upper Saddle River, NJ: Merrill/Prentice Hall.

Smith, P. L. & Ragan, T. J. (2005). *Instructional design, 3rd edition.* New York: John Wiley & Sons.

Whitaker, William. (2006). *Words.* Retrieved from http://lysy2.archives.nd.edu/cgi-bin/words.exe.

Chapter 8

Learning Environments and Instructional Activities

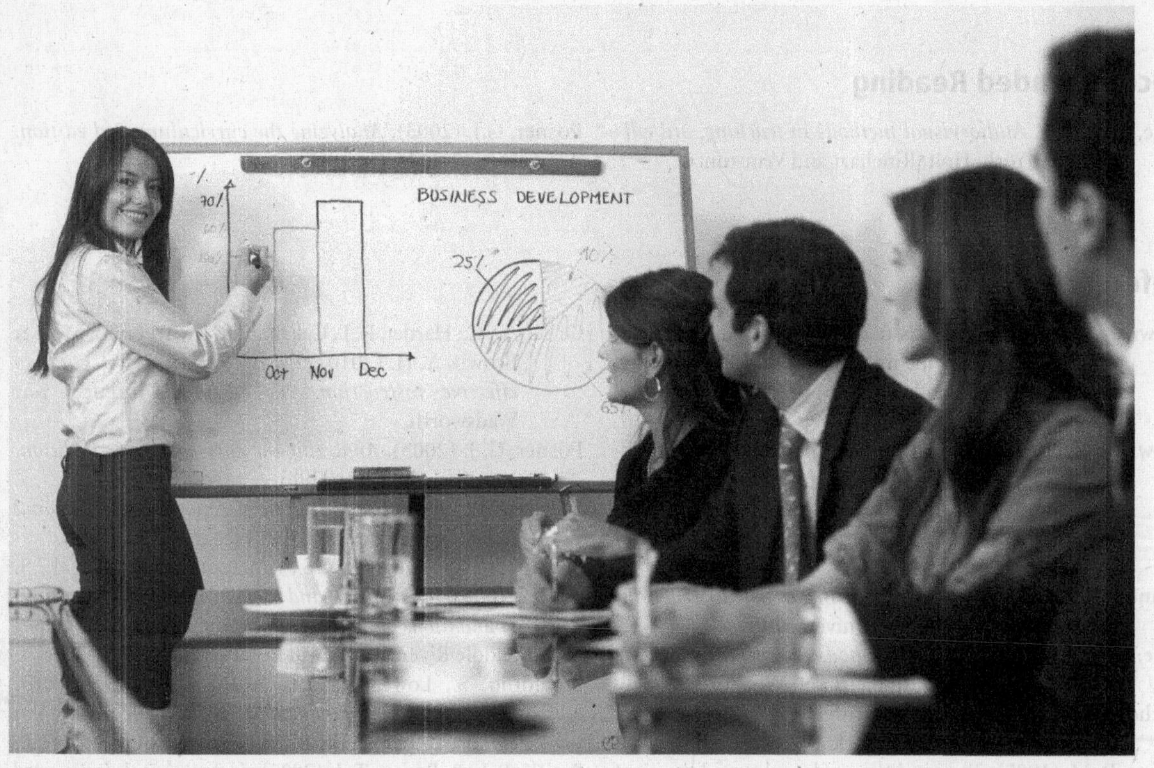

Bill is in charge of developing his community college's new writing center. The college recognizes the need for student writing support. Learner and task analyses have been conducted, and goals and objectives for the center are established. Bill has much of the content organized; he knows what needs to be taught. What Bill needs to do now is decide what kind of learning environment is most appropriate and what instructional activities the center will conduct.

Carol has been put in charge of her company's customer service supervisor training program. The company has articulated a need for the training; Carol has completed her learner and task analyses, and her instructional design team has developed a set of goals and performance objectives as well as the sequence of instruction. Carol now needs to decide the learning environment and activities that will help the students learn the content and meet the objectives.

GUIDING QUESTIONS

- How are learning environments defined and differentiated?
- How are instructional activities defined?
- How does an instructional designer go about choosing appropriate and effective instructional activities?
- Which instructional activities are supported by grounded theory and research?

KEY TERMS

Advance Organizers *125*
Direct Teaching *119*
Directed Learning Environment *118*
Graphic Organizers *125*
Indirect Teaching *120*
Instructional Games *122*
Just-in-time Teaching *123*
Open-ended Learning Environment *121*
Prescriptions *116*
Scaffolding *121*
Simulations *121*

CHAPTER OVERVIEW

Creating learning environments and producing activities that carry out instructional goals and objectives are two of the most exciting and challenging aspects of instructional design. It is important for the novice instructional designer to be familiar with the types of possible learning environments as well as the various instructional activities that can be employed within those environments.

DEVELOPING INSTRUCTION

Once the goals of the instructional event are determined (in traditional systems design situations, objectives would also be specified) and an organizational strategy (a lesson plan, unit, program of study, or curriculum) has been devised, it is time to develop the interactions and events in which the learners will engage. These interactions and events are what the learners actually participate in to gain new knowledge, skill, or insight.

The instructional designer recommends specific activities based on the information gathered through needs, task, and learner analyses and through the development of goals and objectives. This process is similar to how a medical doctor might prescribe treatment for a patient after forming a diagnosis. In fact, the activities an instructional designer recommends are sometimes referred to as **prescriptions**. At the heart of any instructional design are the activities prescribed for the learners. Although it is never recommended, it is possible to avoid all other aspects of preparing an instructional intervention *except* the preparation of activities.

As an example of instructional design in action, consider how schoolteachers incorporate activities into their instructional designs. Teachers in elementary and secondary school settings typically develop daily lesson plans that are divided into five parts: background, goals, objectives, activities, and evaluation (see Figure 8.1). As with any instructional design, the lesson plan includes information about the learners, goals and objectives set by the instructor, and evaluation procedures to determine whether goals were met. Although the activities in which the students participate are just one part of the lesson plan, they are the only part that actually causes learning to occur.

Background: A class of 24 second-grade students. The students have been in school for 2 months and have studied the natural phenomena of magnetism and liquid surface tension through empirical observation. The general concept "Air takes up space" needs to be introduced by using empirical observation techniques to which the class has become accustomed.

Goal: To understand the concept "Air takes up space."

Objectives: By the end of the lesson, students will be able to describe how a parachute works. Students will also perform a demonstration called "Sailboat Submarines" and describe why the top of the sailboat does not get wet when it is submerged.

Activities:

1. *Introductory Discussion:* Students are reminded about making scientific observations and are introduced to the concept that even though humans do not usually perceive air around them, it is matter that takes up space.
2. *Toy Parachutes:* Using clothespins, string, and paper towels, students create their own parachutes. After they see a sample parachute and create their own, students test their parachutes out on the playground. This testing is followed by a discussion of how the parachute works (specifically, how the paper-towel-and-string configuration causes the air to slow the descent of the clothespin).
3. *Sailboat Submarines:* Using walnut shells, toothpicks, construction paper, and glue, students create small sailboats. The boats are then "sailed" underwater in a large tank by submerging them within an upside-down clear plastic cup. Sailing is followed by a group discussion on why the boat "sails" did not get wet when they were submerged.
4. *Summative Discussion about air:* Students are asked to think of other demonstrations of the concept that air takes up space.

Evaluation: Students are asked to create their own demonstrations of the concept "Air takes up space." Acceptable responses range from simple reconfigurations of the activities (e.g., flying an airplane underwater) to new and original demonstrations of the concept.

FIGURE 8.1 A K-12 Teacher's Daily Lesson Plan

Teaching the Way We Were Taught

A pitfall to avoid when designing instruction is to make use of activities that are comfortable to you because they were used on you when you were a student. People tend to teach as they themselves were taught or in a manner that supports their preferred learning style (Cruickshank, Bainer & Metcalf, 1999). Almost everyone who has attended high school or college has experienced a common method of instruction that includes the assignment of a reading in advance (chapters from a textbook, for example), a presentation by the course instructor, the assignment of a paper that synthesizes the information from the reading and the presentation, and preparation for a test on the same material. There is nothing wrong with these activities; however, they are but a few of many possibilities. If you are reading this book as part of a course assignment, chances are good that you are quite comfortable with the traditional instructional activities that include listening to lectures and studying textbooks; you would not be reading this if you had not mastered techniques for achieving success with these types of assignments. As an instructional designer, it is important to think *beyond* what has worked for you personally and consider what will work best for your target audience.

LEARNING ENVIRONMENTS

A learning environment is the milieu in which the instructor, the content, and the learners are placed. A learning environment is the context in which instruction occurs. More than just a physical setting, a learning environment is shaped by the type of instruction that needs to occur, and it is influenced by the attitudes and preferences of those who organize and operate that environment.

Four Perspectives on the Design of Learning Environments

In their book *How People Learn: Brain, Mind, Experience, and School*, Bransford, Brown and Cocking (2003) describe four types of learning environments: learner-centered, knowledge-centered, assessment-centered, and community-centered.

- ***Learner-Centered Environments*** Focus on the attitudes, skills, knowledge, and beliefs that students bring to an instructional setting. In this environment, the instructor uses information about how the learners relate to the content as well as the learners' preconceived ideas or misconceptions to create situations where the learners generate new (and hopefully improved) perceptions of the content.
- ***Knowledge-Centered Environments*** Focus on the information and activities that help learners develop an understanding of disciplines. In this environment, learners are exposed to well-organized knowledge in order to facilitate planning and strategic thinking.
- ***Assessment-Centered Environments*** Focus on providing opportunities for feedback and revision. In this environment, testing and critique are used to provide learners with opportunities to rethink and revise their ideas.
- ***Community-Centered Environments*** Focus on people learning from one another and contributing to the larger societies of people who share common interests and/or goals. In this environment, the connections between the instructional setting and world outside that setting are used to give the content greater meaning and place it in a more global context.

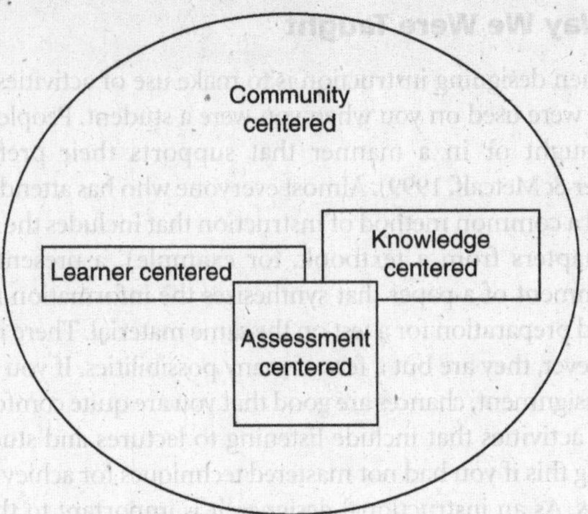

FIGURE 8.2 The Four Learning Environments described by Bransford, Brown and Cocking

It is important to keep in mind that these are not mutually exclusive environments. Bransford, Brown, and Cocking describe these environments as working together (see Figure 8.2), and they can be used to express the various perspectives through which any instructional situation might be viewed.

Directed and Open-Ended Learning Environments

Hannafin, Land, and Oliver (1999) describe two types of learning environments: directed and open-ended. A **directed learning environment** is one in which the instructional designer has determined specific learning objectives and prescribes structured activities in which participants demonstrate that they have learned by meeting the objectives. Most people are familiar with directed learning environments through personal experience. Traditional classrooms are directed learning environments organized around the practice of teaching content in increments through highly structured activities to meet externally generated objectives.

Open-ended learning environments differ from directed learning environments in that the learning goals and/or the method of pursuing those goals are determined in one of three ways (Hannafin, Land & Oliver):

1. Presenting the learner with a complex problem along with a specific task to complete
2. Presenting the learner with a complex problem to explore (with no specific task to complete)
3. Helping the learner articulate a personalized problem to be solved or explored

Both directed and open-ended learning environments operate by establishing instructional goals, but only directed environments require the creation of specific instructional objectives. Directed and open-ended learning environments each have their strengths (see Figure 8.3). Open-ended learning environments can be especially useful in promoting divergent thinking and are helpful in cases where multiple perspectives are valued. On the other hand, directed learning environments are particularly useful in situations where a variety of learners need to develop the same or similar knowledge, skills, or attitudes.

Directed Learning Environments	Open-Ended Learning Environments
Content is broken down and taught in increments.	Opportunities are set up for students to manipulate, interpret, and experiment.
Detection and mastery of specific concepts is simplified.	Concepts are linked to everyday experience.
Structured teaching—learning strategies are used.	Information is explored by looking at "the big picture." Flexible understanding is encouraged, and appreciation for multiple perspectives is fostered.
Learning is promoted through specific activities and practice.	Learning is promoted by supporting the individual learner's personal connections to the material.
Internal learning is activated by carefully directing external conditions.	Cognition and context are linked.
Mastery is achieved by producing "correct" responses.	The importance of understanding through trial and error is stressed.

Source: Adapted from "Open Learning Environments: Foundations, Methods, and Models," by M. Hannafin, S. Land, and K. Oliver, in *Instructional Design Theories and Models: A New Paradigm of Instructional Theory* (pp. 115–140), edited by C. M. Reigeluth, 1999, Mahwah, NJ: Erlbaum. Copyright 1999 by Lawrence Erlbaum Associates. Adapted with permission.

FIGURE 8.3 Directed and Open-Ended Learning Environments

The differences between directed and open-ended learning environments echo two views of what a learner is. An instructor may perceive a learner as either a passive receiver of information or as an active participant in constructing his or her knowledge (see Figure 8.4).

Cruickshank, Bainer, and Metcalf (1999) make a distinction between direct (or expository) teaching and indirect teaching. **Direct teaching** places the instructor in the center of all activity. The instructor presents specific information and decides exactly what students will do and when they will do it. Direct teaching is most commonly employed in directed learning environments.

Passive Reception	Active Participation	Timing
Presentations (lectures, performances)	Simulations and games	The student must keep up with the pace set by the activity.
Displays (textbooks, static Web sites, bulletin boards, dioramas)	Problem-based learning	The student may proceed at his or her own pace.

FIGURE 8.4 Differences Between Passive Reception and Active Participation

Indirect teaching places the instructor in a more peripheral position during learning activities. The instructor offers support and guidance while students approach an assigned problem in the ways that seem best to them. This approach is commonly employed in open-ended learning environments. A common expression that illustrates the two possibilities is the teacher as either "the sage on the stage" (direct) or the "guide on the side" (indirect).

Most educators perceive learners as being at some point on a continuous scale in which "completely passive" (they need to guided through everything) and "completely active" (they can find everything on their own) are the extremes. Most educators recognize that learners fall somewhere in between these two extremes; therefore, activities that comprise both directed and open-ended learning environments almost never exist in complete isolation of one another. For example, a good problem-based learning activity will provide opportunities for learners to receive information presented by experts in a directed manner as well as participate in their own research and analysis, all of which lead to solving the problem. In any sequence of instruction that extends beyond a single instructional activity, it is entirely possible to make use of both direct and indirect approaches. For example, an instructor may spend most of his or her time as "the guide on the side" as students solve a prescribed problem, while on occasion employing direct teaching methods by making presentations or lecturing on a specific topic, thereby providing specific information that may help in solving the problem.

Bill decides that the learning environment will be knowledge-centered. Because the writing center is intended to help students become better writers, Bill wants people to work in an atmosphere that focuses on the many aspects of the writing discipline. Furthermore, since the goal of the center is to provide instruction on a variety of fundamental and advanced writing activities based on individual needs, Bill decides the environment must be open-ended.

Carol decides the learning environment for the customer service supervisor training program will be assessment-centered. Because directed learning is required to help students meet a series of performance objectives, Carol thinks using testing and critique and providing opportunities for students to rethink and revise ideas will work well.

Professionals in Practice

Our instructional plans—for both classroom-based and online learning—are based on the idea that hands-on exposure to our software early and frequently provides the best skill-building and knowledge retention. I developed a little model called "See it, Read it, Do it" [that] reflects this idea well. First, an instructor can demonstrate an idea or concept. Then, there might be some associated reading [or] video/animation observation of the concept or its supporting concepts. Then, the student begins the task(s) actively, either with the real software or a simulation of it in the online world. All instructional activities have a real-world counterpart.

—Erik Novak
distance learning course developer
at Interactive Intelligence, Inc.
Indianapolis, Indiana.

INSTRUCTIONAL ACTIVITIES

Instructional activities are the experiences designed to help students learn. These are the interactions and events in which people participate to gain new knowledge, skill, or insight. A wide variety of different activities are possible for just about any education situation. It is the instructional designer's job to identify those activities that will work best based on the learners' needs and instruction's goals and objectives.

Most people are familiar with traditional instructional activities—such as lecture, presentation, demonstration, drill and practice, and question and answer—but there are also a number of other possibilities.

Problem-Based Learning

Problem-based learning (PBL) activities are open-ended learning situations. Students are usually presented with a problem that needs to be solved and are then encouraged to develop a solution to that problem by using the resources and tools available to them. Once the problem is presented to the class, students work in small groups to decide how to approach the problem and what information is necessary to form a reasonable solution. Students then conduct research individually, returning to the group later to share findings and apply these to developing a solution. In the final phase of a PBL activity, students reflect on both the problem and their methods of developing a solution, summarizing and synthesizing what they have learned (Albion, 2003). As students engage in solving carefully contrived problems, they develop and refine their understanding of the subject matter in a highly personal and meaningful way.

As an example, some Master of Business Administration (MBA) programs employ a PBL approach by informing students at the beginning of a semester that they must submit their answer to a specific question by the end of that semester. The question may be something like, "Should company X acquire company Y?" Students then spend that semester engaging in research to learn more about the problems involved in answering the question, determining the best solution, and presenting their findings in such a way as to convince others that their course of action is best.

According to Hannifin, Land, and Oliver (1999), any **open-ended learning environment** should include four components to support the learners:

1. ***Enabling Contexts*** Articulated perspectives that influence how the approaches are planned and resources are interpreted
2. ***Resources*** A range of sources (print, electronic, human) that provides information about the problem
3. ***Tools*** The means for engaging and manipulating resources and ideas
4. ***Scaffolding*** Processes that support individual learning efforts

These four components are critically important in creating an effective and truly educational problem-based learning situation.

Simulations and Games

Learning through simulation has long been part of human experience. **Simulations** are in essence evolving case studies that allow participants to examine issues and problems that arise in a specific situation (Gredler, 2004). Participants make decisions that affect the situation and experience the results of those decisions in an environment that does not affect the real world.

Professionals in Practice

When I was a public school teacher, I was a member of the executive council of my union. I was involved with negotiating a contract between teachers and the local board of education. Both sides agreed to facilitate the process by undergoing training from the Harvard Negotiation Project. One of the first things the project instructors had all of us do was participate in a simulation game that had all of us working on coming to an agreement over prices and wages for some fictitious community. Although I can barely remember the scenario or the rules, I remember clearly the lessons learned about combating the problem instead of combating the opposing team. That activity helped all of us as we entered into a particularly difficult contract negotiation.

—Abbie Brown
former teacher at George Washington Middle School
Ridgewood, New Jersey

Simulation as an educational tool is particularly appealing for situations where physical safety is an issue. Activities that allow individuals to play out situations without placing anyone at risk have a long and honorable history. As an example, astronauts practice spacewalks in pools that simulate the conditions they will encounter in outer space; this is much safer than letting new astronauts experiment with spacewalking for the first time when they are in orbit around Earth. Proponents of simulations as an educational activity argue that humans have a natural tendency to learn through mimesis, that a simulation offers a safe environment in which to explore possibilities, and that there is a need for opportunities to experiment with decision-making before actually entering certain professional arenas. For example, the personnel of California's San Onofre Nuclear Power Generating Station regularly reviews and explores the best methods of dealing with emergencies by staging simulated crises in a room designed to look exactly like the plant's actual control center. Simulations can also be useful instructional activities for promoting better, more informed decision-making regardless of the relative safety of the real-world event (Brown, 1999). It seems students gain experience as multidimensional problem-solvers while engaged in instructional simulations (Brown, 1999; Gredler, 1996).

Instructional Games

Instructional games are a subset of instructional simulations. A game is an activity in which participants abide by specified rules as they strive (often competing against others) to achieve a specific goal (Smaldino, Lowther & Russell, 2008). According to Gredler (2004), games can support four different instructional purposes:

1. To practice or refine knowledge or skills
2. To identify gaps or weaknesses in knowledge or skills
3. To review or summarize the content presented
4. To illustrate and develop new concepts among concepts and principles

Making use of games as instructional activity has a number of advantages: Games keep learners interested in repetitious tasks (e.g., memorizing); well-designed games are fun to play and attractive to learners; and game play can provide a relaxed atmosphere for learning. However, games can also distract learners from focusing on the content if they are poorly designed or create an atmosphere of intense competition (where the goal of winning the game eclipses that of learning the content) (Smaldino et al.). Depending on the construction and application of an instructional game, it may be oriented toward either a directed or open-ended environment.

One particularly popular game adaptation is based on the *Jeopardy!* television show. Within a directed learning environment, a review activity based on a popular television game show such as *Jeopardy!* can be an engaging and effective content review activity.

Just-in-Time Teaching

Just-in-time teaching or just-in-time instruction is currently a very popular concept among educators. It is a strategy whereby direct instruction is provided based on the immediate needs expressed or indicated by students during a lesson or work period. Just-in-time teaching is adaptive; the instructor may choose from a number of short lessons prepared in advance or the instructor may improvise a brief lesson. The just-in-time approach makes use of direct teaching methods within an indirect teaching environment. The instructor takes the role of facilitator, providing short lessons that cover content the students themselves request.

RESEARCH SUPPORT FOR INSTRUCTIONAL PRACTICES

An instructional designer's job includes making decisions about the instructional activities that are to be used to help learners meet specific goals and objectives. In making these decisions without falling into the cycle of only teaching the way we were taught, where should an instructional designer begin? One of the most valuable ways to think about this question is to look at the literature on teaching effectiveness. In doing so, the following question should be explored: What instructional practices and process have been validated by research data? Three major research studies or research meta-analyses give specific guidance in answering this question. The results of these studies can assist instructional designers in selecting appropriate and effective instructional activities.

One of the earliest and most helpful meta-analysis was conducted by Joyce and his colleagues (2008). They propose systems of instruction (what they call "models") that have research validation (see Figure 8.5). These models work better than other processes in accomplishing certain learning outcomes (goals). They have proposed four categories

Model			
Personal	**Information Processing**	**Behavioral**	**Social**
Nondirective teaching Concepts of self	Inductive thinking Attainment of concepts Scientific inquiry and inquiry training Memorization Synectics Advance organizers The developing intellect	Mastery learning and programmed instruction Directed instruction Simulations	Partners in learning (dyads to group investigation) Role playing Jurisprudential inquiry Adaptation to individual differences

FIGURE 8.5 Models of Teaching Validated by Research (Joyce and Weil)

of models: personal, information processing, behavioral, and social. More than twenty models, which have substantial research validation, are presented in their book *Models of Teaching* (Joyce & Weil, 2008).

Another meta-analysis of research-supported teaching practices appeared in 1993 when Ellis and Fouts published their first analysis involving innovations in education. The second edition of their book (1997) included the results of meta-analyses of twelve educational innovations. They proposed viewing the research on teaching practices on three research levels: basic, comparative, and evaluative.

Level I (basic) is pure research conducted in a laboratory setting. The purpose is to establish a "theoretical construct or idea as having some validity" (Ellis, 2001, p. 20). The research conducted at this stage is extremely useful but must be validated with continued research. This research typically has led to theories about learning, which are often then developed into programs or instructional methods.

Level II (comparative) research is designed to "test the efficacy of particular programs or instructional methods in educational settings. Educational researchers who are interested in applying theories and procedures developed at the pure or basic level generally conduct such studies (Ellis, 2001, p. 22). The research conducted at this level is done in educational settings to determine how effective these particular instructional methods or programs are.

Level III (evaluative) research is designed to determine the efficacy of instructional methods or programs at a much larger level rather than in an isolated educational setting. Large-scale implementation of an instructional model or program is studied to examine its overall effects on various stakeholders (e.g., learners, instructors, customers).

Ellis (2005) continues this analysis. His work indicates that few educational innovations have sufficient research validation (Levels II and III) to prove their effectiveness. There are a few clear winners (teaching practices with research validation) and a few clear losers (teaching practices with little or no clear research validation), with the majority of educational innovations having mixed research support. The educational innovations he analyzed are:

- Setting standards
- Self-esteem and self-efficacy
- Brain research
- Teaching for intelligence
- Thinking skills programs
- Whole-language learning
- Curriculum integration
- Cooperative learning
- Mastery learning
- Direct instruction
- Assessment

Marzano, Pickering, and Pollock (2004) also conducted a meta-analysis of teaching practices research. In their book *Classroom Instruction That Works: Research-Based Strategies for Increasing Student Achievement*, they propose that teaching is rapidly becoming more of a science. The evidence examined so far indicate specific types of teaching practices have strong effects on student achievement and that these practices work well with all types of subject matter. We use Marzano, Pickering, and Pollock's work to organize the recommended instructional activities in the following section.

ACTIVITIES BASED ON PROVEN EFFECTIVE PRACTICES

There are probably as many different kinds of specific learning activities as there are instructors. Every teacher has a few activities that have become his or her favorite through habit or a history of success. As a novice instructional designer developing your own repertoire of instructional activities, it is important to experiment with those that have the greatest potential to positively affect your students' achievement. As mentioned previously, Marzano, Pickering, and Pollock's (2004) categories of instructional strategies are proven through research to have a strong effect on student achievement. The nine categories are:

1. Identifying similarities and differences
2. Summarizing and note-taking
3. Reinforcing effort and providing recognition
4. Homework and practice
5. Nonlinguistic representations
6. Cooperative learning
7. Setting objectives and providing feedback
8. Generating and testing hypotheses
9. Questions, cues, and **advance organizers**

Prescribing activities that employ these general strategies should therefore lead to a more successful and effective instructional design. The following is Marzano, Pickering, and Pollock's list expanded to include descriptions and specific examples of activities that can be prescribed.

Identifying Similarities and Differences

The ability to determine how things are alike and different is critically important and crucial for most forms of understanding. Specific instructional activities that can facilitate this process include:

- ***Examples and non-examples*** The essential instructional strategy activity that explores similarities and differences is the provision of examples and non-examples. It is not enough to simply describe what something is. It is important to also illustrate what something is *not* (for example, "A noun is a person, place, or thing. A noun is *not* an action word nor is it a descriptive word.").

Classifying

Classifying requires the organization of various elements, objects, or concepts according to their similarities. According to Marzano, Pickering, and Pollock, one of the critical tasks of classifying is identifying the rules that govern category relationship. Activities that support skill with classifying include:

- ***Graphic Organizers*** A visual display that illustrates the classification of information can help students better understand the similarities and differences among various elements, objects, or concepts. Venn

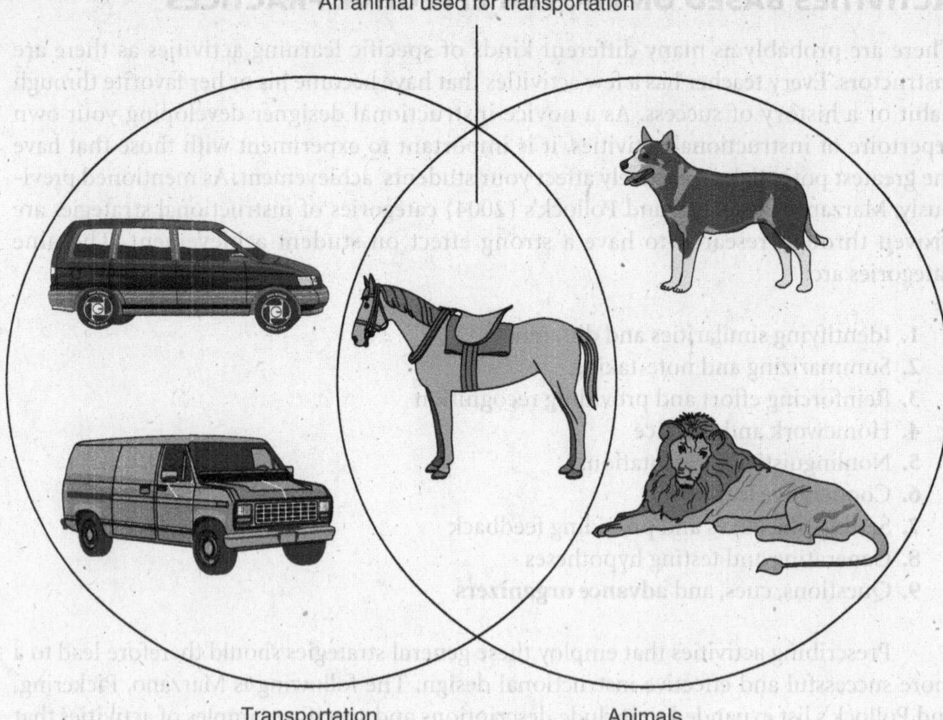

FIGURE 8.6 A Simple Venn Diagram Showing Sets and Subsets

diagrams are popular graphic organizers for the display of sets and subsets. See Figures 8.6 and 8.7.

- ***Scattergrams*** An example of an instructional activity that requires students to organize information according the components' similarities is a scattergram. The instructor provides a randomized display of the various elements, objects, and/or concepts that are the topic of study and asks students to organize them according to their similarities. This is an activity students may do on their own, as a class, or in small groups. Although there is usually no single correct method of organizing the data, a critically important aspect of this activity is the discussion of why

Orders of the reptile class of animals

Lizards	**Snakes**	**Turtles**
Gecko	Boa Constrictor	Box Turtle
Iguana	Cobra	Painted Turtle

FIGURE 8.7 A Simple Classification Chart

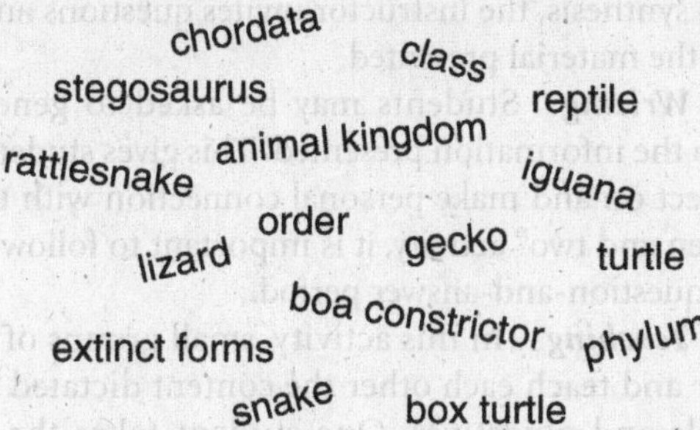

FIGURE 8.8 A Scattergram of Terms and Labels Used in the Order of the Reptile Class of Animals

students organized things as they did (this allows for clarification and guidance from the instructor and from peers). See Figure 8.8.

- ***Analogies, Metaphors, and Similes*** Another activity that explores the similarities and differences of elements, objects, and concepts is the development of analogies ("A is to B as C is to D"), metaphors ("A is D"), and similes ("A is like D"). The exploration of analogies, metaphors, and similes can encourage students to draw on their own experiences to better understand new information.

Summarizing and Note-Taking

While these are often considered study skills and are not often addressed as part of an instructional design after high school, summarizing and note-taking have proven themselves to be highly effective instructional activities for both adolescent and adult learners. Activities that facilitate summarizing and note-taking include:

- ***"Ten and Two"*** Common wisdom among experienced instructors is the rule of "ten and two" (ten minutes of presentation; two minutes of synthesis). During formal instruction, schedule a brief, relatively informal review and synthesis activity after about ten minutes of formal presentation. Students may turn to a neighbor and discuss the information presented or they may review and compare their notes. After this

Professionals in Practice

In teaching instructional design, I often ask students to develop a simile that compares the production process to the students' previous experiences. Asking students to complete a sentence such as, "Instructional design is like . . . " often results in deeply insightful statements that, when shared with the entire class, cause everyone to understand multimedia production a bit better than they did before. It often increases my understanding of how better to describe the process as well.

—Abbie Brown
associate professor at East Carolina University
Greenville, North Carolina

review and synthesis, the instructor invites questions and offers clarifications on the material presented.

- ***Reflective Writing*** Students may be asked to generate a written response to the information presented. This gives students an opportunity to reflect on and make personal connection with the material. As with the "ten and two" activity, it is important to follow reflective writing with a question-and-answer period.
- ***Reciprocal Teaching*** In this activity, small groups of students gather together and teach each other the content dictated by the instructional goals and objectives. One student takes the role of group leader and directs the discussion, but all members of the group are responsible for reviewing, clarifying, and summarizing the information.
- ***Revising and Adding to Notes*** An effective instructional activity that is often overlooked is the revision of notes taken during presentation. Students work individually or in small groups to revise and add to their notes in order to summarize and synthesize the material.

Reinforcing Effort and Providing Recognition

Critically important to student success is the belief that effort ultimately enhances achievement. Students who believe in the importance of effort are much more likely to succeed. Finding ways to recognize and reward effort made is therefore an activity that can increase the efficiency and effectiveness of an instructional design.

- ***Pause, Prompt, and Praise*** This is an activity that can be extremely important in helping students achieve success, but it is not possible to schedule this precisely into an instructional design. If the instructor notices a student or students struggling with a task, the students are asked to pause what they are doing in order to discuss the problems they have encountered. The instructor then offers a prompt, suggesting a way of working around or through the problem (see the description of just-in-time teaching). If the students succeed by implementing the suggestion, the instructor offers praise for a job well done.

Rewards and Symbols of Recognition

An instructional design may have built into it methods of rewarding and recognizing student success. Students may receive tokens (small prizes) or they may see their name highlighted in a place of honor. These extrinsic rewards do not diminish intrinsic motivation if they are given rewards for accomplishing specific performance goals (Marzano, Pickering & Pollock, 2004).

Homework and Practice

Research indicates that homework and practice increase achievement and learning (Marzano, Pickering & Pollock). It is also a natural, intuitive assumption that the more one practices, the better one becomes with just about anything. Assigning activities that promote repeated practice is a recommended component of most instructional designs. Activities that promote practice include:

- ***Speed and Accuracy Reporting*** For instruction that has skill development as one of its goals, requiring students to keep track of their speed and accuracy is a very good idea. Have students keep a progress chart for themselves that tracks individual progress.
- ***Homework*** Assigning activities to be completed outside of formal class time can extend learning opportunities as well as give students a chance for more practice. Assuming the instruction requires multiple class meetings, assign homework that includes a clear statement of the assignment's purpose and outcome; this lets students know why they are performing the task and what they should focus on. Be prepared to offer feedback on homework assignments at subsequent class meetings; offering feedback greatly increases the effectiveness of homework as an instructional activity.

Nonlinguistic Representations

A popular psychological theory known as dual coding (Marzano, Pickering & Pollock, 2004; Pavio, 1990) suggests that humans store information in two forms: linguistic and imagery. The imagery mode is a combination of mental pictures, physical sensations (touch, taste, smell), kinesthetic associations, or sound. The linguistic mode is the one most commonly used to present instructional material (through the use of lecture, assigned reading, and question-and-answer sessions). However, research indicates that the more people make use of both linguistic *and* imagery modes, the better they are able to analyze and recall information. Nonlinguistic representations include:

- ***Illustrations and Animations*** The research of psychologists such as Richard Mayer (2001) suggest that recall is enhanced when learning activities include graphics and animated sequences that illustrate the content. There is evidence to suggest that memory for pictures is generally better than memory for words; this is referred to as the picture superiority effect (Anglin, Vaez & Cunningham, 2004). However, animations should be used judiciously because research indicates that they are effective primarily as attention-getting devices or in situations where the learners are not novices with the content and have some knowledge of how to attend relevant cues and details provided by animation (Anglin, Vaez & Cunningham, 2004).
- ***Graphic Organizers*** Graphic organizers, discussed earlier in this chapter (see the section on classifying), are actually a combination of the linguistic and imagery mode because they use words and phrases organized in descriptive patterns. See Figure 8.9.
- ***Sound*** The use of sound effects and nonspeech audio (music, background noises) can have a profound effect on learners recall. Sound cues support the acquisition, processing, and retrieval of new information in a variety of ways (Bishop & Cates, 2001). The programs of National Public Radio that incorporate background

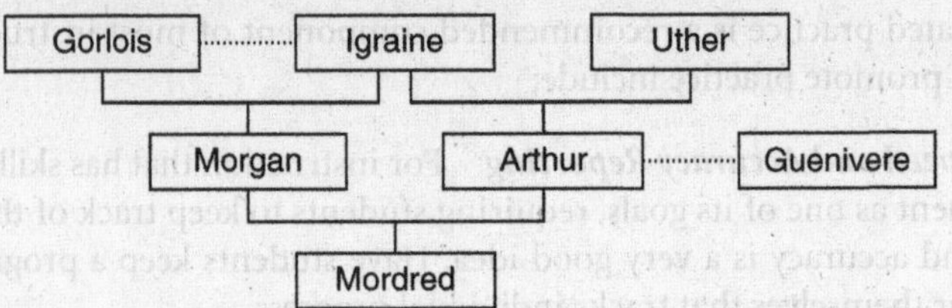

FIGURE 8.9 A Graphic Oillustrating the Rather Convoluted Family Relationships in the Legend of King Arthur

noises and sound effects are good examples of how nonlinguistic sound can be used to enhance the presentation of information in a way that stimulates the listener's ability to attend to and recall the information presented.

- ***Kinesthetic Representation*** Creating physical models or working with manipulative representations (such as the Cuisenaire rods used in elementary math classes) can help learners interpret and understand information through the sense of touch and movement.

Cooperative Learning

Students working together to accomplish a task is currently very popular, and there is research to suggest that cooperative learning is an effective and efficient instructional activity (Marzano, Pickering & Pollock, 2004; Ellis, 2005). Cooperative learning experts David Johnson and Roger Johnson (1999) outline five defining elements of cooperative learning: positive interdependence (everyone working together to succeed); face-to-face promotive interaction (offering help and praise to group members); individual and group accountability (each member contributing to the group's success); interpersonal and small group skills (communication, decision-making, conflict resolution); and group processing (reflecting on how the group functions and how its functioning can be improved). Cooperative learning activities are particularly helpful to low- and middle-achieving learners when the groups consist of heterogeneous combinations of low-, middle-, and high-achieving students. All indications are that cooperative learning works best when groups are kept relatively small (three or four students per group). The best cooperative learning activities are well-structured with clearly defined goals and expectations. Because cooperative learning is particularly popular at this time, it is important not to overuse this type of activity at the expense of independent practice and skill development.

Setting Objectives and Providing Feedback

In Chapter 6, we discussed the importance of determining instructional goals and the common practice of creating instructional objectives that accompanied these goals. It is true that setting instructional objectives (determining the expected outcome of the instructional activity) promotes efficient instruction. However, in some cases, setting objectives may cause the instruction to be too efficient in a limited manner. Research indicates that objectives carefully specified by the instructional designer may actually cause a decrease in students' general learning. Students may focus so completely on the specified objective that they do not explore the material in a way that allows them to develop broader or deeper understanding of the general topic (Marzano, Pickering & Pollock, 2004; Walberg, 1999). If the goal is for students to develop a personalized, broader, and deeper understanding of a topic, they should be encouraged to personalize the instructional goals by creating their own learning objectives. The instructor then works with the student, providing feedback on how well the student's objectives align with the instructional goals and whether the student is meeting his or her objectives. Activities that support setting objectives and providing feedback include:

- ***Contracts*** A popular activity that supports setting personalized learning objectives is the student contract. Students work with the instructor to develop their own individualized learning contracts, stating objectives that relate to both the instructional goals and to the students' personal interests, strengths, or weaknesses.
- ***Critique Sessions*** The instructor, other students, or groups of students offer feedback as to whether the individual or group is accomplishing stated objectives. Group-to-group critique sessions are particularly effective as part of cooperative learning activities. Feedback should be some combination of positive and corrective; formal critique sessions often follow a format that offers three categories of feedback; "What I see" (statements of exactly what the reviewer perceives), "What I like" (statements of what the reviewer is positively impressed with), and "What I think needs improvement" (statements of what the reviewer finds problematic).

Generating and Testing Hypotheses

Having students make predictions and conduct experiments based on those predictions is a good way to improve student achievement (Marzano, Pollock & Pickering, 2004). There are essentially two methods of generating hypotheses: inductive reasoning and deductive reasoning. Inductive reasoning is the process of drawing new conclusions from available information. Deductive reasoning is the process of using general rules (heuristics) to predict a future action or event. In generating hypotheses as a classroom activity, students may use inductive or deductive reasoning or a combination of the two. However, it is important to have students explain their thinking (perhaps even explain whether they are working inductively or deductively) in order to gain the greatest benefit from any hypothesis-generation activity. Although creating and testing hypotheses is most often associated with science, it is possible to make very good use of this activity in many other content areas. For example, high school students studying the short story form might be asked to predict a story's outcome before completing the story. As another example, adults learning a specific administrative process might be asked to predict the follow-up tasks involved upon completing the process. Hypotheses generating activities get students to explore the content of the lesson more thoroughly. They also can cause students to think more about their own thinking process (metacognition), which helps students become better decision-makers and problem-solvers.

Questions, Cues, and Advance Organizers

The strategies of introducing a topic by asking questions about that topic or by providing some type of preview of the topic (cues and advance organizers) are intended to help students retrieve what they already know that is related to the topic and prepare them to receive new information in the best frame of mind. Research on questions, cues, and advance organizers indicates they are an effective and efficient instructional activity (Marzano, Pickering & Pollock, 2004). General rules that apply to all question, cue, and advance organizer strategies are:

1. Focus should always be on what is important about the topic (as opposed to focusing on what is unusual about the topic).
2. Questions and cues that require students to analyze information produce more learning than questions that require simple recall.
3. Having posed a question, waiting briefly before accepting student responses can increase the depth of those responses (teachers are typically instructed to mentally take a slow "three count" before accepting responses from students).

Advance organizers can take a variety of forms. Before proceeding with instruction:

- Students may be encouraged to skim the content.
- The instructor may tell a brief story that relates to the content.
- An agenda or outline may be provided to students.
- A graphic organizer may be provided to students.
- Students may be given a writing prompt related to the content.

The activities described in this section are only a sample of the myriad activities that are used for instruction. However, these activities have the advantage of having some research-based support for their use.

Bill has decided that the writing center will provide activities that include problem-based learning in which small groups of students will edit poorly written sample papers as well as one-to-one tutoring that provide scaffolding for students to improve and increase their writing skills. The center will make available a variety of text and computer-based resources that students may use at any time, and it will conduct workshops throughout the year, the topics of which will be decided by student surveys. The center will also provide progress charts to help students keep track of their development by recording the results of writing evaluations conducted at the center and grades received on written assignments.

Carol has decided that the customer service supervisor training program will consist of a series of presentations and lectures combined with simulations, games, and reciprocal teaching activities in which participants will engage to increase their skills and abilities in order to meet the program's performance objectives. Each training session will begin with an advance organizing activity, and those who complete the training program will receive a framed certificate as a symbol of recognition.

Learning Environments, Instructional Activities, and the Instructional Design Process

Specifying the learning environment and instructional activities is an important part of the instructional design process. It should help you answer the following questions:

- Will the learning environment be open-ended or directed?
- Will the learning environment be oriented toward the learner, knowledge, assessment, community, or some combination of these four?
- What teaching strategies will be employed?
- What will the students do during the instruction that will help them learn the content?
- How are the instructional activities you prescribe supported by research that indicates their effectiveness?

Summary

The activities in which the learners participate to again knowledge, skill, or insight are the single-most important part of an instructional design. Instructional designers prescribe specific activities based on the information gathered during task, learner, and goals analyses. Something to be mindful of is the fact that most people will naturally recommend the instructional activities that they themselves learned from and/or best fits their preferred learning style; an instructional designer does not have the luxury of prescribing only those activities that he or she prefers. The number and order of the activities prescribed define the scope and sequence of the instruction. There are essentially two types of learning environments: directed and open-ended. Directed learning environments are ones in which the instructional designer determines specific learning objectives and prescribes structured activities in which participants demonstrate they have learned by meeting those objectives. Open-ended learning environments either present learners with a complex problem to complete or explore or help the learner determine a personalized problem to be solved or explored. Problem-based learning and instructional simulations are examples of open-ended learning situations. Instructional games—a subset of simulations— are activities that may be applied in either directed or open-ended environments. Instructional activities that have a strong research base to prove their efficacy are identifying similarities and differences; summarizing and note-taking; reinforcing effort and providing recognition; homework and practice; nonlinguistic representations; cooperative learning; setting objectives and providing feedback; generating and testing hypotheses; and questions, cues, and advance organizers.

Connecting Process to Practice

1. **Bill chose to create a knowledge-center environment for his community college's writing center. He might have chosen to create a learner-centered environment instead. What are the advantages and disadvantages to selecting a learner-centered environment in this case? What might be the advantages and disadvantages of creating a blended learner-centered and knowledge-centered environment?**
2. **How might Carol make use of both direct and indirect teaching strategies in her company's customer service supervisor training program?**
3. **You have been contracted by a hospital to develop instruction for new volunteers on how to work with patients and their families. What type of learning environment would you recommend establishing for this group?**

4. As the instructional designer for a large corporation, you have been assigned the task of creating a ninety-minute workshop on office safety and emergency preparedness. What activities might you include in this workshop?
5. You are a fifth-grade schoolteacher. One of your district's objectives for all fifth-grade students is that by the end of the school year, they will be able to correctly identify the nouns, verbs, adjectives, and adverbs used in a paragraph of expository text. What activities might you prescribe for your students throughout the school year to help meet this objective?
6. A professor of American history would like her students to develop greater understanding of what life was like in Chicago during the "Roaring 20s." What instructional activities might you recommend to her?

Recommended Reading

Bransford, J., Brown, A. L., & Cocking, R. R. (2003). *How people learn: Brain, mind, experience and school, 2nd edition.* Washington, DC: National Academy Press.

Hyerle, D. (1996). *Visual tools for constructing knowledge.* Alexandria, VA: Association for Supervision and Curriculum Development.

Marzano, R. J., Pickering, D. J., and Pollock, J. E. (2004). *Classroom instruction that works: Research-based strategies for increasing student achievement.* Upper Saddle River, NJ: Prentice Hall.

National Public Radio. *Audio archives.* http://www.npr.org.

References

Albion, P. R. (2003). PBL + IMM = PBL²: Problem based learning and interactive multimedia development. *Journal of Technology and Teacher Education, 11*(2), 243–257.

Anglin, G. J., Vaez, H. & Cunningham, K. L. (2004). Visual representations and learning: The role of static and animated graphics. In D. H. Jonassen (Ed.), *Handbook of research for educational communications and technology, 2nd edition* (pp. 865–916). Mahwah, NJ: Lawrence Erlbaum Associates.

Bishop, M. J. & Cates, W. M. (2001). Theoretical foundations for sound's use in multimedia instruction to enhance learning. *Educational Technology Research and Development 49*(3), 5–22.

Bransford, J., Brown, A. L., & Cocking, R. R. (2003). *How people learn: Brain, mind, experience and school, 2nd edition.* Washington, DC: National Academy Press.

Brown, A. (1999). Simulated classrooms and artificial students: The potential effects of new technologies on teacher education. *Journal of Research on Computing in Education, 32*(2), 307–318.

Cruikshank, D. R., Bainer, D. L. & Metcalf, K. K. (1999). *The act of teaching, 2nd edition.* New York: McGraw-Hill College.

Ellis, A. K. (2001). *Research on educational innovations, 3rd edition.* Larchmont, NY: Eye on Education.

Ellis, A. K. (2005). *Research on educational innovations, 4th edition.* Larchmont, NY: Eye on Education.

Gredler, M. (1996). Educational games and simulations: A technology in search of a (research) paradigm. In D. H. Jonassen (Ed.), *Handbook of research for educational communications and technology* (pp. 521–540). New York: Simon and Schuster Macmillan.

Gredler, M. (2004). Games and simulations and their relationships to learning. In D.H. Jonassen (Ed.), *Handbook of research for educational communications and technology, 2nd edition* (pp. 571–581).

Hannafin, M., Land, S., & Oliver, K. (1999). Open learning environment: Foundations, methods and models. In C. M. Reigeluth (Ed.), *Instructional design theories and models: A new paradigm of instructional theory.* Mahwah, NJ: Lawrence Earlbaum Associates.

Johnson, D. W., & Johnson, R. T. (1999). *Learning together and alone: Cooperative, competitive and individualistic learning.* Boston: Allyn & Bacon.

Joyce, B. & Weil, M., (2008). *Models of teaching, 8th edition.* Boston: Allyn and Bacon.

Marzano, R. J., Pickering, D. J. & Pollock, J.E. (2004). *Classroom instruction that works: Research-based strategies for increasing student achievement.* Upper Saddle River, NJ: Prentice Hall.

Mayer, R. (2001). *Multimedia learning.* Cambridge University Press.

Pavio, A. (1990). *Mental representations: A dual coding approach.* New York: Oxford University Press.

Smaldino, S., Lowther, D. L. & Russell, J. D. (2008). *Instructional technology and media for learning, 9th edition.* Upper Saddle River, NJ: Merrill/Prentice Hall.

Walberg, H. J. (1999). Productive teaching. In H. C. Waxman & H. J. Walberg (Eds.), *New directions for teaching practice and research* (pp. 75–104). Berkeley, CA: McCutcheon Publishing Corporation.

Part IV

EVALUATION: DETERMINING THE EFFECT OF THE INTERVENTION

Once you have decided on the goals and objectives of the instruction and have organized the instructional environment and activities, you will need to decide how to measure the learners' development and evaluate the success of the instructional design. Conducting carefully planned evaluation activities helps the instructional designer revise and improve the instructional intervention in order to better serve the learners.

Chapters 9 and 10 describe the principles, processes, and practices of assessment and evaluation that instructional designers use to determine learner success and the success of the instructional design process. Chapter 9 focuses on the principles, processes, and practices of **evaluating learner achievement**. Chapter 10 explains how to go about determining the success of the instructional design product and process.

Chapter 9

Evaluating Learner Achievement

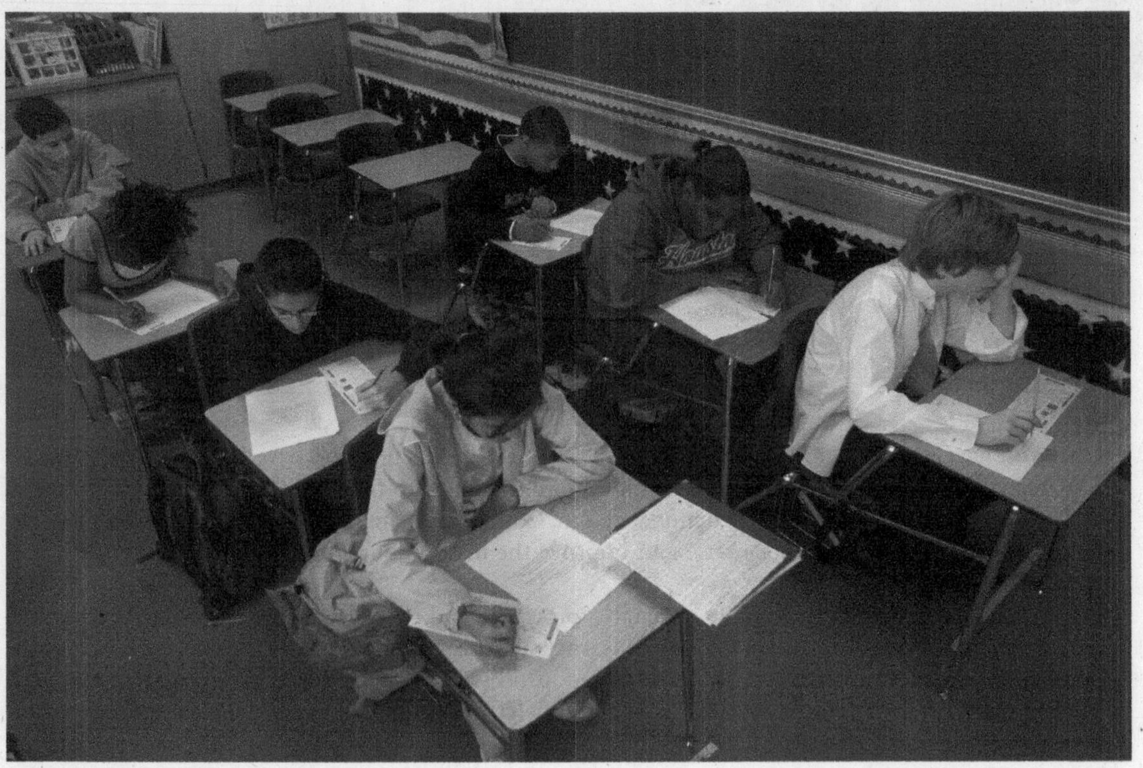

Jake's eighth-grade students need to demonstrate their ability to meet the following California math standard: "Students know the definitions of the mean, median, and mode of a distribution of data and can compute each in particular situations." As Jake works on creating instruction to help his students meet this standard, he is considering how he will assess his students. Jake needs to determine what type of assessment(s) will allow him to best determine if his students have met the standard.

Ian is responsible for determining the effectiveness of a new performance incentive program that has been implemented in his division. The program was designed to boost employee morale, with the outcome being a decrease in employee absenteeism and an increase in sales. Ian needs to determine how to assess whether the program has met its goals.

GUIDING QUESTIONS

- What is evaluation?
- How do evaluation and assessment differ?
- What role does evaluation play in the instructional design process?
- What is learner evaluation?
- What types of learner evaluations exist?
- How are learner evaluations designed and developed?
- How do you determine when a learner evaluation has been successful?

KEY TERMS

Assessment *138*	Instrument *138*	Norm-referenced *141*
Criterion-referenced *141*	Learner Evaluation *139*	Reliability *139*
Evaluation *138*	Measurement *138*	Validity *139*

CHAPTER OVERVIEW

An important part of the instructional design process is determining how well the design worked. Success can (and should) be measured at different stages and on different elements throughout the process. Varied and sustained evaluation helps ensure that the intervention created during the instructional design process meets the needs of everyone involved.

There are three major evaluation types that you will typically use as an instructional designer: learner, formative, and summative. Each has its own specific purpose and distinct techniques; the techniques are procedures used to gather data. An experienced instructional designer has a solid understanding of each of these three evaluation types and the techniques associated with each and is capable of designing and conducting evaluations using all three. With this in mind, the goal of Chapters 9 and 10 is to provide an overview of these evaluation types as they relate to the instructional design process.

In this chapter, the focus is exclusively on learner evaluation. The goal of learner evaluation is described, along with the role it plays in instructional design. The development and implementation of learner evaluations are discussed, as is how to determine if a learner evaluation has been successful.

EVALUATION, ASSESSMENT, AND MEASUREMENT

There are two terms related to evaluation that are important for you to be familiar with: assessment and measurement. **Assessment** refers to procedures or techniques used to obtain data about a learner or product. **Measurement** refers to the data collected, which is typically expressed quantitatively (i.e., numbers). The physical devices that are used to collect the data are referred to as **instruments** (e.g., rating scales forms, observation sheets, checklists, objective tests). Evaluation refers to the process for determining the success level of an individual or product based on data and then making decisions based on this success level. We use the term "evaluation" in this book; in doing so, we are referring to a process that includes assessment and measurement. We will also use the term "assessment" to refer to the techniques used during evaluation to gather data.

PURPOSE OF EVALUATION

Worthen, Sanders, and Fitzpatrick write that the purpose of evaluation is the "identification, clarification, and application of defensible criteria to determine an evaluation object's value (worth or merit), quality, utility, effectiveness, or significance in relation to those criteria" (2004, p. 5). In essence, evaluation is used to determine the success level of

Professionals in Practice

Students attend our live classes in order to get certified on our software. Students who are enrolled in our online education program are either already certified or are building their skills in related areas. Consequently, a written exam and a practical exam are sufficient to determine whether or not someone has the knowledge for certification. Informally, our evaluations break down into three categories, although not always neatly:

1. Human reaction to the course. (This was great; I learned a lot. This was terrible; I want my money back).
2. Skills, concept, or knowledge mastery and retention. (This is exactly what I need to do my job.)
3. Greatly improved job performance.

We use two kinds of formal evaluations to assess if a student has retained a concept:

1. If the student attended a live class, [he or she] first must pass a written exam that includes multiple choice and essay questions.
2. After the written exam, [he or she] must pass a practical exam, in which [he or she] must use our software to successfully configure a telephone system from scratch. Depending on the class [he or she is] taking, [the student] must demonstrate that [he or she] know how to install our software and its related components, configure it, test for dial tone, demonstrate some programming knowledge to route telephone calls to a person or to allow a user to enter data (a credit card number, for example), and handle the call accordingly. Students enrolled in online classes must pass a written exam that includes multiple choice, matching, true/false, and fill-in-the blank questions.

—Erik Novak
distance learning course developer
at Interactive Intelligence, Inc.
Indianapolis, Indiana.

something; this *something* is typically an individual or a product, such as a lesson, project, or program (although, a process can also be evaluated). A properly designed and implemented evaluation provides an instructional designer with appropriate data that can be analyzed to determine the success level of whom or what is being evaluated. Once this is determined, an instructional designer decides if changes need to be made. These changes vary based on whom or what is being evaluated and when the evaluation is taking place. Changes could include such things as learner remediation, redesigning the instructional materials, or abandoning the entire instructional intervention. Changes made are done so to help improve the likelihood that a learner will reach a high level of success.

THE GOAL OF LEARNER EVALUATION

Determining if a learner has reached a high level of success is accomplished through learner evaluation. Learner evaluation helps determine the level of performance or achievement that an individual has attained as a result of instruction. This is established by the extent to which a leaner is able to meet instructional goals and objectives.

Chapter 6 discusses in detail what instructional goals and objectives are and how they are developed. As a reminder, instructional goals describe the general intentions of instruction, while instructional objectives describe more specific outcomes of what a learner should be able to demonstrate once instruction has been completed. An effective and appropriate learner evaluation is based directly on the instructional goals and objectives. The next section describes how this is accomplished.

DEVELOPING LEARNER EVALUATIONS

The development of a learner evaluation begins with examining the instructional goals and objectives that were created as a result of the needs and task analyses. An instructional designer examines the instructional goals and objectives to determine what change the instruction is meant to bring about. Is it a change in learner knowledge, skill, or attitude? In addition, the instructional designer determines how the success of a learner will be judged. Will a learner be compared to other learners or will a learner's level of success be determined based on competence? The answers to these questions will help an instructional designer develop an effective learner evaluation that includes appropriate assessment activities.

Validity and Reliability

Two key concepts are important to understand and keep in mind when developing a learner evaluation: validity and reliability. A learner evaluation is considered to have validity if it helps determine whether the intended outcomes of instruction (based on the instructional objectives) were actually met by the learners. In other words, did the learners meet the instructional objectives? A learner evaluation that allows this to be determined is considered to be valid. Validity of a learner evaluation (especially tests) is not always easy to determine.

There are various types of validity; face validity and content validity are two that an instructional designer should be familiar with. Face validity is concerned with how a learner evaluation appears. Experts are asked to judge whether they believe the learner evaluation is reasonable, well-designed, and likely to be capable of gathering appropriate data. If experts believe these to be true, then the learner evaluation is said to have face validity.

Professionals in Practice

The following is an example of an instructional design project where two different types of evaluation were used and how changes were made as a result of the evaluations. The example is provided to give context for where evaluation fits into the instructional design process.

I was contracted by a hospital to help design and implement an intervention that would help a particular population of nurses employed by the hospital pass a mandatory state examination on anatomy and physiology. Each nurse was returning to the profession after an absence of a year or more. Based upon data provided by hospital administrators and data from analysis (task and learner) conducted by the instructional designer, it was determined that a four week, self-paced training system delivered through the Web would be developed and implemented as the intervention. The nurses from this group, who did not pass the examination the first time, would participate in the training to pass a subsequent examination.

Working with a team that included a Web developer, graphic artist, and two nurse trainers (subject matter experts), I developed the training. As the training was being developed, several nurses were asked to try out portions of it. I observed several using the training. In addition to the observations, I solicited feedback from the nurses by conducting a group interview protocol after they had gone through parts of the training. Several open-ended questions were asked during the group interview. I analyzed my observation notes and the nurses' responses. This formative evaluation revealed that several changes probably should be made to the training. One such change was to add review quizzes more frequently throughout the content. I implemented this change, along with several others.

Once the training was completely developed, it was piloted with twenty-five nurses. The results of the training were encouraging; twenty-two of the nurses passed the examination the second time! Based upon the learner evaluation results (the high percentage of nurses who passed the examination), the hospital administration made it mandatory that all nurses needing to take the examination would participate in the training prior to doing so. If the successful results continued, then additional training would be developed using the same self-paced, Web-based format. It was also decided that the nurses who failed the second examination would go through the training again.

Two types of evaluation were used in this instructional design example: formative and learner. Each was used to provide unique data that allowed me to make decisions on how to develop and implement an efficient, effective, and satisfying intervention that helped meet the goal of my client.

—Tim Green
former director of distance education
California State University–Fullerton

Content validity is similar to face validity. However, what is being determined with content validity is the extent to which the specific intended domain of content is addressed in the evaluation (Carmines & Zeller, 1991, p. 20). For example, the questions in a test should represent the important content and/or skills that the instruction covered. Evidence of content-related validity is generally determined by having subject matter experts look at the test items and make judgments about the appropriateness of each item and how well the domain was covered. Additionally, the instructional designer can create a table of specification to help determine the content validity.

Reliability is the extent to which a learner evaluation will provide similar results when conducted on multiple occasions. If a test is given to the same learner at different times without the learner receiving any additional preparation and similar results occur, then the test is considered to be reliable. There are a variety of statistical methods for determining reliability; however, they are beyond the scope of this book.

Criterion-Referenced and Norm-Referenced: Simplified

Most learner evaluations you will help develop will be criterion-referenced (also referred to as minimum-competency or mastery). A learner evaluation that is criterion-referenced indicates that a learner is being judged based on his or her level of competence. Competence is determined by specific criteria, such as being able to answer a specified number of questions or the ability to demonstrate certain skills in a specific amount of time. If you have a driver's license, remember back to when you first earned it. Part of earning the license was passing a driving test, which consisted of you demonstrating to an examiner that you could safely operate a car. As you drove the car, the examiner asked you to perform various tasks and checked off how successful you were at completing these tasks. At the end of the driving test, the examiner tallied your score to determine the level of competence you obtained. If your score was high enough, you passed the driving test. Passing the test indicated that you had met certain criteria set by the Department of Motor Vehicles or Secretary of State and therefore had demonstrated competence.

A learner evaluation that is norm-referenced indicates that the results of the evaluation are being used to compare or rank learners. There are numerous norm-referenced examinations that as a student you are familiar with. Most graduate students are required to take the Graduate Record Exam (GRE) and include the score as part of their program's admissions application. The GRE is designed to provide a spread of test scores that are ranked in comparison to others who have taken the same test. This information assists admission officers in making decisions about individuals that will be admitted into graduate programs.

Although both serve useful purposes, criterion-referenced learner evaluations generally provide more useful information. This information can help instructors and instructional designers in making decisions about where a learner may have gaps in his or her learning. Knowing this type of information will allow for changes to be made to instruction that will benefit the learner. A norm-referenced learner evaluation does not measure competence. Knowing how a learner ranks in relationship to other learners does not provide the necessary information about how competent the learner is or what changes need to be made to help improve instruction. Our treatment of learner evaluation in this chapter focuses on criterion-referenced learner evaluation.

Starting with the Instructional Objectives

It is extremely important to understand that instructional objectives are a key element in the development of an effective learner evaluation. The learner evaluation should be derived from the instructional objectives. There needs to be a direct relationship between the instructional objectives and learner evaluation. If there is, the learner evaluation will be authentic; in other words, the learner evaluation will help the instructor and instructional designer determine if a learner has or has not met the intended instructional outcomes.

Well-written instructional objectives will describe the outcome a learner should be able to achieve after instruction has been completed. Three typical outcomes are possible; the outcome could be a change in a learner's knowledge, skill, or attitude. The task of an instructional designer is to identify what type of outcome is expected and then develop an assessment technique that will determine whether this outcome has been achieved. Each of these outcome types requires a different approach. We will take a look at how each outcome can be addressed.

INSTRUCTIONAL OBJECTIVES AND INSTRUCTIONAL OUTCOMES How can you determine whether the intended outcome of an instructional objective is a change in knowledge, skill, or attitude? Take a look at the action (the verb) that is part of the instructional objective. For example, read the following and identify the action:

The learner will be able to list the three major warning signs of a heart attack.

The action in the instructional objective is *to list*—more specifically, to list the three major warning signs of a heart attack. The outcome of the instructional objective is for the learner to be able to identify when an individual might be having a heart attack.

We have now identified the action and the outcome, but what type of outcome is this? To help answer this question, refer back to the learning taxonomies we discussed in Chapters 2 and 6. Three types of learning taxonomies were discussed: cognitive, psychomotor, and affective. As you look at these taxonomies, does the action seem to fit into one of these taxonomies? The action fits into the cognitive learning taxonomy (Bloom's taxonomy of the cognitive domain, as it is referred to) at the comprehension level. Because it fits into the cognitive domain, the outcome of the instructional objective is a change in a learner's knowledge. Knowing this information will help you develop an appropriate assessment technique that will determine whether a learner has achieved the outcome.

As you gain more experience with instructional objectives, determining whether the intended outcome is a change in knowledge, skill, or attitude will become second nature.

A CHANGE IN KNOWLEDGE For a learner to be competent in a given field, he or she must possess fundamental knowledge that relates to that field. For example, a nurse needs to know anatomy and physiology before being able to treat a patient, a mechanic needs to know the different parts of an engine before fixing it, and a basketball referee must know the rules of the game before officiating it. Because knowledge is such an important element in all fields, being able to determine the level of knowledge a learner has is a critical part of instruction. Determining a learner's knowledge level and whether it has changed as a result of instruction is typically done through the use of either an objective or constructed-response test (Morrison, Ross & Kemp, 2007). These types of tests are often referred to as paper-and-pencil tests.

An objective test includes questions (referred to as items), such as true/false, multiple choice, and matching, that have one correct answer. Constructed-response tests include short-answer and essay items, which focus on the learner constructing an answer rather than selecting one that is provided. Objective tests deal with low-level cognitive abilities—knowledge and comprehension—while constructed-response tests often deal with higher-level cognitive abilities, such as application, analysis, synthesis, and evaluation.

Writing well-designed objective or constructed-response tests requires skills that few have mastered. There are textbooks and university courses that specifically deal with this topic; it is important to realize that what we provide in this chapter is a basic treatment of the topic. We only provide guidelines for how to develop different types of test items.

Test Development Plan. Millman and Greene (1985) state that answers to several questions need to be obtained before a test is developed. The combination of these answers will help an instructional designer create a test development plan. This plan will help guide the development and eventual implementation of the test.

- What is the purpose of the test?
- Who will be taking the test?
- How much time will be used for testing?
- How will the test be administered?
- What will the test cover?
- What sources of content will be used?
- What are the dimensions of the content?
- Which types of item formats are to be used?
- How many items are available in the item pool, and how many need to be constructed?
- What is the appropriate difficulty and taxonomy level for the items?
- How will the items be grouped and sequenced?
- How will the items/test be scored?
- How will the test be evaluated?
- Will an item analysis be performed?
- Will the reliability and measurement error of the test be assessed? (p. 180)

Hopkins (1998) provides guidelines for developing and implementing tests. The guidelines are:

- Prepare a table of specifications to guide item development and selection and maximize content validity.
- It is usually desirable to include more items in the first draft of the test than will be needed in the final form.
- The item should be phrased so the content rather than the form of the statement will determine the answer.
- The difficulty level of the items should be appropriate to the group of examinees.
- Before the test is given, it is impossible to estimate the difficulty of the items accurately.
- The items should reflect several taxonomy levels.
- Classroom tests should be power tests, not speed tests. Learners should be rewarded for their knowledge rather than their ability to take tests.
- The reading level should be relatively easy.
- It is often desirable to use more than one type of item.
- All items of a particular kind should ordinarily be placed together in the test.
- The directions to the learner should be as clear, complete, and concise as possible.
- Before the actual scoring begins, answer keys should be prepared and scoring procedures outlined.
- Every reasonable precaution should be taken to ensure excellent testing conditions.
- If the test is to be used for program evaluation, research, or important student decisions, it should be field-tested with a group of comparable students. (pp. 226–230)

After examining the standard and the learning objectives associated with it, Jake has determined that he needs to create two assessments. The first assessment will focus on his students' ability to demonstrate their understanding of the definitions of mean, media, and mode. The second assessment will focus on his students' ability to compute the statistics when given a set of data.

Ian has determined that he has three distinct data types to collect: employee morale, the number of employee absences, and the number of sales. Assessing employee morale will be difficult because it is highly subjective. However, Ian believes he will be able to create an instrument that allows him to measure it. Gathering data on employee absenteeism and sales does not require an assessment. This data is readily available to him through various departments in his company.

Developing Objective Test Items

True/False Items. True/False items are written as statements that a learner determines to be either correct (true) or incorrect (false). The knowledge that is tested with a true/false item is limited to factual information (the knowledge and comprehension level of Bloom's taxonomy). The use of true/false items should be kept to a minimum because it is difficult (if not impossible) to determine whether a learner knew the correct response or guessed it (a learner has a 50% chance of guessing the correct answer).

Guidelines for true/false items:

- Use them sparingly, if at all.
- They should be completely true or completely false.
- They should be restricted to only one thought or idea.
- They should not need additional qualification or clarification to answer.
- Avoid negatively worded items.

Examples:

- Sacramento is the capital of California.
- An employee who is late to work more than three days in a row will be terminated.
- At the collegiate level, a player will be disqualified from a basketball game after committing his or her fourth personal foul.

Multiple-Choice Items. Multiple-choice items are considered to be the most useful items used in objective tests. Unlike true/false items, multiple-choice items can be used to judge higher-level thinking, such as application and analysis. A multiple-choice item consists of a stem, alternatives, and distractors. The stem is a question or incomplete sentence. The alternatives are the possible answers to the question, which includes the correct answer and incorrect answers called distractors.

Guidelines for multiple-choice items:

- The content should be meaningful and not deal with trivial information; this can be accomplished by relating the item directly to an instructional objective.
- The stem should be clearly written and should only include enough information to allow the learner to understand the item.
- The stem should be a question ending with a question mark or a statement that ends with a colon.
- Stick to four alternatives.
- Each alternative should be distinct; avoid overlapping alternatives.
- The correct answer should clearly be the best possible response.

- The correct answer should not include irrelevant clues, such as having it include more words or being more precise than the distractors..
- Alternatives should be grammatically consistent with the stem.
- Avoid negatively stated stems.
- Avoid using "all of the above" or "none of the above" as alternatives; "all of the above" can often be simply eliminated by a learner who knows that one of the alternatives is incorrect; "none of the above" does not necessarily indicate that a learner knows the true answer. A learner may correctly choose "none of the above" but would be unable to supply the correct if asked.
- Randomly select the position of the correct answer.

Examples:

- Norm-referenced learner evaluations are used to
  A. determine the competence of learners.
  B. rank or compare learners.
  C. assess the skill level of learners.
  D. make decisions about instructional objectives.
- The primary function of a Notary Public is to
  A. act as an impartial witness.
  B. verify the originality of documents.
  C. authenticate the accuracy of a signature.
  D. bear witness to the signing of loan documents.
- Until 1962, Jamaica was a former colony of what country?
  A. Germany
  B. Great Britain
  C. Spain
  D. United States of America
- In which of the following ways could 180 pencils be packaged for delivery?
  A. 10 boxes with 17 pencils each
  B. 13 boxes with 11 pencils each
  C. 15 boxes with 12 pencils each
  D. 19 boxes with 11 pencils each

Matching Items. With matching questions, a learner is being asked to determine the relationship between two different lists of information. The most appropriate use of matching questions is when the information in each column forms a homogenous group. A few common examples of information that is tested using matching questions are terms and definitions, events and persons, events and dates, and rules and examples. Matching questions are typically used to test knowledge level instructional objectives.

Guidelines for matching items (see Figure 9.1):

- Providing more items in the answer column (the right-side column) reduces the chance of a learner guessing successfully.
- Make certain that learners fully understand the rationale for how the items match.
- Place items on the left with numbers; place the options on the right and assign them with letters.
- Arrange items and options in a logical order.
- Place all the items and options on a single page if possible.
- Limit the list to not more than ten to fifteen items.

	Theorist	Theory
___1.	Bruner	A) Cognitive and affective development of children
___2.	Dewey	B) Cognitive growth
___3.	Gagne	C) Component display
___4.	Gardner	D) Conditions of learning
___5.	Pavio	E) Dual coding
___6.	Piaget	F) Gestalt
___7.	Skinner	G) Multiple intelligences
___8.	Vygotsky	H) Operant conditioning
		I) Progressivism
		J) Zone of proximal development

FIGURE 9.1 Matching Items

Short-Answer Items. A short-answer item is a question in the form of a direct question, a specific problem, or an incomplete statement or question (this type is also known as a fill-in-the-blank item). It requires that a learner provide a response rather than identifying the correct response from a list of possible answers, thus helping to eliminate guessing. A short-answer item differs from an essay item in that it requires a more concise and constricted answer. Short-answer items are particularly useful where computation is required to determine the answer.

Guidelines for short-answer items:

- A direct question is preferable to a statement.
- The question should be written so the response is as brief as possible; this allows the scoring of the question to be more objective.
- Avoid phrasing the items with wording that comes directly from materials learners will have read.
- Avoid grammatical or other clues that give away the correct answer.
- When using incomplete statements or questions, avoid deleting too much information; for example, "The major export of ______, ______, and Venezuela is ________?"

Examples:

- The two major types of graphic file formats used on the Web are called .gif and _____?
- Ian scored 45 out of 47 on a test. What percentage of correct responses did he make?
- What planet is closest to the sun?

Constructed-Response Tests. Constructed-response tests differ from objective tests because the answers to questions making up constructed-response tests do not necessarily have one correct response. Due to this, constructed-response tests are considered to be subjective tests and are therefore generally more difficult to score. The major item used in constructed-response tests are essays. This type of question allows for higher-levels of cognition (e.g., analysis, synthesis, and evaluation) to be assessed.

Essay Items. As mentioned, essay questions are useful for determining a learner's higher-level cognitive abilities (e.g., analysis, synthesis, and evaluation). Essay questions can provide insight into the understanding a learner has on the content that was taught. Additionally, insight can be gained on how well a learner writes. However, a caution needs to be provided: A learner with poor writing skills or whose native language is not being used to answer an essay question may be unfairly evaluated as not understanding content that was taught because he or she lacks adequate writing skills. It is important to take this into consideration when using essay items.

Guidelines for essay items:

- They should be carefully focused.
- Several shorter questions—rather than fewer longer questions—tend to provide a better assessment of a learner.
- Do not give students a choice of questions to answer; have all learners answer the same questions.
- Inform learners of how the questions will be graded; if spelling is important, inform the learners. Understanding how a question will be graded will help learners focus on what is important. This can be accomplished by providing students with a rubric prior to completing the essay questions.
- The length of time needed to answer essay questions can vary greatly among learners.
- Learners need preparation for taking essay questions.
- Before grading, review the major points that should or could be discussed in each answer.
- When grading, read through and grade the same question for each learner before moving on to the next question.
- When grading, it is always desirable to have more than one grader.
- When grading, read through the entire answer once and then check it over for factual information.

Examples:

- In your opinion, what is the most important element of the instructional design process? Support your answer with at least two examples. (3-page limit; 20 points)
- Describe how behaviorist and constructivist theories could be used to teach an individual how to design and develop a website. Treat each theory separately in your answer.

A CHANGE IN SKILL Evaluating whether a learner has had a change in skill is done through examining actions or behaviors that can be directly observed. This is often called performance assessment. Typically, what is being examined is a learner's ability to perform a particular task or series of related tasks that make up a particular skill. An example is taking blood from an individual who is donating blood. This general skill can be broken down into a series of precise skills. The learner is not only being judged on his or her ability to meet the general skill but also on the more precise skills that make up this general skill. It is important to note that what we are calling the general skill can also be considered the instructional goal. The more precise skills would be considered instructional objectives.

Guidelines for evaluating a skill:

- When evaluating a skill, both process and the product can be evaluated. Determine whether both or just one will be evaluated; generally, both are evaluated. The product is the end result or outcome of the skill (for example, a filled vile of blood correctly labeled and stored).

- When evaluating the process, the following elements can be included: following a proper series of steps, using tools or instruments properly, completing the skill in a certain timeframe.
- When evaluating the product, the quality and quantity of the product can be assessed.
- Evaluate the skill under the most realistic conditions possible.

Evaluating a learner's change in skill can be done by using a variety of assessment techniques, such as direct testing, performance ratings, observation and anecdotal records, and portfolios. It is important to note that evaluating a learner's change in skill often includes the use of more than one of these assessment techniques.

Direct Testing. There are certain skills that can be directly tested to determine how well a learner can perform the skill. What is primarily being evaluated is the final outcome (i.e., the product) that is a result of performing the skill. In addition, the process or processes of how the learner performed the skill can be evaluated; this can provide important information about areas in which a learner needs improvement.

Examples:

- A nurse drawing blood from a patient
- A postal worker sorting letters
- A track and field athlete running the 110-meter high hurdles
- A carpenter using a power tool

Guidelines for the direct testing process:

- Start by reviewing the task analysis results; this will help determine the steps of the skill the learner will need to perform. The steps will serve as the individual criteria that the learner will be evaluated on.
- Determine the level of proficiency that is considered acceptable for the outcome; for example, a track and field athlete who is able to run the 110-meter high hurdles in 14 seconds or less will make the team.
- Determine where the testing will take place, what equipment, materials, and personnel are needed, and what safety precautions should be taken.
- Write the test instructions that inform the learners of how the test will be conducted.
- Establish how the results will be recorded.
- Conduct the test, judge the learner's level of proficiency, and provide feedback to the learner.

Performance Ratings. Performance ratings and direct testing are similar techniques. However, the main focus of each is different. The focus of a performance rating is on a learner's ability to perform certain actions, not on the product, as it is with direct testing. Although this is the case, the product resulting from the actions completed during a performance rating is also evaluated—often in terms of both quantity and quality.

Two common techniques used as part of a performance rating are checklists and rating scales. A checklist is used to determine the sequence of actions taken by a learner while performing a task. No qualitative judgment is being made on how well the actions were performed when using a checklist; all that is being determined is if the action was performed or not.

1	2	3	4	5
Poor	Below average	Average	Above average	Excellent

FIGURE 9.2 A Likert-Type Scale

A rating scale is designed to provide a rating of how well a learner performs different actions. The rating is typically identified on a numerical scale that indicates performance from low to high, poor to excellent, or unacceptable to acceptable. This is called a Likert-type scale. See Figure 9.2.

When developing a rating scale, it is important to pilot-test the scale with several learners from the target group (or those who closely resemble the target group) to determine how the rating scale will work. Additionally, it is important that if multiple individuals are using the rating scale that they understand and agree on the rating scale criteria. This helps bring about consistency with how the learners will be rated (known as "interrater reliability").

Examples of performance ratings:

- Applying cooking techniques for making a soufflé
- Developing black and white photographs in a darkroom
- Using interrogation skills to gather information from a suspected felon
- Debating skills

Guidelines for the performance rating process:

- As with the direct testing technique, start by reviewing the task analysis results; this will help determine the steps of the skill the learner will need to perform. The steps will serve as the individual criteria on which the learner will be evaluated.
- Develop the rating scale that will be used:
  1. Typically, it is most appropriate to include five levels on the rating scale; this will help clearly differentiate a learner's performance. Scales of two or three items can also be used.
  2. When defining the numerical rating points, verbal descriptions should be used; the descriptions should not be overlapping.
  3. Clear and distinct wording should be used to express the item that is to be rated.
  4. Only one idea should be included in each item.
- Pilot-test the rating instrument with at least two learners from the target group or from a closely representative group.

Observations and Anecdotal Records. An anecdotal record is developed as a result of observing a learner perform a skill. Typically, the skill is performed in the exact (or a representative) setting in which the skill will generally be used. During the observation of the skill, notes are taken that reflect how well a learner performed. Once the observation has concluded, the notes are expanded into a narrative that describes the learner's performance and areas in which the learner needs to improve. For the most useful results, the notes should be written into narrative form soon after the observation has finished.

It is important to understand that using observations and anecdotal records can be time-consuming, especially when the number of learners that need to be observed is large. In addition to the time involved, subjectivity can also be an issue. Subjectivity can be minimized if the observer directly reports on what he or she sees—staying away from interpretation until after the observation has been completed. Additionally, rubrics and checklists (both described later in this chapter) can be used during the observation to focus the observer on what he or she should be looking for.

Examples of observation and anecdotal records:

- Observing a student teacher in a classroom
- Observing an instructor conducting a training session
- Following a supervisor for a day to determine how she manages her employees
- Riding along on shift with a police officer to assess how the officer interacts with the public
- Closely monitoring a student as he interacts with other students during several class periods

Guidelines for the anecdotal records process:

- Determine what skills the observation will focus on; this will help guide the observer during the observation.
- Determine whether recording devices will be used during the observation, such as a video camera or tape recorder; permission will need to be obtained from the individual being recorded and from the organization where the observation is taking place; if other individuals, such as students, coworkers, or customers, will be recorded (whether planned or not), permission must also be obtained from each of them.
- Obtain permission to observe the learner at the organization. Organizations have different policies about this, and it can take days to weeks to gain permission to access certain organizations; prepare for this.
- Decide whether the observation will be announced or unannounced.
- Notes taken during the observation should be brief and directly about what is taking place; avoid interpretation of the events until after the observation is over; expand on the notes soon after the observation has finished.
- Determine whether follow-up observations are necessary; although time-consuming and often costly, multiple observations can provide data that will more accurately depict a learner's level of skill.
- If multiple instructors will use the rating scale, make certain they understand and agree to the criteria.

Portfolios. A portfolio is a collection of artifacts that depicts a learner's ability. "Well-designed portfolios represent important, contextualized learning that requires complex thinking and expressive skills" (Herman and Winters, 1994). The focus of a portfolio is on the products a learner creates as a result of skills the learner has acquired over a given period of time. Therefore, a portfolio is meant to show the progression of learning that has taken place. It can directly indicate how well the learner is applying skills learned during instruction by indicating areas of strengths and weaknesses. "The goal is to produce richer and more valid assessments of students' competencies than are possible from traditional testing" (Novak, Herman & Gearhart, 1996).

Examples:

- The collection of paintings from an artist
- Songs written and performed by a musician
- Short stories written by a writer
- A collection of different products created by a fourth-grade student on a specific topic
- A set of instructional design project examples created by an individual or group
- Scholarly and creative works (e.g., articles, presentations, multimedia projects) by a university professor

Guidelines for the portfolio process:

- Determine what skill(s) the portfolio will cover and over what period of time; the skills should be directly related to instructional goals and objectives.
- Identify how the artifacts will be evaluated; rubrics should be developed that provide criteria for judging their quality.
- Clearly identify how the entire portfolio will be evaluated; how will a learner's change in skill be determined?
- In consultation with the instructor, a learner should determine what artifact samples are included in the portfolio; typically, a learner and instructor meet during the development of the portfolio, allowing the instructor to provide feedback to the learner to determine how the learner is progressing.
- The instructor judges the completed portfolio.

Rubrics. We have mentioned several times in this chapter that rubrics can be used in conjunction with various learner evaluation techniques. Let us look at what a rubric is. A rubric is an assessment instrument that is used to evaluate a learner based on the learner's performance of specific criteria. Specifically, a rubric is a printed set of scoring guidelines (criteria) that is used to evaluate a learner's performance or product. Rubrics can be used with knowledge-, skill-, and attitude-related instructional objectives. When a rubric is used to evaluate a learner, he or she is provided with an overall score based on how well the learner performed on the entire mixture of criteria. The rubric will also indicate how well the learner performed on each of these individual criteria. A rubric looks similar to a rating scale; however, a major difference is that a rubric is more descriptive. Rubrics also take a more holistic approach to evaluating a learner's performance by looking at the entire learner outcome.

A rubric can work as a guide for learners and instructors. If provided to a learner before instruction begins, a rubric will guide the learner by helping him or her focus on the specific areas he or she will be evaluated on. A rubric also helps guide a teacher by focusing the teacher on the areas that will be evaluated. Rubrics allow evaluation to be more objective and consistent by clarifying the criteria to be evaluated in specific and descriptive terms. Rubrics provide a much higher level of detail on how a learner has performed than do rating scales.

Rubrics have become very popular in recent years—especially with K–12 teachers—due in part to the standards-based education movement. Many K–12 teachers have turned to rubrics as evaluation tools because they: 1) can be matched directly to state standards and instructional objectives, 2) provide a much greater level of detail than do letter grades and numerical scores for how a student is performing, 3) can save evaluation time (once they are developed; development of rubrics can be time-consuming), and 4) can help make evaluation more objective and consistent. Rubrics are also popular with non-K–12 teachers because of many of these same reasons.

There are numerous rubric development software and websites that can be used to help develop rubrics. We suggest that you conduct a Web search for rubric development software and websites in order to try out a few different types. You will be able to find a tool that meets your needs.

A CHANGE IN ATTITUDE The most difficult outcome to determine whether a learner has achieved is a change in attitude. Attitudes are based on feelings, emotions, and perceptions, which are highly subjective, often subtle, and are very difficult to evaluate directly. A learner's attitude is typically evaluated by examining his or her behaviors and what he or she says. Assessment techniques used to examine these are observations and anecdotal records, surveys and questionnaires, self-report inventories, and interviews.

Examples of determining a change in attitude:

- An employee's feelings about a change in policy about accumulating time off for sick leave
- A learner's interest in listening to classical music
- A doctor's attitude toward his patients
- A customer's perceptions about a new product
- A change in a learner's eating habits

Observations and Anecdotal Records. For determining attitude change, observations and anecdotal records work much like they do for determining whether a learner has had a change in skill. An instructor observes a learner in an authentic environment (e.g., classroom, job site) and writes notes about what the instructor observes as it relates to affective outcomes (i.e., attitudes and behaviors). For example, an instructor may be looking at how a learner treats others or how enthusiastic a learner may be to participate in a certain activity. Soon after the observation is completed, the instructor expands on the notes to provide a more complete picture of what took place.

Surveys and Questionnaires. Observations and anecdotal records are often not feasible. Let us look at an example dealing with healthy eating. After participating in a workshop dealing with losing weight, a learner is expected to change his behavior by planning and eating healthy meals that include certain foods. Direct observation of whether the learner's behavior has changed toward certain types of food would be almost impossible to determine through direct observation. An instructor would not have the time (nor the inclination) to follow the learner around to see what he eats through the day. Instead of observing the learner, a survey or questionnaire could be used to gather data about the learner's behavior and attitudes toward healthy foods.

Surveys and questionnaires generally include two types of items: open-ended questions where a leaner writes answers to the questions and questions with fixed responses where a learner chooses the answer that best indicates their opinion. Open-ended questions can provide data that requires a significant amount of time to analyze; however, the data provided may be highly informative and insightful about the learner. Questions with fixed responses are easier and quicker to analyze. However, they do not provide the same level of depth that open-ended questions provide.

Rating scales are often used in surveys and questionnaires. As a reminder (see the section on "Rating Scales"), a rating scale item is one that allows the user to select from several choices—generally, from two, three, or five choices. A rating scale that consists of five choices is known as a Likert-type scale.

Self-Reporting Inventories. A self-reporting inventory generally consists of a series of structured questions or statements that are to be answered with yes or no.

- I usually turn in my homework on time.
- Finishing high school is important to me.

Self-reporting inventories are similar to Likert-type or rating scales. Often, self-reporting inventories use Likert or rating scale formats.

Interviews. Interviews are one of the most widely used assessment techniques. An interview can provide an opportunity for a wide-range of topics to be discussed. It can also be a useful technique for allowing a learner to clarify and expand on answers given through other assessment techniques (e.g., a survey or questionnaire). Because of the potential for increased amounts of data to be collected, interviews can take significant amounts of time to analyze.

Unstructured interviews are usually not advisable to conduct because too much time is used up on a limited number of topics; additionally, the learner and not the instructor often determine these topics. A skillful learner will develop a series of open-ended questions that guide the interview. A skillful interviewer will also provide few clues about the *right* answers to questions. The interviewer refrains from being too active in the interview process and therefore will not help "shape" a learner's responses.

Learner Evaluation and a Change in Attitude. When conducting a learner evaluation to determine a change in attitude, there are problems that can occur. These problems are related to the responses learners provide on rating scales, surveys, questionnaires, self-reporting inventories, and during interviews. The most common problems are social-desirability responses, self-deception, and semantic problems.

Social-desirability responses are those that a learner gives because he or she believes they are the ones that he or she is expected to give (hence, they are "socially desirable" responses). Self-reporting inventories are highly susceptible to social-desirability responses. Self-deception is a "common adjustment phenomenon in human behavior" where the "tendency to want to like what we see when we look at ourselves" impacts how we respond (Hopkins, 1998, p. 296). A learner may respond in certain ways because he or she wants to appear a certain way and therefore feel good about him or herself. Semantic problems deal with the meanings a learner may attach to words. For example, a rating scale may use the words "rarely," "seldom," "average," "frequently," and "usually" as choices for an item that asks a learner how often he or she chooses to listen to classical music over other types of music. As the learner answers this item, he or she wavers between selecting "rarely" or "seldom" because he or she is unsure of the difference.

CONDUCTING A LEARNER EVALUATION

When should a learner be evaluated? As a beginning instructional designer, a common mistake is to think that learner evaluation is only performed at the end of instruction. Although this is an appropriate time to do so, there are additional times that a learner can be evaluated. The three most common are before instruction has begun, during instruction, and at the conclusion of instruction. Data gathered at these times can provide very different information about the learner.

Pre-Instruction

Evaluating a learner before instruction has begun allows data to be gathered about a learner's ability related to the instructional objectives and content that makes up the instruction. This evaluation will not determine how well a learner has done, but it can help to determine how well a learner will do. By understanding what a learner knows or does not know about the objectives and content, the instructor will be able to make adjustments to the instruction that will help the learner to be successful and satisfied.

Depending on the objectives of the instruction, various assessments can be developed to use in a pre-instruction learner evaluation. These are commonly referred to as pre-assessment activities. An objective test or quiz is often used as a pre-assessment activity for instruction that focuses on producing a change in a learner's knowledge. For instruction focusing on a change in skill, a learner may be asked to perform tasks that relate to the skill. Instruction focusing on a change in attitude can be done through a questionnaire or short essay that a learner completes. A role-play scenario can also give insight into a learner's attitude.

When developing pre-assessment activities, it is important to keep in mind that the purpose is to gather data about the current abilities of a learner, which will allow for decisions to be made about how instruction might be altered. In addition to gathering data about a learner's ability, pre-assessment activities can be useful as a way to gain learner attention at the start of instruction. A pre-assessment activity can be used to focus a learner on the instruction by providing an overview of what outcome the learner is expected to obtain.

During Instruction

Evaluation during instruction provides data that indicates how a learner is progressing. There are numerous assessment activities that can be used during instruction. Many of these can be done quickly and without a great deal of advanced preparation.

One such assessment activity that can be extremely effective is observation. The instructor can observe a learner as he or she participates in the instruction. The instructor can modify the instruction based on what is observed. The instructor can also take notes about the learner, which can then be looked at and analyzed after instruction is over. This is a useful technique if the instruction continues over multiple sessions. However, it may be difficult—if not impossible—to effectively take notes in some instructional environments. Observing and taking notes on multiple learners during instruction is difficult.

Other assessment activities, such as a quick-write or a random-call, can be used throughout instruction to provide data on how a learner is progressing. A quick-write can be accomplished by having a learner write a response to either a question the instructor has asked or on the major ideas he or she has learned up to that point in the instruction. A random-call is conducted by selecting several learners at random to respond to a question about the content or to demonstrate a skill. It is important to realize that some learners may not react favorably to being asked to share what they have learned to a group of learners. A supportive environment is necessary if this type of assessment activity is to work effectively.

Post-Instruction

Post-instruction evaluation can be considered summative evaluation because it happens at the end of instruction. The goal of post-instruction learner evaluation is to determine how successful a learner was. What level of achievement did the learner have? Did it produce a change in learner knowledge, skill, or attitude? Was the learner able to meet the instructional objectives?

A common assessment technique used during post-instruction evaluation to determine a change in knowledge is a paper-and-pencil test—an objective or constructed response type test. Determining a change in skill is done through a performance assessment where both the process and the product are evaluated. A change is attitude is the most difficult to determine. It is typically accomplished by using assessment techniques, such as observations, self-reporting inventories, and surveys and questionnaires, which focus on the words and behaviors of a learner.

Formative and Summative Evaluation

Although formative evaluation and summative evaluation will be dealt with formally in Chapter 10, we believe it is important to provide a brief discussion of these two evaluation types to show how they relate to learner evaluation. While learner evaluation focuses directly on the learner, formative evaluation and summative evaluation tend to focus on the instructional design process and the intervention created as a result of this process. Morrison, Ross, and Kemp (2007) write: "Formative evaluation is quality control of the development process" (p. 242). Formative evaluation is used throughout the instructional design process to ensure that the intervention being developed is tested and revised to meet the needs of the client. As the name implies, formative evaluation is used as the intervention is forming. Summative evaluation is conducted at the end of instructional design process to determine how successful the process was in helping meet the major goals. As the name implies, summative evaluation is used to provide a summary of what occurred.

Although we have described how both formative and summative evaluations do not specifically deal with learner evaluation, it is important to note that learner evaluation can be formative and summative in its approach. What does this mean? As you have read in this chapter, learner evaluation can take place at different times during instruction—typically, prior to instruction, during instruction, and after instruction has been completed. Conducting learner evaluation prior to and during instruction is formative learner evaluation because we are trying to determine how learners are progressing. Learner evaluation conducted after instruction is completed is summative learner evaluation to determine how successful a learner was. A well-designed learner evaluation will include both formative and summative elements.

BRAIN-BASED ASSESSMENT

We provided an overview of the major ideas and theories behind brain-based education in Chapter 2. As a reminder, brain-based education is a comprehensive approach to teaching and learning that draws heavily on current research—particularly in neuroscience—about how the brain functions and develops over time. Assessment that follows a brain-based approach will take into consideration an individual's learning style and that achievement is best demonstrated over time (rather than through a one-time assessment).

What does brain-based assessment typically look like? Brain-based assessment often consists of various instruments that are administered to a learner over a period of time. The instruments allow for multiple measurements to be taken that can provide a holistic picture of learner achievement. This is often accomplished through the creation of a portfolio that includes artifacts (i.e., writing samples, tests, surveys) that demonstrate student achievement and growth in learning. With brain-based assessment, the assessment process should also allow the learner to monitor his or her own learning and how he or she is progressing (Jensen, 1998, 2000).

As an instructional designer, it may be difficult to approach assessment through the use of a portfolio for several reasons—the amount of time required being one of the most significant. Despite this, as an instructional designer, there are several key ideas regarding brain-based assessment you should be aware of: 1) Individuals learn differently; thus, one assessment approach will not work effectively for all individuals; 2) learning is a complex process that takes place over time; thus, true demonstration of learning achievement often requires multiple assessments administered at different times; and 3) learners should be encouraged and given the opportunity to monitor their own learning.

A SUCCESSFUL LEARNER EVALUATION

A successful learner evaluation is one that provides adequate data that helps those involved in the instructional intervention (e.g., instructor, instructional designer) make decisions about what took place and what should subsequently be done. Generally, what is being established by looking at the data is whether a learner was able to meet the instructional objectives and to what degree.

Much of the learner evaluation—after it has been developed—is out of the hands of the instructional designer. The instructor plays a crucial role in executing the assessment activities and then making decisions based on the data collected. An instructional designer should be available and willing to assist an instructor to look at the data and make recommendations based on the data. If a learner evaluation indicates that a learner was not able to meet instructional goals and objectives, then the instructor—possibly with the help of the instructional designer—will attempt to find out why. Finding out why will help establish what appropriate next steps need to take place for a learner. It could indicate that such things as remediation is needed for the learner or that the instructional materials need to be improved.

If adequate data was not collected during the learner evaluation to allow for the learner to be properly evaluated, then the learner evaluation needs to be examined. An examination of the leaner evaluation could indicate that the assessment techniques used to gather data were inappropriate. Most likely, this would result if the instructional objectives were not properly matched with the proper type of assessment technique (e.g., an objective test was used to evaluate a change in a learner's attitude). If the instruction were to be used again, then the learner evaluation would need to be redone. Another possible issue with the learner evaluation could be in how it was implemented. If the assessment techniques were not properly implemented, inadequate data may have been collected. Those responsible for implementing the learner evaluation may need training.

AN INSTRUCTIONAL DESIGNER'S ROLE

The role of an instructional designer is to help create and execute a plan of action to design, develop, and implement an efficient and effective learner evaluation. An efficient and effective learner evaluation is one that provides appropriate data that helps determine the success level an individual has achieved as a result of instruction. This plan of action should include the following elements:

- Analyze the instructional goals and objectives; determine the intended learning outcome(s).
- Based on the instructional objectives and learning outcome(s), determine the appropriate type of learner evaluation needed.
- Design and develop the appropriate assessment techniques that will be used to gather data about the learner.
- Assist, as necessary, in the implementation of the assessment techniques; this can include analyzing the data, determining if the learners have been successful, and deciding what steps need to take place based on the results of the data analysis.

Jake has decided that he will conduct assessments at two phases during the instruction. The instrument Jake has created is a brief quiz of short answer questions that he will administer to his students at the pre-instruction phase. The assessment will determine what his students' current knowledge is regarding mean, medium, and mode. The assessment will help guide his instruction. Jake will also give a post-instruction assessment. The instrument he will use has two types of item: multiple-choice questions and open-ended problems. The instrument will help determine whether his students are able to accurately pick out the appropriate definitions in the multiple-choice questions and calculate the correct statistics in the open-ended problems. The post-instruction assessment will help Jake determine if he needs to reteach the entire class, provide remediation for some students, or if the class can move on to more difficult concepts.

Ian has created a multipronged approach to assessing whether employee morale has changed since the incentive program was started. Even though this approach will take a significant amount of time, he feels it is important to gather multiple data that will allow him to make an accurate and informed decision. Ian also understands the problematic nature of the assessment he is conducting. Ian has chosen to conduct observations (and keeping anecdotal notes) of the employees, administer a self-reporting inventory on them, and interview a random selection of the employees. Using the absences and sales data, Ian believes he will have enough data to make an accurate decision on the effectiveness of the incentive program.

EVALUATING LEARNER ACHIEVEMENT AND THE INSTRUCTIONAL DESIGN PROCESS

Evaluation is a process for determining the success of an individual, product, or process. Evaluating learner achievement helps to determine if the intervention created and implemented is successful in meeting the specific learning goals and objectives set out for the learner. As an instructional designer, you should be able to answer the following questions as you approach evaluating learner achievement:

- What are the goals and objectives of the intervention?
- What data needs to be gathered in order to measure whether the learning goals and objectives have been met?

- What instruments are needed to gather this data?
- Are there instruments currently available or do the instruments need to be made?
- During what phases of instruction should assessment take place?
- What is the process for how the instruments will be administered?
- How will the data that is gathered be used?

Summary

Evaluation is a process for determining the success of an individual, product, or process. There are three main types of evaluation that an instructional designer will use: learner, formative, and summative. Each is used at different times in the instructional design process to gather data. The data gathered is analyzed to determine the level of success that has been obtained. Based on the success level, various decisions can be made. A common decision made by an instructional designer (often in consultation with an instructor, subject matter expert, or client—or possibly all three) is to make changes to the instruction that was developed. Properly designed and implemented evaluations allow instructional designers to create effective and efficient interventions.

Learner evaluation is often considered to be the most critical type of evaluation. It is used to determine the success level a learner has achieved by participating in instruction. The success level is based on the extent to which a leaner is able to meet the instructional goals and objectives. The results of a learner can be compared against a set of standards (criterion-referenced) or to other learners (norm-referenced). A criterion-referenced learner evaluation is used to determine learner competence. A norm-referenced learner evaluation is used to compare and rank learners. Most learner evaluations an instructional designer helps develop will be criterion-referenced.

Assessment techniques, which are part of a learner evaluation, are typically implemented at three varied times: prior to instruction, during instruction, and after instruction has finished. The data collected during these three times provide very different information about the learner. Prior to instruction, data is gather to determine what a learner may or may not know about the instructional objectives. Data gathered during instruction helps determine how a learner is progressing. Data gathered after instruction has finished helps determine what a learner achieved.

Developing a learner evaluation starts by examining the instructional goals and objectives and determining the expected outcome—a change in knowledge, skill, or attitude. The expected outcome will influence the type of learner evaluation that will be developed. Assessments are developed and implemented to determine whether the expected outcome occurred.

A properly designed learner evaluation will provide appropriate data that will allow an instructor to determine if a learner was successful. If a learner was not successful (that is, did not meet the learning objectives and the intended outcome), then decisions are made about what needs to be done. An instructional designer will often work with an instructor to determine what the appropriate next steps are, such as learner remediation or a change in the instructional materials.

Connecting Process to Practice

1. Consider the assessment approaches of Jake and Ian. Do you see any potential problems with the approaches they have taken?
2. How might you approach Jake's situation differently? Create a different assessment plan that includes when you would assess the students and the instruments you would use.
3. How might you have approached Ian's situation differently? Create a different assessment plan that includes the instruments you would use and how you would go about gathering the appropriate data you need to make an informed decision.
4. Compare and contrast learner evaluations that are criterion-referenced and norm-referenced.

5. Describe the process you would go through to develop a learner evaluation for an instructional design project you are working on. List the steps, and describe what you would do during each step.
6. When is it most appropriate to use
   - an objective test?
   - a constructed-response test?
   - a performance assessment?
7. The instruction you have helped design has the following instructional objectives:
   - The nurse will be able to explain the difference between the natural rhythmicity of the heart and breathing.
   - The nurse will be able to explain why it is important that the control of breathing involves both automatic and conscious aspects.
   - The nurse will be able to list the muscles involved in both normal and hard (labored) breathing.
   - The nurse will be able to name three chemical factors that influence respiration.
   - The nurse will be able to assess a patient's breathing to determine if any significant breathing problems exist.
   - The nurse will be able to articulate the assessment of the patient to the nurse's supervisor.
   - The nurse will be able to help a patient control his or her breathing through the use of proper breathing techniques.

   What type(s) of learner evaluation would you develop to determine whether a learner was successful?
8. Why are validity and reliability—as they relate to learner evaluation—important concepts for an instructional designer to understand?

Recommended Reading

Aiken, L. (1995). *Rating scales and checklists.* New York: John Wiley & Sons.

Aiken, L. (1997). *Questionnaires and inventories: Surveying opinions and assessing personality.* New York: John Wiley & Sons.

Carmines, E. G. & Zeller, R. A. (1991). *Reliability and validity assessment.* Newbury Park: Sage Publications.

Gardner, H. (1993). *Multiple intelligences: the theory in practice.* New York: Basic Books.

Hopkins, K. D. (1998). *Educational and psychological measurement and evaluation.* Boston: Allyn & Bacon Publishers.

Medina, J. (2009). Brain rules: 12 principles for surviving and thriving at work, home, and school. Seattle: Pear Press.

Worthen, B., Sanders, J., and Fitzpatrick, J. (2004). *Program evaluation: Alternative approaches and practical guidelines.* Boston: Allyn & Bacon.

References

Carmines, E. G. & Zeller, R. A. (1991). *Reliability and validity assessment.* Newbury Park: Sage Publications.

Hopkins, K. D. (1998). *Educational and psychological measurement and evaluation.* Boston: Allyn & Bacon.

Jensen, E. (1998). *Teaching with the brain in mind.* Alexandria, VA: Association for Supervision and Curriculum Development.

Jensen, E. (2000). *Brain-based learning.* San Diego: Brain Store Incorporated.

Morrison, G. R., Ross, S. M. & Kemp, J. E. (2007). *Designing effective instruction, 5th edition.* New York: John Wiley & Sons.

Worthen, B., Sanders, J. & Fitzpatrick, J. (2004). *Program evaluation: Alternative approaches and practical guidelines.* Boston: Allyn & Bacon.

Chapter 10

Determining the Success of the Instructional Design Product and Process

Tobias is the lead instructional designer for a company that is developing training materials for Web-based software. Although his team is making progress toward completing the project, he feels there are some issues that need to be resolved within the design and production team if the beta version of the training is going to be released on time. He wonders whether he should conduct a formative evaluation to determine issues that might be resolved to help improve the group's working relationship.

Elizabeth works for a faculty development center at a university. Her university has spent significant amounts of money over the past two years on two Web-based synchronous communication and learning tools. Elizabeth was asked to create and deliver a three-part workshop on integrating the tools in order to increase faculty use of them. After conducting the workshop over two semesters, she was asked to evaluate the workshop's effectiveness.

GUIDING QUESTIONS

- What information can formative and summative evaluations provide to improve the instructional design process?
- Why is it important to include various types of evaluation in the instructional design process?
- How can the success of formative and summative evaluations be judged?
- How can an instructional designer use evaluation to improve an instructional design team's effectiveness?

KEY TERMS

Formative Evaluation *162*
Group Processing *174*
Program Evaluators *169*
Rapid Prototyping *166*
Summative Evaluation *168*
Usability Testing *167*

CHAPTER OVERVIEW

Evaluation is a crucial part of instructional design. As we discussed in Chapter 9, evaluation is a process that allows for data to be gathered that helps determine the level of success of someone or the worth of something. In instructional design, a major purpose of evaluation is to help determine how successful a learner has been as a result of participating in instruction. This type of evaluation is called "learner evaluation." Although learner evaluation is extremely important, there are two other important evaluation types: formative and summative. These two types concentrate on the instructional design process and the instruction developed as a result of the process. This chapter's focus is on defining formative and summative evaluations, describing specific approaches of instructional design experts, and how formative and summative evaluations can be designed and implemented.

FORMATIVE AND SUMMATIVE EVALUATION

It is a common misconception of beginning instructional designers that evaluation only takes place at the conclusion of instruction to evaluate learners. Evaluating the learners is only one of several types of evaluation that instructional designers must understand how to design and implement. In reality, evaluation should also take place at various stages of the instructional design process through the use of formative and summative evaluations. Knowing when and how to use various evaluation types helps instructional designers develop instructional interventions that are efficient and effective.

Formative Evaluation

Formative evaluation is used throughout the instructional design process to gather data that can be used to provide feedback on how the process is going. It is especially useful during the early stages of the instructional design process. The feedback allows an instructional designer to make improvements to the instruction before it is completely developed. This helps ensure that high-quality instruction is developed. In addition to helping improve the instruction, data gathered through a formative evaluation can be shared with a client to indicate how the project is progressing. Periodic communication with your client about how the project is progressing helps make certain that project goals and expectations will be met.

Approaches to Formative Evaluation

Instructional design experts take a variety of approaches to formative evaluation. Despite their differences, they all have in common the goal of helping improve the instruction that is being developed. Let us begin by looking at three different approaches to formative evaluation.

Smith and Ragan (2004) write that formative evaluation is conducted to "determine the weakness in the instruction so that revisions can be made to make them more effective and efficient." This helps an instructional designer know "whether the instructional materials are 'there' yet, or whether she needs to continue the design process" (p. 388). The stages that Smith and Ragan advocate for formative evaluation are design reviews, expert reviews, learner validation, and ongoing evaluation.

The first stage—design reviews—is completed prior to the development of instruction. Stage two—expert review—typically occurs after the instruction is completed but before it is used with learners. The final two phases include the use of the actual instruction with learners that represent the intended learners.

Design reviews are conducted after various phases of the instructional design process, such as the needs analysis, task analysis, goals and objective analysis, and learner analysis. Design reviews help to verify the accuracy of information at each stage of the instructional design process before instruction is developed. Smith and Ragan advocate revisiting the data gathered during these instructional design phases to determine how accurate they are.

Expert reviews are conducted to gather information about the instruction to determine if it is accurate and current. Various experts—such as content experts, instructional design experts, pedagogical experts, and experts on the learners—can be used to provide various perspectives on the instruction. The instruction provided for expert reviews is typically at the draft stage. Smith and Ragan suggest that expert reviewer comments should be divided into three categories: 1) revisions that need to be made immediately, 2) suggested revisions that require additional data that can be gathered during the final two stages of the formative evaluation, and 3) suggested revisions that should be ignored.

Learner validation includes three levels: one-on-one evaluation, small-group evaluation, and field trials. The three levels are identical to those promoted by Dick, Carey, and Carey. We refer you to the previous section if you need to refresh yourself on how these are conducted.

The final stage—ongoing evaluation—includes gathering data on the long-term effectiveness of instruction. Smith and Ragan state that if instruction is meant to be used multiple times, then provisions need to be made in a formative evaluation plan to collect effectiveness data. This data, which is similar to data collected during a field trial, provides feedback on what revisions needed to be made to instruction based on its actual use and whether the revisions made have been effective.

Morrison, Ross, and Kemp (2007) advocate a basic model for formative evaluation based on the work of Gooler (1980). Gooler's approach follows these eight steps:

1. Purpose
2. Audience
3. Issues
4. Resources
5. Evidence
6. Data-Gathering Techniques
7. Analysis
8. Reporting

There are three main phases to this approach: planning, conducting, and reporting. Phase one includes steps one through five, while phase two includes steps six and seven. Phase three is the eighth and final step, reporting the results.

Phase one includes determining the evaluation purpose, the primary audience the results will be disseminated to, the issues that need to be addressed, the resources that are needed to address the issues, and the types of evidence that will be acceptable to address these issues. It is extremely important to work closely with the client during phase one in order to clearly articulate and manage expectations.

The first step—determining the purpose or purposes of the evaluation—is done in consultation with the client. The two most common purposes are to improve the instruction that is being developed and to satisfy administration requirements of the client you are working for. Many corporations and institutions require evaluations to be conducted. Most state agencies are required to include an evaluation component to help ensure that project goals are being met and to report how monies have been spent.

The audience of the evaluation is important to determine because it will establish the types of information that need to be collected and reported. The client will be able to help determine who the intended audience will be. Conducting an evaluation for multiple audiences should be avoided because it will be difficult to satisfy varying needs within a single report. It is best to try and narrow the audience down as much as possible.

After determining the purposes of the evaluation and the intended audience, it is time to determine the issues that need to be addressed. The issues are generally stated as questions that need to be answered. For example, in the case of an interactive, instructional kiosk:

- Are learners able to successfully utilize the kiosk after completing the instruction?
- What elements of the kiosk do learners find most understandable and least understandable?

Or in the case of Web-based instruction:

- What is the average time spent on the summary exercises?
- Do the learners find the Web-based self-instructional materials helpful in learning the content?

Once questions have been developed based on the evaluation issues, resources should be identified that are needed to answer the questions. People, artifacts, and equipment are common types of resources that are often needed to address evaluation issues. It may be difficult to actually secure all the resources needed to address the evaluation issues. If this situation occurs, the instructional designer needs to communicate this with his or her client. Issues may need to be adjusted if the necessary resources cannot be secured. The final step in phase one is to identify the types of evidence that are needed to satisfy the evaluation issues.

Phase two—conducting the evaluation—includes determining the data-collecting techniques that will be used, gathering the data, and analyzing the data. When determining the data-collecting techniques to be used, Morrison, Ross, and Kemp (2007) state: "Two key, and often opposing, factors need to be weighed: precise measurement versus feasible or practical measurement" (p. 310). For example, during the planning stage of a formative evaluation of a nurse-training program, an instructional designer determined that all participates would have specific skills evaluated by using hospital patients. However, due to logistical impracticalities (e.g., amount of time required), the nurse's skills were tested on other nurses in the training program. An instructional designer must often make a choice between what is ideal and what is practical when gathering data.

The various data collecting techniques that can be used are the same as those presented in Chapter 9. They included observations, questionnaires, interviews, paper and pencil tests, and performance tests—to name a few. It is highly recommended to use a variety of techniques to gather multiple sources of data. This can help to triangulate the findings.

Step seven—analyzing the data—should reflect the purpose of a formative evaluation: to provide usable and useful information that helps instructional designer improve instruction. Complex statistical analyses are typically not required. Morrison, Ross, and Kemp recommend the following typical analysis procedures:

- Frequency distributions
- Frequency graphs or histograms
- Descriptive statistics, such as percentages, means, and medians
- Listing of actual comments made by respondents (p. 311)

The final phase—step eight—is reporting the results of the evaluation to the primary audience. This is typically done as an evaluation report, with the format of the report tailored to the audience the report will be disseminated to. A typical evaluation report is formatted in the following way:

1. ***Executive summary*** An abstract that outlines the major findings, conclusions, and recommendations.
2. ***Evaluation purpose***
   - Evaluation issues—stated as questions
   - Description of the instruction being evaluated
3. ***Methodology used***
   - Participants
   - Instruments used to gather data

4. ***Results***
   - Analysis
   - Findings
5. ***Conclusions and recommendations***

It is not uncommon that, in addition to a written report, an oral report of the project will be requested. The oral report can either be conducted one-on-one with the client or more formally to a larger group. It is important to remember that the purpose of the evaluation is to provide recommendations based on the data collected. When disseminating a final report, be certain to highlight the conclusions and recommendations.

Dick, Carey, and Carey (2009) write: "The emphasis in formative evaluation is on the collection and analysis of data and the revision of instruction" (p. 258). They provide three basic phases of formative evaluation: 1) one-to-one or clinical, 2) small group, and 3) field trial. It is important to note that the type of formative evaluation Dick, Carey, and Carey advocate is designed to work specifically with self-instructional materials. Despite this, elements of their approach can be used with other types of instruction and materials.

During phase one, the instructional designer works with individual learners to gather data that is used to revise the instruction. The purpose of the phase is to remove obvious errors and omissions in the instruction, gauge initial learner performance, and determine learner reactions to the content. Dick, Carey, and Carey suggest that the instructional designer work with at least three learners (with varying abilities, attitudes, and/or experiences) who represent the target population the instruction is intended for. However, only one learner at a time should be worked with during a one-on-one evaluation. The instructional designer should be actively involved during this phase.

After selecting the learners who will participate in the one-on-one evaluation, the steps to this phase are:

1. Explain to the learner that you would like his or her reactions to new instructional materials that have been developed.
2. Give a pretest on the content.
3. Encourage him or her to talk about the materials as he or she goes through the instruction and to be candid about what he or she likes, does not like, what makes sense, and what does not make sense.
4. Give a post-test; discuss the results with the learner by asking his or her to explain the responses he or she made.
5. Note the time it takes him or her to go through the instruction.

Phase two has two primary purposes: 1) to determine how effective the changes are that were made as a result of phase one and 2) to determine if learners can go through the instruction without the assistance of the instructor. For this phase, eight or more learners should be selected who are a representative sample of the entire intended group of learners. After selecting the learners who will participate in the small group evaluation, the steps to this phase are:

1. Explain to the group of learners that you would like reactions to new instructional materials that have been developed; you want them to work through the material on their own as best as they can.
2. Conduct the instruction as it is intended to be used in its final form; give a pretest if that is part of the instruction.

3. Observe what is taking place without involvement unless the learners are unable to continue the instruction; make note of the difficulties learners have in completing the instruction.
4. Conduct a post-test once the instruction is finished.
5. Administer an attitude questionnaire.
6. Debrief the group of learners.

The final phase—the field-trial evaluation—is intended to help determine how effective the changes made during the small-group evaluation are and whether the instruction is capable of being used in its intended environment. A representative group of thirty learners should be used for this phase. The environment chosen for the field-trial evaluation should be similar to an environment in which the instruction is being developed for.

The steps to this phase are similar to the small-group evaluation. The major difference is that an instructor, not the instructional designer, should administer the instruction. The role of the instructional designer is to observe and take notes of what takes place. The outcome of a field-trial evaluation is to determine the attitudes of the learners toward the instruction as well as the learners' achievement.

In addition to these three phases, Dick, Carey, and Carey advise that the instruction should be given to subject matter experts and/or instructional experts to note whether it is accurate and current. This information—along with the data gathered during the three phases—should provide an instructional designer with enough information to make necessary revisions to the instruction being developed.

Rapid Prototyping and Usability Testing

In addition to the three approaches we described in the previous section, two additional—and related—approaches to formative evaluation are important for instructional designers to understand and have as part of the instructional design skill repertoires: **rapid prototyping** and usability testing. Both are often overlooked as formative evaluation approaches because they are traditionally thought of as "product processes" rather than formative evaluation processes. However, built in to each approach is formative evaluation, which allows the instructional designer to determine how well the instructional intervention is being designed.

Professionals in Practice

We have several methods of evaluating the success of the instruction. One of the primary methods is an evaluation form used for all classroom instruction. We also use a similar form for online training. We also evaluate the success of the instruction by collecting data before the instruction and comparing the performance results after the instruction has been implemented. For example, if the problem statement is that consistent training is leading to increased tool downtime and increased costs, then we collect that data at the beginning of the instructional design method. Once the instructional plan has been implemented, we will watch the costs and tool downtime issues to see if they improve. If so, we can associate our training with that event if no other variables exist.

— Jona Titus
senior training specialist
Intel Corporation

As we discuss in Chapter 1, the essential idea behind rapid prototyping is to arrive at a final product through the creation of a series of prototypes. Each prototype is evaluated by some combination of experts and end users; each successive prototype is more like the final product; that is, "fidelity" of the prototypes increases with each new one until a working product is achieved. A rapid prototyping approach requires that the design environment allow for the relatively quick and easy creation of instructional materials (Tripp & Bichelmeyer, 1990).

Rapid prototyping suggests that each member of the design/development team is a "co-inquirer" (Rathburn, Saito & Goodrum, 1997) and that there is a social process of design and development in which everyone offers feedback and criticism to each other. With rapid prototyping, each time a new version of the product is tested, it provides a way to critically reflect on what the final product should actually look like (Rathburn, Saito & Goodrum). The analysis of learners' needs and the content of the final product depends in part on the knowledge that is gained by actually building and trying out a prototype (Tripp & Bichelmeyer, 1990).

Usability testing is a concept originally borrowed from engineering that has gained popularity among software developers, multimedia producers, and instructional designers. Usability testing is a type of formative evaluation, which consists of evaluating the product by observing it in action with potential end users. Typically, a usability test consists of evaluators observing a user or users interacting with the product under controlled conditions. The user(s) interact with the product for a specified amount of time, having been asked to complete a set of tasks determined in advance by the evaluation team. The tasks are based on the goals and objectives the product is designed to meet. Results of a usability test inform the production team of the problems inherent in the design (e.g., the graphic for a button is not well-understood or the instructions are worded in a manner that is confusing) and suggest—through observation of end users in action—ways to effectively eliminate those problems.

Professionals in Practice

Usability testing has become an integral part of the software development life cycle at The Home Depot. The Home Depot Information Technology department works on dozens of projects every year, most of which have a user interface component that requires periodic input from end users. Required at several stages throughout the development process, usability testing primarily takes the form of qualitative data collection based on observations of users interacting with an application in the usability lab. We are fortunate to have a permanent in-house usability lab and internal resources to support testing and usability analysis work. The usability team works with various project teams to plan and conduct usability tests of applications during design, late in development, and during testing.

By putting an application in front of users at these various stages, particularly during design, we have a better chance to provide a high-quality product and positive user experience, which translates into everything from increased productivity to higher sales and better associate retention rates.

Usability testing for internal applications is unique in several ways from usability for the Web, for example. Most of the applications The Home Depot deploys are for internal use, meaning that we have a well-defined and available user group to draw from when usability testing is conducted. Users are a more homogeneous group than the general population, and we have a better understanding of them. The environment, hardware, software, and network speed are predefined.

(*continues*)

We use a relatively informal process in our usability cycles in order to conform to aggressive development timelines and to provide rapid feedback to project teams. A usability strategy and protocol are formulated in hours or days, users are brought in as soon as schedules allow, and an analysis document is produced immediately. Usability problems are listed in order of importance, and solutions are suggested. For a small or mid-size application, a single usability cycle can be completed in a few days. For larger and more complex applications or for applications that are in late stages of development and are database-driven, more time is required for technical setup. However, even those tests—once scheduled—are completed in days.

Since we are all part of the same organization, usability is more of a collaborative process that evolves as the IT department evolves, and as we do more and more testing, our understanding deepens in regards to our organization and the IT systems that support it. One critical issue that the usability team stresses is that each application can't be tested in isolation; one must consider how it works in relation to other applications a particular user group would use. Given the dozens of applications that are built, updated, or changed every year, an overall picture of usability and user interface design must be maintained.

— Lisa Hansen
former usability lead at The Home Depot
Atlanta, Georgia

Tobias realizes that after talking separately to various members of his instructional design team that they need to formally engage in some group processing. There seem to be some misconceptions regarding team member responsibilities. Although the group processing will most likely be initially uncomfortable for everyone and it will take time away from working on their product, Tobias believes it will help refocus the team.

Elizabeth believes that she needs to conduct a formative evaluation to determine if the workshops had a positive impact on participants. She is specifically interested in determining if and how faculty are using the Web-based synchronous communication and learning tools in their courses.

Designing and Conducting a Formative Evaluation

Seasoned instructional designers understand the importance of formative evaluation in helping create efficient and effective instruction. Because of this understanding, they consistently include plans for formative evaluation when starting out ID projects. The approach to formative evaluation an instructional designer will take is dictated by the scope of the ID project. It may not be feasible for every ID project to conduct a complete formative evaluation by using one of the three approaches that was described in this chapter. A less robust formative evaluation may need to be developed and carried out for smaller instructional design projects. No matter what the scale of an ID project is, it is extremely important that some form of formative evaluation is carried out.

Summative Evaluation

As part of the instructional design process, **summative evaluation** takes place after an instructional intervention has been implemented. The major goal of a summative evaluation is to gather data that allows for its effectiveness to be determined. Did the instruction bring about the desired changes? Were the goals of the client met? These are two major questions that summative evaluations help answer.

The results of a summative evaluation are described in a formal report outlining the impact of the instructional intervention. The evaluation report will typically outline who participated in the instructional intervention, what activities impacted them, and what changes occurred from their participation. The evaluation report will often include the costs and benefits of implementation, descriptions of the essential conditions necessary to continue the program or reproduce it, and recommendations on whether the instructional intervention should be modified, discontinued, or continued as is.

Approaches to Summative Evaluation

For the beginning instructional designer, summative evaluation can be a daunting task. It is a complex process that takes a great deal of skill and experience to successfully carry out. There are evaluation experts whose sole professional activity is to conduct summative evaluations; they are typically referred to as **program evaluators**. A program evaluator uses various approaches to conduct a summative evaluation. In *Program Evaluation: Alternative Approaches and Practical Guidelines,* Worthen, Sanders, and Fitzpatrick (2004) describe six such approaches (see Figure 10.1). It is beyond the scope of this book to describe the intricacies of these approaches and how to become a program evaluator.

Criterion	Formative Evaluation	Summative Evaluation
Purpose	To determine value or quality	To determine value or quality
Use	To improve a program or instruction	To make decisions about the instruction's future or adoption
Audience	Program administrators and staff	Program administrators and/or potential consumer or funding agency
By Whom	Primarily internal evaluators, supported by external evaluators	External evaluators, supported by internal evaluators in unique cases
Major Characteristics	Provides feedback so program personnel can improve it	Provides information to enable program personnel to decide whether to continue it, or consumers to adopt it
Design Constraints	What information is Needed? When?	What evidence is needed for major decisions?
Purpose of Data Collection	Diagnostic	Judgmental
Measures	Sometimes Informal	Valid and Reliable
Frequency of Data Collection	Frequent	Infrequent
Sample Size	Often small	Usually Large
Questions Asked	What is working? What needs to be improved? How can it be improved?	What results occur? With whom? Under what conditions? With what training? At what cost?

FIGURE 10.1 Differences Between Formative and Summative Evaluation

Adapted from Worthen, Sanders, and Fitzpatrick (2004)

If you wish to learn more about summative evaluation than what is presented in this chapter, we suggest that you start by reading their book and by taking a course on program evaluation. The knowledge and skills gained as a result will certainly help you as an instructional designer.

We focus our discussion of summative evaluation on four different approaches that instructional design experts advocate. The purpose is to introduce how summative evaluation is approached in instructional design; it is not to make you an expert.

One of the most cited approaches to summative evaluation in instructional design is Kirkpatrick's Four Levels of Evaluation. Kirkpatrick developed this model to evaluate the effectiveness of training programs—specifically, training programs in industry. The four levels of his model are: 1) reactions, 2) learning, 3) transfer, and 4) results. According to Kirkpatrick, evaluation should always begin with level one and then progress through the remaining levels as time and the budget allows. However, to truly evaluate the effectiveness of a training program, all four levels should be used.

Each of Kirkpatrick's levels requires more time and rigor than previous levels. Data collected from each level serves as a base for the next level and the evaluation that takes place at that level. As each level is conducted, more precise measures of the effectiveness of the training program are gathered.

Level 1—reactions—attempts to provide data on how participants reacted to the training. Did participants enjoy the training? Was the training relevant to the participants? Kirkpatrick indicates that all training programs should at least include this minimum level of evaluation in order to provide data that will help improve the training (1994). A typical method used to gather data at this level is an attitude survey where participants indicate how satisfied they were with the training. If students indicated negative feelings toward the training, this typically indicates that little to no learning took place (however, positive reactions do not necessarily indicate that learning took place).

Level 2—learning—is conducted to determine whether participants' skills, knowledge, or attitudes changed as a result of the training. Determining this is much more laborious than Level 1 because it requires gathering data at multiple times. Typically, pretests and post-tests are used to measure these changes.

Level 3—transfer—attempts to answer the question of whether the newly acquired skills, knowledge, or attitudes are being used by participants in their real-world environments. In other words, have participants transferred what they learned in the training into their everyday environment? This is often considered to be truest measure of a training program's effectiveness. Evaluating at this level is complicated because it is difficult to determine when a participant will actually display what he or she learned. Therefore, decisions will need to be made on when, how often, and how long the evaluation will take place in order to determine if transfer has taken place.

Level 4—results—attempts to evaluate a training program's effectiveness in business measures, such as increased sales, improved product quality, fewer on-the-job accidents, and so forth. Evaluation at this level must be long term in nature in order to determine trends that have taken place. Data that helps support the effectiveness of training at this level is often gathered through methods such as interviews with managers, focus group meetings with customers, and post-training surveys.

Smith and Ragan (1999) write: "Within the context of instructional design, the purpose of summative evaluation is to collect, analyze, and summarize data to present to decision makers in the client organization so that they can make a judgment regarding the effectiveness, and perhaps appeal and efficiency, of the instruction" (p. 352). The judgment that is being made is whether the use of the instruction should be continued. The specific question being asked is, "Does the instructional adequately solve the 'problem' that was identified in the needs assessment and that resulted in the development of the instructional materials?" (p. 353).

They provide an eight-step process for conducting a summative evaluation:

1. ***Determine the goals of evaluation*** Identify the questions that should be answered. The questions should be developed in consultation with the client. Typically, more questions will be developed than can be answered during the course of the evaluation. It is important to come to an agreement on the exact questions that are feasible to answer given the available resources.
2. ***Select indicators of success*** Where will data be gathered? What needs to be looked at in order to answer the evaluation questions? Again, in consultation with the client, these issues need to be addressed and agreed on.
3. ***Select the orientation of evaluation*** Will the evaluation be objective or subjective? An objective orientation focuses on answering the evaluation questions based on data collected through quantitative methods (e.g., questionnaires, paper-and-pencil tests, performance tests). The advantage of this orientation is that results are generally replicable. A subjective orientation is based on the perspective of the individual conducting the evaluation. Qualitative methods (e.g., interviews and observations) are used to gather data that describe the impact of the instructional intervention. The advantage of this orientation is that a rich description is provided that describes the impact the instructional intervention has had. The downside to this orientation is that the results can be influenced by the biases of the evaluator. Most summative evaluations do not strictly follow one or the other orientation; typically, a combination of the two orientations is used.
4. ***Select design of evaluation*** Determine how the data will be collected, when it will be collected, and under what conditions.
5. ***Design or select evaluation measures*** Determine what measures will be looked at to determine effectiveness of the instructional intervention. Learning transfer, learning outcomes, attitudes, level of implementation, and costs are all measures that can be used to determine effectiveness.
6. ***Collect data***
7. ***Analyze data***
8. ***Report results*** A summative evaluation report should include the following sections: summary, background information, description of the evaluation study, results, and conclusion and recommendations. The background information will come from the analyses conducted early on in the instructional design process (e.g., needs, learner). The description of the evaluation study includes the purpose of the evaluation, the evaluation design, and the outcome measures. The results will include a discussion on how well the outcomes were met.

The approach taken by Morrison, Ross, and Kemp is similar in many ways to the approach described by Smith and Ragan. Morrison, Ross, and Kemp (2007) write: "A summative evaluation permits a designer or instructor to reach unbiased objective answers to evaluation questions concerning expected program outcomes and to then decide whether the program is achieving those outcomes" (p. 318). A summative evaluation can help examine the following issues:

- Effectiveness of learner or trainee learning
- Efficiency of learner or trainee learning
- Cost of program development and continuing expenses n relation to effectiveness and efficiency
- Attitudes and reactions to the program by learners, instructors, and staff
- Long-term benefits of the instructional program (p. 320)

These issues fall within three major areas: program effectiveness, program efficiency, and program costs. A program is referring to the instructional intervention that has been designed and implemented. Evaluating program effectiveness is the major issue that is dealt with by a summative evaluation. The program effectiveness helps answer this question: "How successful have learners been in meeting the learning objectives?" Specifically, what is being determined is whether change has taken place with the learners. For example, are employees able to do their jobs more efficiently and effectively after participating in an instructional intervention?

Morrison, Ross, and Kemp list the major steps of a summative evaluation process as:

1. ***Specifying program objectives*** Revisit the instructional goals and objectives of the instructional intervention that was developed.
2. ***Determining the evaluation design for each objective*** How will data be collected that will help determine if the learning goals and objectives have been met? Determine what types of data are needed.
3. ***Developing data collection instruments and procedures for each objective*** Appropriate data collection instruments and procedures were discussed earlier in this chapter. Pretests, post-tests, questionnaires, and observations are all examples of data collection instruments or procedures.
4. ***Carrying out the evaluation*** It is advised that data are collected from the beginning stages of the project. This will ensure that the necessary data are collected, especially data regarding costs and time involvement. Data collection may need to be schedules.
5. ***Analyzing the results from each instrument***
6. ***Interpreting the results***
7. ***Disseminating the results and conclusions*** Develop a summative evaluation report (refer to the previous section on Smith and Ragan to see how an evaluation report can be formatted). Individual discussions and group presentations are often useful (and required by the client) to disseminate evaluation findings.

The approach Dick, Carey, and Carey (2009) advocates a very different approach than the two previous approaches we described. Despite the different look and how it is conducted, the fundamental goal is the same as the other two approaches: to determine the effectiveness of the instructional intervention. Dick, Carey, and Carey define summative evaluation as "the design of evaluation studies and the collection of data to verify the effectiveness of instructional materials with target learners" (p. 320). Its major purpose is

Professionals in Practice

Generally, the success or failure of a person to install and use our system after spending five days in class is a good indicator of whether or not the instruction was successful. To throw a little twist into things, we have a session called "Break-Fix" on the fourth day in which one student deliberately "breaks" some software or hardware component in the system of another student (either by introducing a configuration error or by something as simple as unplugging a telephone from its jack, for example). The "victim" then needs to figure out what the problem is. This type of problem-solving is a great way to measure if a concept has been retained because it doesn't allow a person to react to a problem by rote response.

Due to the constant evolution of software, we must conduct formative evaluation in every class to ensure that the course content is valid. We rely on support engineers, software developers, and the students themselves to do this. Often, we use addendums to books, paper handouts, or other alterations to adapt to changing software. The simple question "Are our facts accurate today?" drives this process.

Measuring the success of online learning materials is different. Formative evaluation is much more difficult because of the lag between production time and SME [subject matter expert] input. Consequently, we rely on written test scores and student feedback (using a survey and e-mail feedback.) We use summative evaluation when we have the luxury of time to really revise course content according to SME input.

— Erik Novak
distance learning course developer
Interactive Intelligence, Inc.
Indianapolis, Indiana

to decide whether currently used instructional materials should continue to be used or whether new instructional materials need to be adopted that have the potential to meet the instructional needs of an organization.

They state that a summative evaluation has two main phases: an expert judgment and a field trial. The purpose of the expert judgment phase is to determine whether instruction that is currently being used or instruction that is being considered for use has the potential to meet the instructional needs of an organization. The field-trial phase has the purpose of documenting the effectiveness of "promising instruction" given to learners from the intended target group given in the actual setting. There are a series of steps that take place during each phase that help reach these purposes.

Designing and Conducting a Summative Evaluation

In an ideal situation, the instructional designer would be directly involved in designing the summative evaluation but would not be responsible for conducting it. The evaluation would be conducted by an evaluator outside of the organization that contracted the instructional design project. Having the instructional designer responsible for designing and conducting the summative evaluation is often seen as a conflict of interest because the instructional designer is biased and has a tremendous stake in the project's success. However, this is not to imply that an instructional designer cannot be unbiased; it only complicates the situation.

As we mentioned, conducting a successful summative evaluation is a complex process that takes a great deal of skill and experience. If at all possible, we advise that beginning instructional designers do not take on the role of primary evaluator for a summative evaluation. However, the reality is that as an instructional designer, you will be required to conduct a summative evaluation. If this is the case, it is important to plan for a summative evaluation at the beginning stages of an instructional design project. Discuss with the client what the expectations are for the summative evaluation. Especially important to discuss are the summative evaluation goals. Although these may change once the summative evaluation is formally developed, the goals will help an instructional designer know what the client expectations are for the ID project. In addition, planning in advance will allow for data to be gathered through the formative evaluation that can be used in the summative evaluation.

The evaluation goals will dictate the remaining steps that are to be taken in the summative evaluation. A process, such as the one advocated by Smith and Ragan, can be used as a guiding model for a beginning instructional designer. As with successful instructional design projects, continual and consistent communication with the client is a key element in determining the level of success an instructional designer will have in conducting a summative evaluation.

GROUP PROCESSING: EVALUATING THE INSTRUCTIONAL DESIGN TEAM

It is rare for an instructional designer to work alone. Most projects require that instructional designers work in teams that often consist of individuals with various roles, such as subject matter expert, programmer, graphic artist, content editor, Web developer, or media developer—to name a few. In addition to working with these individuals on a team, instructional designers are often called on to be the project manager and manage the team. Being the project manager requires that the instructional designer is able to manage all aspects of the instructional design process, including how the team works together.

Although project management is formally dealt with in Chapter 11, one aspect of project management that we will focus on now deals with evaluating how well a team is working together. A technique that can be used to accomplish this is **group processing**. Group processing can be considered a type of formative evaluation. Group processing refers to the reflections that group members have on their work and interactions with team members. The reflections help the team focus on improving the working relationship of the group to ensure that the team effectively meets project goals. It allows team members to voice concerns, share successes, and provide feedback that will help the team to complete projects successfully.

Johnson, Johnson, and Holubec (1998) have written much about group processing. Although their work focuses on teams in a classroom environment, what they have written is appropriate for instructional design teams. We have often used group processing in the instructional design projects we have worked on. It has allowed us to form positive working relationships within our teams. According to Johnson, Johnson, and Holubec (1998), group processing helps:

- improve the quality of how the team approaches tasks;
- increase individual accountability of team members by focusing attention on the tasks a team member must complete;

- learn from each other by spending time discussing the tasks individuals are completing;
- eliminate problems that may be occurring.

Group processing is a time where team members can share information. Four different parts of processing should be included: feedback, reflection, goal improvement, and celebration. Feedback should be given to team members about how well they are completing their tasks and how well the team is working together. Team members should then have time to reflect on the feedback they have received. If improvement needs to be made on how the team is working together, then the team should discuss ways to improve and come up with a plan of action. Additionally, the team members should help each other and set goals for improving the quality of their work. Finally, the team should celebrate the hard work of the team members and the team's success (Johnson, Johnson & Holubec, 1998).

Tobias decided to approach group processing with his team by using a multipronged approach. The initial phase was carried out during a weekly team meeting, where Tobias described the situation as he currently saw it. He allowed team members to voice concerns about how the project was progressing and how the team was working together. The second phase consisted of individual meetings with team members, where Tobias provided direct feedback to each member on his or her work and the contributions each is making. During these meetings, Tobias clarified team member duties and expectations. The third phase took place at a team meeting. He clarified to the group the various team member roles and expectations. Tobias also provided a time for praises and wishes. The praises included successes of the team and team members. The wishes consisted of constructive criticism of how the team needed to progress and what was expected for the team during the upcoming week.

Elizabeth settled on Kilpatrick's Four Levels of Evaluation as a framework to guide her evaluation. This framework would allow Elizabeth to gather data on multiple levels to provide a holistic picture of how effective her workshops were in influencing participants to use the synchronous tools in their courses. Elizabeth hoped to answer the following questions as part of the evaluation:

- *Did the workshops Elizabeth conducted provide faculty with the incentives, knowledge, and skills faculty needed?*
- *Did faculty members take what they learned and apply it to their own courses?*
- *If so, did the use of these tools positively influence the teaching and learning processes in the courses?*

The data gathered from the evaluation will allow Elizabeth to determine the success of her workshops. She will be able to use the data to improve her workshops.

PRODUCT AND PROCESS EVALUATION AND THE INSTRUCTIONAL DESIGN PROCESS

Determining the success of the instructional design product and process is a significant task that can help lead to an improved instructional design product and process. Although there are various approaches to conducting an evaluation, the questions an instructional designer will need to answer before beginning an evaluation are the same. These are:

- What is the goal of the evaluation?
- Who is asking for the evaluation?
- What type of evaluation is needed?
- When does the evaluation need to take place?
- What are the questions that need to be answered?
- What types of data need to be gathered?
- Does the data currently exist?
- What instruments are needed to gather the data?
- How will the data be gathered?
- How will the data be analyzed?
- How will the data be reported?
- How will the results be used to improve the instructional design product or process or both?

Summary

Sustained and varied evaluation is a crucial element of the instructional design process. Evaluation provides information that allows decisions to be made about learners, instruction, and the instructional design process. Formative, summative, and learner evaluations are three types of evaluation that instructional designers commonly employee.

Formative evaluation is used throughout the instructional design process to gather data that can be used to provide feedback on how the process is going. Typically, formative evaluation is used to provide feedback on the instruction being developed. Feedback obtained during a formative evaluation can help instructional designers make changes to the instruction that makes it more efficient and effective. Formative evaluation should be built into an instructional design project from the beginning stages.

Although instructional design experts conduct formative evaluation for a common reason, the approaches they take are different. We described three approaches to formative evaluation. Dick, Carey, and Carey advocate three basic phases of formative evaluation: 1) one-to-one or clinical, 2) small group, and 3) field trial. Smith and Ragan provide a four-step approach to formative evaluation: design reviews, expert reviews, learner validation, and ongoing evaluation. Morrison, Ross, and Kemp recommend Gooler's eight-step process: purpose, audience, issues, resources, evidence, data-gathering techniques, analysis, and reporting.

Summative evaluation takes place after an instructional intervention has been implemented. The major goal of a summative evaluation is to gather data that allows for its effectiveness to be determined. Two main questions are to be answered: "Did the instruction bring about the desired changes?" and "Were the client's goals met?"

It is often considered a conflict of interest to have the instructional designer conduct a summative evaluation on an ID project he or she has worked on. If at all possible, an instructional designer should not be the primary evaluator. He or she should act in a supporting role by helping design the evaluation and provide necessary data. However, reality dictates that instructional designers are asked to conduct summative evaluations on projects they have worked on. To ensure success of a formative evaluation, the instructional designer should meet with the client early on in the ID project to discuss expectations of the evaluation, especially the evaluation goals. A process—such as the one advocated by Smith and Ragan—is a good model to be used by a beginning instructional designer.

An additional type of formative evaluation called "group processing" should be included as part of the instructional design process. Group processing allows for instructional design team members to regularly reflect on and communicate how well the team is working to meet project goals. It consists of four areas: feedback, reflection, goal improvement, and celebration. Group processing helps to build healthy and productive instructional design teams.

Connecting Process to Practice

1. How would you describe to your client the differences between learner, formative, and summative evaluations?
2. What decisions are being made with each type of evaluation?
3. What are the major issues associated with conducting an evaluation on an instructional design product?
4. What are the major issues associated with conducting an evaluation on the instructional design process that an instructional design team has gone through (or is currently going through)?
5. Consider Elizabeth's scenario. What issues do you see with the approach she advocated? Explain.
6. Could Tobias have taken a different approach to examining the situation with his instructional design team? Explain the approach.
7. Your client asks you to justify why you have suggested multiple evaluations throughout the instructional design process. What do you tell your client?
8. You have been contracted by a large law firm (approximately fifty employees) to design its intranet. The firm would like the following initial functionalities built into the intranet: client billing, document uploading and retrieval, and a calendar of firm events (e.g., court and deposition dates and times, scheduled vacations). As part of the contract, you have been asked to provide training to the paralegals and legal secretaries working at the firm. What type of evaluation(s) do you include in your plan? What do you anticipate using, and how do you communicate this to your client?
9. You are the lead instructional designer on a project team that has six members. Why is it important to include group processing as part of this instructional design project? Describe how you would incorporate group processing.

Recommended Reading

Flagg, B. N. (1990). *Formative evaluation for educational technologies.* Hillsdale, NJ: Lawrence Erlbaum Associates.

Kirkpatrick, D. L. (1994). *Evaluating training programs: The four levels.* San Francisco: Berrett-Koehler.

Rathburn, G. A., Saito, R. S., & Goodrum, D. A. (1997). Reconceiving ISD: Three perspectives on rapid prototyping as a paradigm shift. Proceedings of Selected Research and Development Presentations at the 1997 National Convention of the Association for Educational Communications and Technology. Washington, DC: AECT, pp. 291–296.

Tripp, S. D. and Bichelmeyer, B. (1990). Rapid prototyping: An alternative instructional design strategy. *Educational Technology Research and Development, 38*(1), pp. 31–44.

Worthen, B., Sanders, J., & Fitzpatrick, J. (2004). *Program evaluation: Alternative approaches and practical guidelines.* New York: Longman Publishers.

References

Dick, W., Carey, L. & Carey, J. (2009). *The systematic design of instruction.* New York: Longman Publishers.

Flagg, B. N. (1990). *Formative evaluation for educational technologies.* Hillsdale, NJ: Lawrence Erlbaum Associates.

Johnson, D., Johnson, R. & Holubec, E. (1998). *Cooperation in the classroom.* Boston: Allyn & Bacon.

Kirkpatrick, D. L. (1994). *Evaluating training programs: The four levels.* San Francisco: Berrett-Koehler.

Morrison, G. R., Ross, S. M. & Kemp, J. E. (2007). *Designing effective instruction, 5th edition.* New York: John Wiley & Sons.

Rathburn, G. A., Saito, R. S. & Goodrum, D. A. (1997). Reconceiving ISD: Three perspectives on rapid prototyping as a paradigm shift. Proceedings of Selected Research and Development Presentations at the 1997 National Convention of the Association for Educational Communications and Technology. Washington, DC: AECT, pp. 291–296.

Smith, P. & Ragan, T. (1999). *Instructional design.* Hoboken, NJ: John Wiley & Sons.

Tripp, S. D. & Bichelmeyer, B. (1990). Rapid prototyping: An alternative instructional design strategy. *Educational Technology Research and Development, 38*(1), 31–44.

Worthen, B., Sanders, J., & Fitzpatrick, J. (1997). *Program evaluation: Alternative approaches and practical guidelines.* New York: Longman Publishers.

Part V

MEDIA PRODUCTION: MANAGING THE MEDIA DEVELOPMENT PROCESS

Chapter 11 introduces the concepts of **project management**. It includes information on how media is produced, managing media production teams, and communication and conflict resolution.

Chapter 12 describes **visual design** and explains the basic principles that apply to creating easy-to-read and attractive visual displays.

Chapter 11

Instructional Media Production Management

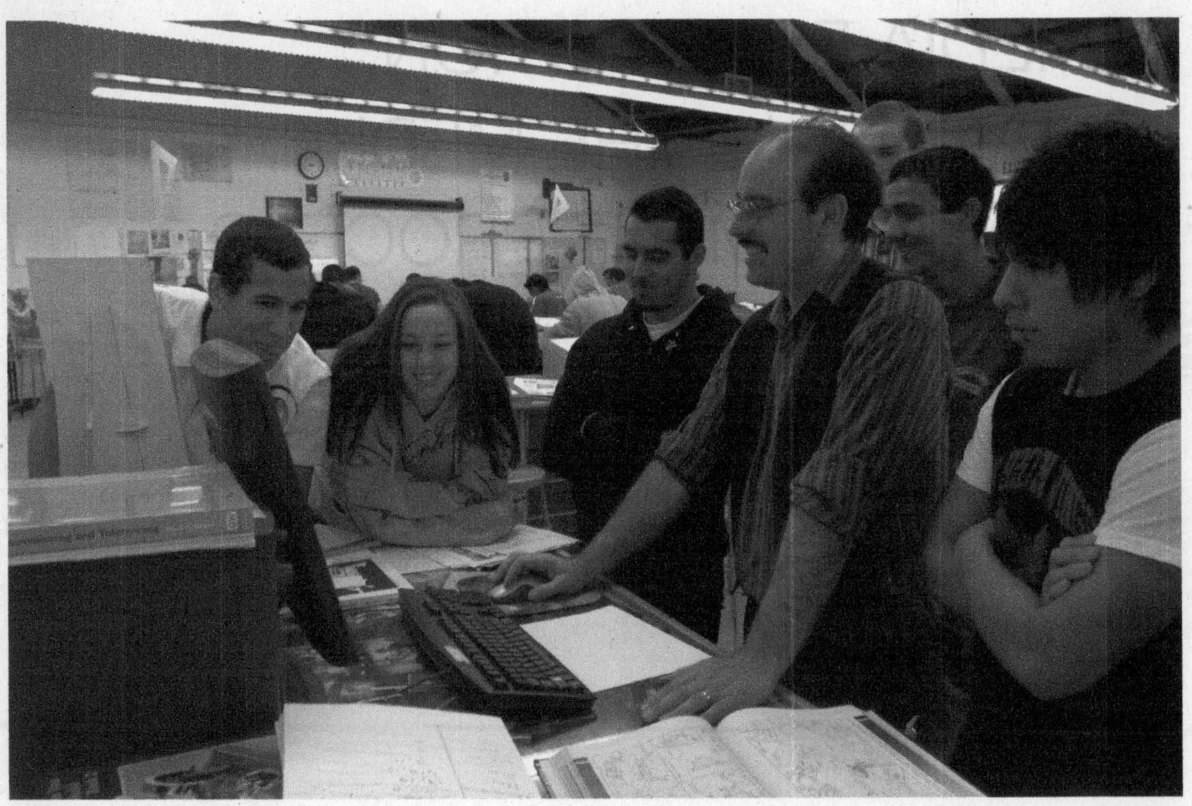

Part of the instructional design process is the production of the materials students and teachers use in a learning environment. These materials range from simple handouts to sophisticated computer simulations. Instructional media production is a series of processes that requires planning and careful follow-through. More sophisticated designs often rely on the coordinated efforts of a team. This chapter explains the media production process and recommends management approaches that make that process effective and satisfying for all concerned.

GUIDING QUESTIONS

- What are the phases of the production process?
- What are the roles and responsibilities of production team members?
- How does one manage a production project?
- What are recommended methods of minimizing and resolving conflict among production team members?
- How does one evaluate an instructional media product?

KEY TERMS

Client *184*	Navigation Layout *189*	Post-Production *182*
CPM Chart *187*	Milestones *185*	Production Calendar *185*
Drop-Dead Date *185*	Peer Review *193*	Prototyping *190*
Expert Review *193*	PERT Chart *187*	Storyboard *185*
Gantt Chart *187*	Pre-Production *182*	Style guide *187*

CHAPTER OVERVIEW

Instructional media production is the process of bringing to life the instructional designer's plans and specifications. Once an instructional designer or design team conducts the necessary analyses, develops the goals and objectives, specifies the activities, and determines the appropriate evaluation procedures, some person or group must actually create the media that will provide the instruction or instructional support. This media can take many forms. It can be print-based (e.g., worksheets, textbooks), audiovisual (e.g., film, video, slide presentations, sound recordings), interactive (e.g., software), or any combination of the three.

In some work environments, the instructional designer is separated from the media production team, but just as often, the instructional designer is an active participant in the production process. Often, the instructional designer for an organization is also in charge of the team that produces and delivers the instruction. Depending on the setting, the instructional designer may also take on a number of media production roles.

Regardless of whether you as an instructional designer have specific production responsibilities, it is helpful to have some idea of how media is produced in order to have appropriate expectations in terms of the production team's capabilities and the quality of the finished instructional products. Therefore, it is important to you as a novice instructional designer to become familiar with instructional media production processes.

This chapter focuses on the practical aspects of managing and working with a production team. Topics in this chapter include the specific functions of media production team members, methods of organizing a project, methods of group management and communication, and methods of evaluating the finished product.

THE PRODUCTION PROCESS

There are essentially three phases to any media production project: **pre-production**, production, and **post-production**. Pre-production is the planning phase; production involves design and development; and post-production includes distribution, integration, and archiving of the product.

In the pre-production phase of a media project, a clear description of what the product will be when it is finished is developed. Also, all the resources necessary to realize the project are determined, and a timeframe for completing the various production tasks is worked out. With instructional media, instructional designers provide the description of what the product will be through needs, task, learner, and goals analyses and the specification of activities and evaluation strategies. The production team must now determine what resources are available to realize the vision of the instructional design (this is sometimes called *planning and costing*) and how best to deploy these resources over a specified period of time.

In the production phase, the final design of the project is developed, and all the necessary components for its completion are created and integrated. Depending on the type of media being produced, this may include the creation of specific graphic elements, typeset text, soundtracks, video footage, and/or computer software.

In the post-production phase, the finished product is made ready for distribution to those who are going to use it. Often during post-production, the product is also archived so future production teams have access to the product and its components.

Although each phase of the production process can be viewed separately, there are no hard-and-fast rules for defining the components of each phase. Individual production teams will have their own ideas about what constitutes pre-production, production, and post-production. However, most media producers will agree that pre-production is that time when the team looks at what needs to be accomplished and decides how to make it happen; production is when plans are put into action and the final product is completed; and post-production is when the product is formatted for distribution.

ORGANIZING A PRODUCTION TEAM

A production team takes the raw material resources available and uses those resources to create a finished product. Good production teams consist of people with a variety of skills and talents. Teams may be large and highly specialized or they may be small, with each member assuming a broad range of responsibilities. Regardless of the number of individuals involved, there are three essential components to any production team: management, direction, and artists.

Management is the organizational aspect of the production. Managers take responsibility for getting things accomplished within the constraints of the resources available. Direction is the guiding force that suggests how the resources available will be used to create the finished product. Directors are the individuals who establish the artistic guidelines and style for the product. Artists are the human component of the resources available.

Artists are also those individuals who apply their creative skills to the product (during production, actors—who by definition fall within the "artist" category—are referred to separately as *talent*).

The roles and responsibilities of the members of any production team depend on the type of product being created. For example, a team responsible for producing computer-based multimedia might include the following:

Production Manager: Responsible for the organization and timing of the production. The production manager ensures that everyone knows what he or she should be doing and when specific tasks need to be accomplished. The production manager may also be called on to resolve conflict within the team.

Subject Matter Expert (SME): An individual who is a specialist and authority in the content area of the product (e.g., an astronomer helping with a product that teaches the basics of stellar cartography).

Writer: Responsible for generating text, scripts, and documentation.

Art Director: Responsible for the product's "look and feel" by specifying such things as color schemes, artwork, and typefaces. The art director oversees the efforts of the graphic artists.

Graphic Artist: Responsible for creating the graphic elements specified by the art director.

Sound Designer: Responsible for designing and producing audio elements.

Video Director: Responsible for gathering and/or creating video elements.

Video Editor: Responsible for preparing video elements specified by the video director.

Interface Designer: Responsible for specifying the product's human-computer interactions. The interface designer oversees the efforts of the programmers.

Programmer: Responsible for making a working version of the software.

Talent: The actors whose bodies, faces, and/or voices interpret the writer's scripts.

In many cases, members of a production team take on multiple roles. The production manager might take on direction or artistic responsibilities; the interface designer might also be the artistic director as well as the programmer. Any combination of roles is possible. However, in order for a production to run smoothly, there has to be some agreement among the team as to who has final responsibility (and authority) for management, for each aspect of direction, and for the production of each necessary element.

Professionals in Practice

Our team is comprised of a director, consultant, two instructional designers, a web developer, a media production specialist, and a graphic artist. The projects themselves are typically managed by the instructional designer that is working on the course, but they are all handled differently.

—Kara Andrew
instructional designer in distance education
California State University–Fullerton

Perhaps the most important role in any production project is that of **client**. The client is typically the person for whom the project is being created. Anyone with whom the producer or production team has entered into an agreement to create a specific product is a client. In a large business organization, the instructional media production unit may view other units (i.e., customer service or human resources) as clients. In a school setting, faculty members or departments may be considered the clients of the instructional media specialist. If you are participating in a course on instructional design, the course instructor might be considered the client for any instructional media projects assigned to you. No matter who it is specifically, the client in general is that person who has requested the product, and the client's satisfaction is in large part a measure of the project's success.

As part of a production team, you have a responsibility to your teammates. In some ways, you are each other's clients because there are things you are responsible for that your team is counting on. Depending on how you define the word in the context of creating instruction, you may also consider the target audience (the learners) as clients for your work. By the same token, you may consider the instructor or organization that plans to implement your design as a client. If you are working on a production project as part of a course you are taking, you may want to identify the person who will evaluate the project for a grade as a client.

Once you have a list of the clients involved, you may want to arrange the list in order of priority. A prioritized list of this kind can help when design and implementation decisions have to be made.

PRODUCTION MANAGEMENT

Production management includes the establishment and execution of those tasks and procedures that facilitate the completion of a project within a set of specified parameters. The parameters include a timeframe and a given set of available resources (including access to tools, the skills of production team members, and money). Management also includes maintaining communication among a project's participants and stakeholders. Establishing and maintaining communication reduces the risk of misunderstandings and increases the potential for successfully completing a project. The goal of any good production manager is to complete a project that is of the highest quality "on time and under budget." This is not an easy task. It requires careful planning, organization, and supervision to keep a production project on task.

The Media Production Triangle: Time, Resources, and Quality

The media production triangle represents the interplay between time, available resources (often, this is the money available to pay for services), and quality. The ideal is to always produce a high-quality product quickly and inexpensively. However, the adage among experienced media producers is that at any one time, you can only choose two of three choices: fast, cheap, or good. This means that there are always three less-than-ideal choices. A product may be created quickly and well, but it will not be cheap; it can be created inexpensively and well, but it will take time; or it can be created quickly and inexpensively, but it will not be very good.

Planning for Success: The Production Calendar

Given a finite amount of time to complete a production project, it is perhaps possible to create a high-quality product without planning in advance what will be accomplished at various points between the beginning and end of the project . . .

. . . but it is *highly unlikely.*

One of the critically important aspects of production management is time management. Even a production "team" consists of a single individual benefits from developing early on a timeline that anticipates the completion of various tasks. When a production is the responsibility of more than one person, a timeline is also helpful as a means of communication among team members; anyone may refer to it to see what and when specific tasks need to be completed. Most production teams establish a *production calendar* during pre-production. The production calendar establishes when specific tasks are to be completed and often includes notes on who is specifically responsible for the completion of each task. Figure 11.1 is an example of one month from a production calendar.

The production calendar consists of a combination of **milestones** and **drop-dead dates**. Milestones are the dates when important activities are to be accomplished; these include finalizing the style guidelines, the completion of **storyboards** or prototypes, production team meetings, and meetings with the client. Drop-dead dates are when a specific task must be completed (or abandoned if it is not complete); these include completion of filming, final artwork, programming, and submitting the completed product to the client.

Many production plans include a list of critically important dates, along with a description of who is responsible for approving elements of the design prior to

Progress Meeting | Production Plan | Storyboards | Development | ALPHA | BETA | Final Product

Sunday	Monday	Tuesday	Wednesday	Thursday	Friday	Saturday
1	2	3	4	5	6	7 Production
8 Production Calendar	9 ...	10 ... • Meeting after EDEL 515 -	11 ...	12 ...	13 ...	14
15 Storyboards	16	17 • Meeting after EDEL 515 -	18	19	20 • Meeting with • Production	21
22 Storyboards	23	24 • Meeting after EDEL 515 -	25	26 ...	27 ... • Meeting Paul and • Storyboards	28
29 Development	1	2 • Meeting after EDEL 515 -	3	4	5 • Meeting with Abbie Location:	6

FIGURE 11.1 A Sample Production Calender

production. The person responsible for approving an element needs to be informed that once he or she signs off on a design, that element is going into production as is (this may also be applied to the instructional designer, the subject matter expert, or any other member of the production team that is responsible for making pre-production and/or production specifications). Getting everyone to agree to these "milestone" dates in advance is highly recommended.

Establishing milestone dates goes hand in hand with determining *dependencies*. In any production situation, there will be some activities that completely depend on finishing other activities. For example, a video production using live actors in period costumes cannot begin shooting until the costumes have been obtained or created and fit to each actor. Shooting the video depends on the costumes being completed by the shooting date. It is critically important to determine which production activities depend on each other in order to prepare a reasonable production calendar.

Very often, the first item placed on a production calendar is the deadline date for the finished product. This is because it is usually the one date agreed on before even pre-production begins. It is common practice—and highly recommended—to begin with the finished project deadline date and work backward from there to establish the other deadlines and milestones that comprise the entire production cycle. See Figure 11.2.

Production Stage	Task
Pre-production	Review project parameters Determine budget and resources (cost and plan) Establish team assignments Create production calendar
Production	Complete the text components Establish style manual or guide for product elements Completion of initial prototype (a 'rough draft' that outlines the product's final form) Get client feedback and approval for the initial prototype Complete graphic elements Produce video elements Produce audio elements Completion of an *Alpha* version (a functional prototype) Get client feedback and approval for the *Alpha* version Completion of a *Beta* version (a functional prototype ready to be tested with end-users) Submit finished product to the client
Post-production	Distribute or deploy the product Archive product and project elements Review production process with the team (what worked; what needs improvement)

FIGURE 11.2 Typical Production Milestones and Deadlines for a Multimedia Project

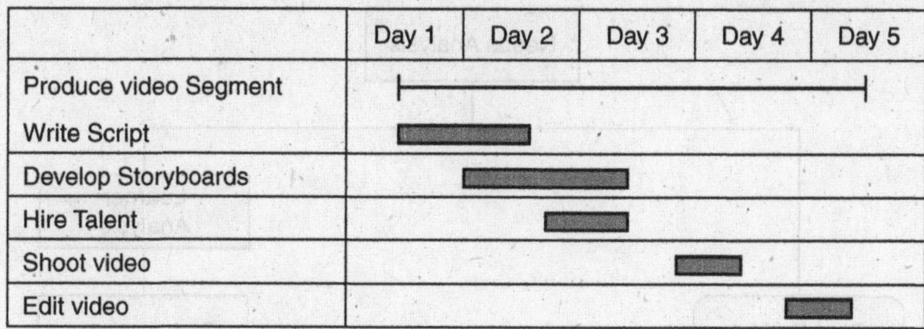

FIGURE 11.3 An Example of a Simple Gantt Chart

WHEN A SIMPLE CALENDAR IS NOT ENOUGH: GANTT, PERT, AND CPM CHARTS For small projects producing a single piece of instructional media, a simple production calendar is usually more than sufficient. For very large or complex projects or when the same production team handles multiple projects simultaneously, more specialized methods of keeping track of time and resources may be necessary. Three of the most popular project management charting techniques are *Gantt, PERT*, and *CPM*.

Gantt charts, named for project management expert Henry Laurence Gantt (1861–1919), are used to show the scheduled and actual progress of various elements of a project. On the vertical axis is a list of all the tasks to be performed. The horizontal axis lists the estimated task duration and may also list the skill level necessary to complete the task and the individual assigned to that task. See Figure 11.3.

PERT (Program Evaluation and Review Technique) and **CPM** (Critical Path Method) charts visually display task, dependency, and duration information. PERT and CPM charts begin with a horizontal line that indicates the first task in the project, the task's duration, and the number of people assigned to complete it. Successive horizontal lines drawn below the first one supply the same information for each successive task, illustrating where tasks may overlap on the timeline. See Figure 11.4.

When managing large, complex production projects or multiple projects that employ the same team members, Gantt, PERT, or CPM charts can prove to be valuable tools. Microsoft's MS Project software is considered the industry standard for producing and maintaining these management tools, providing a vast array of options and simplifying a number of repetitive setup tasks. However, we caution against using such specialized software for smaller projects because the time it takes to gain mastery of the software itself may prove counterproductive.

Style and Technical Guides

Creating and/or agreeing on a few **style guides** that everyone uses as they contribute to the project is highly recommended. Style guides help to unify the project, providing standards for the product's visual look, feel, and functionality. We recommend starting by deciding what style you will use for documentation. A team member may take on the role of documentation editor. The editor makes all the final decisions on how the documentation looks.

Depending on the project and the roles assigned to team members, you may also want to establish technical guidelines. For example, "The colors used in all graphics are to be reduced to a Web-safe palette," "The operating platform for the finished product is

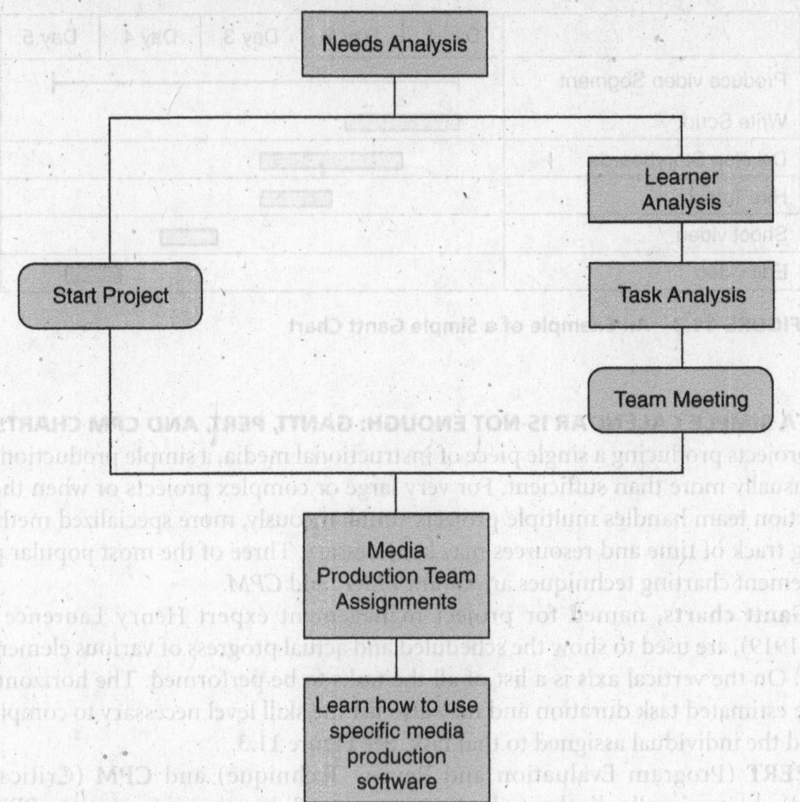

FIGURE 11.4 An Example of a PERT Chart.
The Rectangles with Rounded Corners Indicate Milestones.

Windows 2007," or "All sound files are to be 16-bit stereo." It may seem overly prescriptive, but agreeing and adhering to a set of technical guidelines in the pre-production phase can save everyone a great deal of trouble during production.

As the project progresses, it is advisable to create a style manual for all media that will be incorporated into the final product. A style manual often contains specific details for:

- Fonts (typefaces) and font sizes (there may be specific guidelines for headings, body text, captions, etc.)
- Color scheme (the background color, font color(s), palettes, etc.)
- Graphics (the type of graphic—cartoon, iconographic, photorealistic, etc.). In the case of computer-based instructional media, this may (and probably should) also include specifications for the pixel depth and resolution of images.
- Sound (bit depth, stereo/mono, MIDI or analog recording, etc.)

Storyboards

In the earliest stages of production, virtually all film, video, and animation projects are translated from a script to a *storyboard*. The storyboard visually depicts the script. Traditionally, a storyboard is indeed a big board on which are posted rough sketches that visually "tell the story." The entire project can then be seen as a series of pictures, allowing everyone working on the project to share a single vision of what the product should look like in its final form.

Some wonderful examples of storyboards are available as "extras" on the DVD versions of films and animated features. The DVD of Pixar's animated feature *Monsters, Inc.* includes a brief feature that shows the process of taking an idea from script to storyboard to finished animation. The DVD of The Beatles' *Yellow Submarine* allows one to watch the finished animation and the original storyboard simultaneously on a split screen.

Computer-based multimedia projects are also often translated into a storyboard early in the production process. The storyboard of a multimedia project gives a screen-by-screen view of how the finished product should look. Multimedia storyboards are often accompanied by a **navigation layout**. A navigation layout (see Figure 11.5) is a visual display of the possible choices one may take in navigating the multimedia presentation; this

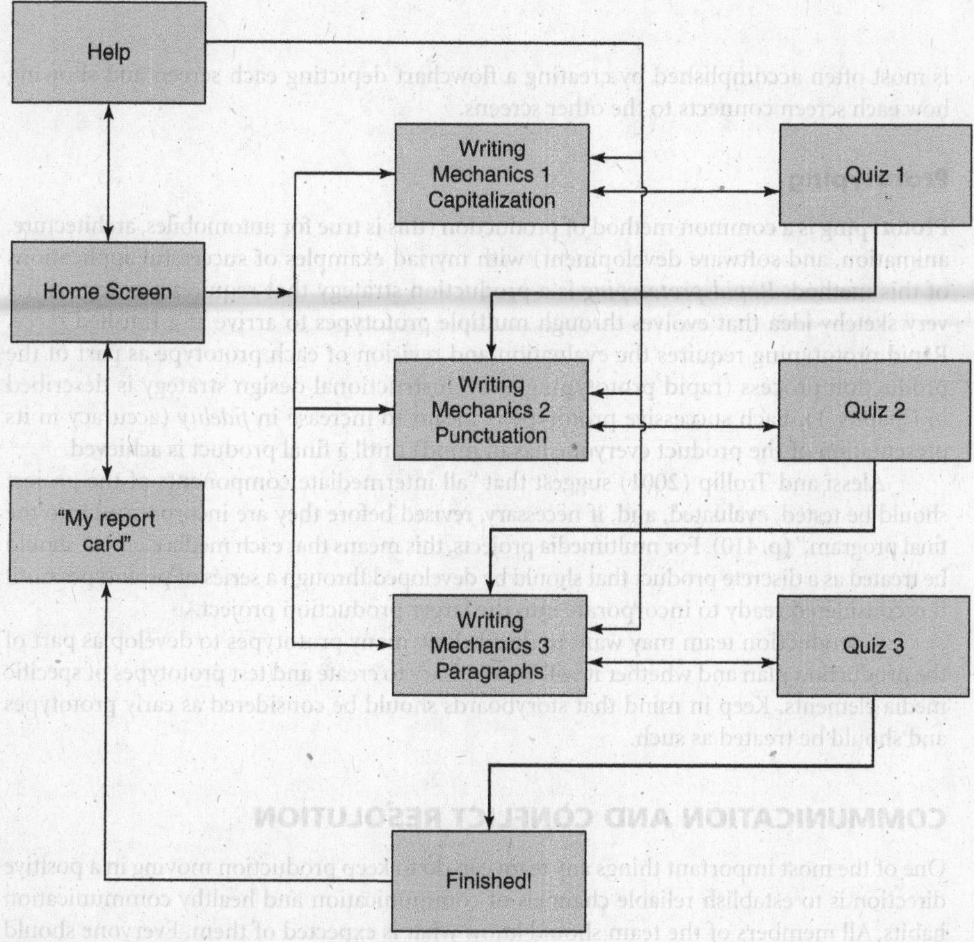

FIGURE 11.5 An Example of Navigation Layout.
Each Rectangle Represents a Full Screen in the Design.

Professionals in Practice

When I create instructional software, I make a list of the functions that are specified for the product that I have never before attempted. I then make a small mockup piece of software that employs only that function to test whether it will meet the design specifications. I think of this as a mini prototype for one portion of the finished product. For example, I was once asked to author a program in Macromedia Director that would allow students taking a test to save their answers on to a floppy disk—something I had never attempted. The final product had to be cross-platform, so this function had to work equally well in Macintosh and Windows environments. I began by creating this function alone (one platform at a time) and testing it to be sure it was stable. Incorporating the function into the final product was then largely a matter of cutting and pasting.

—Abbie Brown
instructional media producer
Greenville, North Carolina

is most often accomplished by creating a flowchart depicting each screen and showing how each screen connects to the other screens.

Prototyping

Prototyping is a common method of production (this is true for automobiles, architecture, animation, and software development) with myriad examples of successful applications of this method. *Rapid-prototyping* is a production strategy that requires starting with a very sketchy idea that evolves through multiple prototypes to arrive at a finished piece. Rapid prototyping requires the evaluation and revision of each prototype as part of the production process (rapid prototyping as an instructional design strategy is described in Chapter 1). Each successive prototype is meant to increase in *fidelity* (accuracy in its presentation of the product everyone has in mind) until a final product is achieved.

Alessi and Trollip (2001) suggest that "all intermediate components of the project should be tested, evaluated, and, if necessary, revised before they are incorporated into the final program," (p. 410). For multimedia projects, this means that each media element should be treated as a discrete product that should be developed through a series of prototypes until it is considered ready to incorporate into the larger production project.

A production team may want to decide how many prototypes to develop as part of the production plan and whether it will be necessary to create and test prototypes of specific media elements. Keep in mind that storyboards should be considered as early prototypes and should be treated as such.

COMMUNICATION AND CONFLICT RESOLUTION

One of the most important things any team can do to keep production moving in a positive direction is to establish reliable channels of communication and healthy communication habits. All members of the team should know what is expected of them. Everyone should also have a reliable means of voicing and dealing with problems as they arise. Keeping good and reliable channels of communication open with the client is also critically important to the success of a project. Four key communication strategies that can help are *respect, regular consultation, specificity,* and *paper trail maintenance* (Brown, Green & Zatz, 2001).

Respect: Individuals must realize that each member of the team brings to the project a set of unique skills and talents as well as a unique perspective. It is important to the health of any project that everyone recognizes the value of each team member's contributions by listening to them and accepting critical comments in the spirit in which they are intended.

Regular Consultation: Regular meetings, phone conversations, or correspondence are an important part of the production process. These allow team members and the client to share ideas, provide clarifications, and ensure that the product is being designed to match everyone's shared vision.

Specificity: Everyone involved in the production process should strive to be as specific as possible. For example, the term "a clever animation" does not adequately describe how a finished animation should look (one person's "clever" is another's "trite"). Clarify and show specific examples as often as possible.

Paper Trail Maintenance: During pre-production and in the early stages of production, have everyone share layouts, sketches, and storyboards as much as possible to establish a shared vision of the finished product. During the later stages of production, establish signoff dates when the production manager, team members, or the client must sign an authorization that the product component is acceptable for incorporation into the final product. Establish signoff dates for the alpha and beta prototypes when the client gives authorization that the prototype is acceptable.

Watch Out for Cowboys

One classic problem that many instructional design teams face is sometimes referred to as the *cowboy* (or *hero* or *superhero*) syndrome. A *cowboy* is someone who is usually highly competent but does not work well with others. The cowboy tends to make statements like, "I'll take care of that—no one else on the team needs to worry about it." The cowboy does not take direction well and does not share what he or she is doing until it is completed—often at the last minute, when there is little or no time for changes. Many times, cowboys are people who have previously been rewarded for their expertise and their ability to work independently. This is very common among specialists who often have no one else around who understand what it is they do. It is important to recognize the good intentions of cowboys; they have no doubt spent a good deal of their professional lives "riding in to save the day." However, there really is no room for cowboys or superheroes on a team that is functioning well. The old saying is true: "There is no 'I' in team." The trick is to develop the right balance between independently dealing with tasks and collaborating with team members.

The importance of good communications among team members cannot be overstressed. It takes awhile for teams to form into effective working groups, and much of why teams operate effectively is still a mystery to us. However, one thing we know from experience is that effective teams have effective communication strategies in place.

Tips for Successful Teamwork

In the introduction to the chapter on collaborative problem-solving in the book *Instructional Design Theories and Models: A New Paradigm of Instructional Theory Volume II*, (Reigeluth, 1999), Laurie Miller Nelson writes:

> Often in our daily lives we find ourselves working in small groups, whether it be in the context of a work project, a civic group, a classroom, or a family. Group problem solving is one of the most common and natural situations in which we accomplish the work of society. (p. 244)

Working in teams is commonplace, and most of us operate as members of a variety of teams during any given week. We are members of departments, faculties, workgroups, classes, etc., and we take on specific roles within those groups in order to accomplish tasks that are important to us as individuals and important to the group as a whole.

Teamwork has its benefits and its drawbacks. As you begin to form teams and plan for completing a production project, you may want to take the following into consideration:

1. Teamwork requires communication. Make sure your team knows how to communicate effectively (e.g., specific days or times of day when everyone should have checked e-mail, weekly meetings, or phone conferences).
2. Teams should consist of people with explicit roles. Members of the team should take specific responsibilities. These should include project manager (the person who coordinates everyone's efforts), subject matter expert (the person who decides the content of the instruction), and media producer. Other roles teams may want to assign include editor (the person responsible for making all the documentation flow together), artistic director (the person who designates the "look and feel' of the instructional media) and assessment director (the person who develops and implements the assessment protocols).
3. Teamwork requires consensus. Team members must discuss and agree on critical elements of successful project completion. Team communication protocols and assigned roles are something that all team members must agree to (therefore, all team members should have input into the decision processes). The team should come up with a roster of the specific roles of each team member as well as a timeline that indicates when each team member's production obligations are to be met.

EVALUATING THE PRODUCT

In describing the production of instructional software, Alessi and Trollip (2001) write: "Although there is much research in learning and instruction to guide us in developing instruction, the best guarantee that a program will be effective is to try it out, revise it, try it again, and so on until you get it right" (p. 408). In trying it out, the critically important evaluative activity involves close attention to the reactions and responses of the clients and the end users. The question to constantly consider is, "Is this product meeting the specified instructional goals and objectives?"

We recommend ongoing, iterative evaluation of the product as it develops. In the earliest stages of pre-production and production, product ideas and rough sketches can be evaluated through **expert review**. An expert review is soliciting input from a person or persons with a great deal of experience with the type of instructional media under development. Because of his or her experience, an expert can gain a sense of the production team's vision from very rough drafts (a cocktail napkin with a few sketches and a verbal description is often enough to give an expert an idea of the finished product).

In the middle and later stages of development, the product can be evaluated through **peer review**. Other producers and/or instructional designers may be asked to review the product in its storyboard or alpha prototype form in order to get an "informed outsider's" opinion of the product (often, a fresh pair of eyes can see potential problems that the design team cannot).

At the later stages of development, potential end users may effectively review the product. As the product takes on its final shape, those who will use the product can test it out and offer advice or criticism. This is often accomplished through *usability testing*.

Usability Testing

A concept originally borrowed from engineering that has gained popularity among software developers, multimedia producers, and instructional designers is *usability testing*. Usability testing consists of evaluating the product by observing it in action with potential end users. Typically, a usability test consists of evaluators observing a user or users interacting with the product under controlled conditions. The user(s) interact with the product for a specified amount of time, having been asked to complete a set of tasks determined in advance by the evaluation team. The tasks are based on the goals and objectives the product is designed to meet. Results of a usability test inform the production team of the problems inherent in the design (e.g., the graphic for a button is not well-understood or the instructions are worded in a manner that is confusing) and suggest—through observation of end users in action—ways to effectively eliminate those problems.

Mission Creep

It is often said among media production specialists that no multimedia project is ever completed; it is merely abandoned. One of the problems faced by a team that successfully creates a prototype product is that once it becomes evident that the product will work, those contributing to the project will want to add components and make improvements. This very natural wish to add to a successful product often results in the product never reaching completion. At some point, someone must declare the product completed.

FINAL THOUGHTS

All aspects of production management and evaluation should serve the project, not the other way around. Think of the calendar, priority list, prototypes, and evaluation strategies as support pieces that aid in creating a high-quality piece of instructional media. If at some point any of these support pieces creates more problems than it solves, then it may be time to re-evaluate it and create a modified or new support piece to replace the one that is not actually offering support. Think of each production planning item as a small contract—if it becomes impossible to honor that contract, it may be time to renegotiate it. Using the "contract" metaphor is deliberate on our part. Contracts are generated to protect the interests of all parties; one person having trouble with a contract is still bound by it if the other parties insist on honoring it.

MEDIA PRODUCTION MANAGEMENT AND THE INSTRUCTIONAL DESIGN PROCESS

Coordinating the production of the media and working effectively with all members of a production team is an important part of instructional design. As an instructional designer, you may be called on to work with a diverse group of professionals or you may have to take on a number of production roles yourself. No matter what role you play in the production process, your goal is to deliver instruction that suits the needs of the client and the learners. An understanding of the media production process should help you answer the following questions:

- What is my role during pre-production?
- What is my role during production?
- What is my role during post-production?
- Who do I report to, and who reports to me?
- How do I plan out a successful media production project?
- How can I best communicate with my production team?
- What can I do to resolve conflicts as they arise?

Summary

Depending on the work setting, an instructional designer may either submit plans and specifications to an instructional media production team or may be an integral part of that team. In either case, an instructional designer must have some idea of how instructional media is produced in order to maintain appropriate expectations for the finished product.

There are three phases to any production project: pre-production, production, and post-production. In pre-production, a production team is formed that consists of managers, directors, and artists. Management is responsible for project organization, timing, and the deployment of resources. Directors are responsible for the "look and feel" of the product. Artists create the elements necessary for the project's completion. A project is usually instigated at the request of a client, and the client's satisfaction with the project is in large part a measure of its success.

Production projects typically begin with the creation of a production calendar that includes milestones and deadline dates critical to the project's success. Style guides are then created and/or agreed on to unify the product. The project is then produced through a series of prototypes, often beginning with a script, progressing to a storyboard, then on to alpha and beta prototypes in preparation for a final release product.

While conflict is almost inevitable among any team, maintaining good communication among team members can facilitate resolving problems. Four strategies that contribute to good communication are: respecting the input of each team member, regular consultation among team members, careful use of specific terms to describe aspects of the production, and the maintenance of a complete "paper trail."

Evaluating the instructional media product is best accomplished as an ongoing, iterative process. This process includes expert review, peer review, and usability testing (observation of the product in action).

It is important to keep in mind that all aspects of production management and evaluation should contribute to the success of the project. If any supporting activity creates more problems than it solves, it may be necessary to modify the existing activity or create a new one to replace it.

Connecting Process to Practice

1. You have been put in charge of a new production team that consists of yourself as instructional designer, a commercial artist, a computer programmer, and a writer. The computer programmer comes to you on your first day and explains that she is used to working on her own and that she will be more productive if left on her own to develop products without team input. How do you respond?
2. You are part of a team creating interactive instructional media for a prominent museum. In a pre-production meeting, the account executive representing the museum asks about the evaluation portion of your production plan. He is concerned about both the time and the cost of this part of production. What do you tell him about the need for expert and peer review and usability testing?
3. You are assigned the task of producing a booklet that contains information about your organization's options for health insurance. What are the critically important activities of pre-production, production, and post-production for this project?
4. You are the manager for a large video production project. The client is a philanthropist who would like to create something that inspires young people to choose biochemistry as a career path. The client has very specific ideas about what she would like a specific video segment to look like, but the video production team is not sure it can match her vision and stay within the budget. What do you do?
5. You are part of a five-person instructional media production team that works for a large university. Each member of the team is an experienced instructional design and has extensive media production skills. The team has been assigned a project that requires the development of instructional software for a chemistry professor (the project is being paid for by a grant the professor has received). What are the roles and responsibilities that each team member will need to be assigned? What roles or responsibilities would the chemistry professor assume?
6. You are part of a team developing computer-based interactive instruction that supports reading skill development for second-grade students. The team has three months to complete the project. What activities would you build into the production calendar to be sure the finished product is both effective instruction and well-received by the students?
7. You are the manager of an instructional multimedia project. The member of your production team responsible for completing the project's graphics is not ready on the day all graphics are to be turned over to the software author. What do you do?

Recommended Reading

Alessi, S. M. & Trollip, S. R. (2001). *Multimedia for learning: Methods and development, 3rd edition.* Boston: Allyn & Bacon. (Chapters 12 through 15 address design and development of instructional multimedia.)

Dumas, J. S. & Redish, J. C. (1999). *A practical guide to usability testing, Revised edition.* Portland, OR: Intellect.

Elin, L. (2001). *Designing and developing multimedia: A practical guide for the producer, director, and writer.* Boston: Allyn & Bacon.

Kuniavsky, M. (2003). *Observing the user experience: A practitioner's guide to user research.* San Francisco: Morgan Kaufman Publishers.

References

Alessi, S. M. & Trollip, S. R. (2001). *Multimedia for learning: Methods and development, 3rd edition.* Boston: Allyn & Bacon.

Brown, A., Green, T. & Zatz, D. (2001). Developing and designing multimedia production projects: A set of guidelines. *EDUCAUSE Quarterly, 2*(4), 26–29.

Carrigan, D. (Director). (2002). *Monsters, Inc.* United States: Pixar.

King Features (Producer) & Dunning, G. (Director). (1968). *Yellow Submarine.* [Motion picture]. Great Britain: Apple Films.

Microsoft Project. (2003). Redmond, WA: Microsoft Corporation.

Nelson, L. M. (1999). Collaborative problem solving. In Reigeluth, C. (Ed.), *Instructional design theories and models: A new paradigm of instructional theory, Volume II* (pp. 244–267). Mahwah, NJ: Lawrence Erlbaum Associates.

Chapter 12

Visual Design for Instructional Media

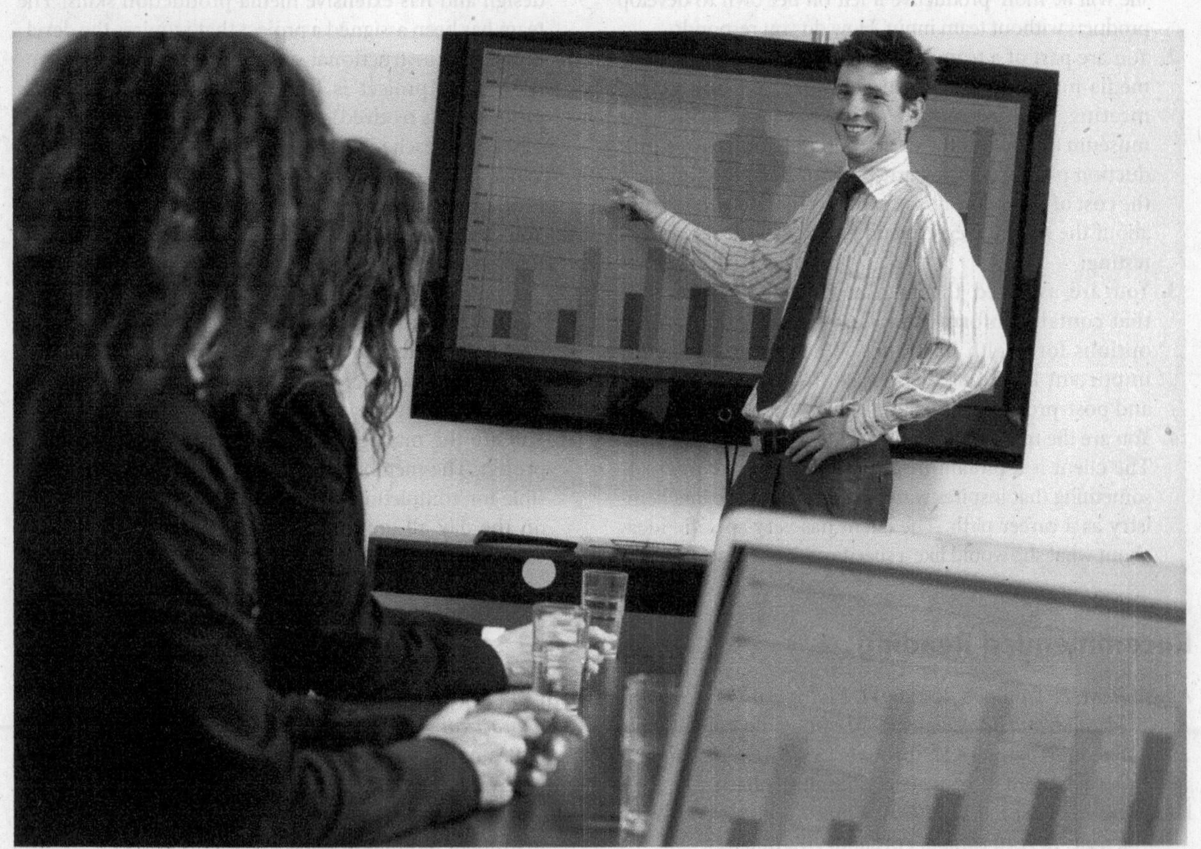

Instructional designers are responsible for communicating ideas efficiently and effectively. This often includes being able to produce visual media. Educators—including K–12 classroom teachers, corporate trainers, and college professors—often find themselves producing their own media, including slideshows (e.g., PowerPoint presentations), Web pages, bulletin boards, posters, and handouts. Computer software and hardware provide the necessary tools for media production, but to create professional-looking materials, one must understand and apply the rules of visual design.

GUIDING QUESTIONS

- Why is it important for an instructional designer to have some knowledge of visual design?
- What are the basic principles of visual design?
- What are common strategies commercial artists use to make visual displays attractive and appealing?
- How does one select an appropriate type or font?
- What are the most effective color combinations of background and text?
- How does one evaluate a visual design?

KEY TERMS

Additive Color Model *203*
Alignment *199*
Contrast *199*
Decorative Typefaces *202*
Four-Color Process Model *203*
Negative Space *201*
Polarity *204*
Proximity *199*
Repetition *199*
Sans Serif Text *201*
Serif Text *201*
Squint Test *204*
Subtractive Color Model *203*

CHAPTER OVERVIEW

There was a time when professional commercial artists and print specialists took care of designing and producing almost all the print materials instructional designers used. Now, more often than not, instructional designers make many of their own print materials by using computer-based word-processing, image manipulation, Web-editing, and desktop publishing tools. The final product may not be as good as it would be if it were produced by an experienced commercial artist, but do-it-yourself materials have the advantage of being quick and inexpensive to make.

Computers and desktop publishing software give us the freedom to use different typestyles, type sizes, and graphics in a way that can look truly professional. However, the freedom to do anything with type and graphics sometimes leads to some "unusual" (to put it politely) results. Random selection and placement of graphics and text or a design based solely on one's personal taste often leads to instructional materials that are difficult to comprehend.

While you might not become a skilled commercial artist without years of dedicated study and practice, you can produce effective and visually pleasing materials by following a few essential rules. Ideally, any flyer, Web page, or brochure should be easy to read and attractive. Understanding and following a few basic visual design principles will help to meet this goal.

This chapter explains the essential elements of visual display and describes fundamental rules of visual design. Topics covered in this chapter include an introduction to the basic principles of visual design, suggestions for making designs attractive, choosing the best type and font size for a design, and examples of readable and legible designs.

WHY INSTRUCTIONAL DESIGNERS NEED TO LEARN ABOUT VISUAL DESIGN

When desktop publishing tools first became available in the 1980s, professionals of all types made widespread but indiscriminate use of them to add graphics and styled text to their work. Graphic designers trained in the complexity of visual thinking criticized the use of these tools and expressed concern that software companies were overselling their products' capabilities (Schriver, 1997). Today, desktop publishing and Web-editing software are even more sophisticated, but the situation remains the same. Although many programs are available that allow one to "dump" text and graphics into a ready-made template, this is not a reasonable substitute for understanding and applying visual design principles.

The tools currently available to most instructional design professionals (e.g., PowerPoint, Word, Dreamweaver) offer their users the capability of producing sophisticated media products (products that once would have been produced only by professionals with some visual design expertise). While these products offer the user a great deal of control over the medium, they cannot make design decisions for you. Even when making use of the design templates that abound (for example, Microsoft provides an astounding number of templates for products such as PowerPoint and Word), you will make better use of them if you understand and apply visual design principles. Without some understanding of visual design, you are likely to create materials that are less than optimal. The pop-culture-driven viewpoint that anyone is a media producer as long as he or she has access to the right software and hardware is not appropriate for instructional design professionals. Maintaining this attitude may hamper an instructional designer's ability to function well in a professional setting (Brown, 1999).

Creating displays that are easy to read and understand is a skill one can develop. There is a body of literature that addresses issues that include optimal color combinations, type size and style, and placement of images and text. There is also a body of experiential knowledge among commercial artists and designers from which everyone can learn.

Few instructional design students have an extensive background in visual design, but most are interested in learning more about it (Brown, 2004). It will never be possible to do more than scratch the surface of visual design in an introductory textbook chapter such as this. However, we can offer an explanation of the general practices of visual design as well as a few of the more important design concepts to give you a better understanding of the discipline and some appreciation for your own potential as a visual designer.

Even if you are not going to be making visual design decisions (for example, if you work as an instructional designer in an environment that employs commercial artists for production), you still should know enough about visual design to make appropriate recommendations and assess the work of others. More often than not, instructional designers have to make visual design decisions, and these decisions should be made based on knowing at least the basic concepts of visual design.

BASIC PRINCIPLES OF VISUAL DESIGN

In *The Non-Designer's Design Book* (2008), author Robin Williams presents four basic principles of visual design: **alignment**, **contrast**, **repetition**, and **proximity**. Williams points out that these four principles are interconnected, and one does not often see one of these four aspects of design applied independently. In creating an effective and appealing design, you apply all four principles simultaneously.

Alignment

Alignment is what leads the reader through the design (this is sometimes called "flow"). Nothing should be incorporated into the design without careful consideration of its placement. One common alignment strategy is to have all the headings line up with each other, with indented subheadings and/or body text beneath each heading. See Figure 12.1.

Contrast

Contrast distinguishes different elements of a design. For example, make headings stand out from body text by using very different typefaces for each. Bold and italic text contrasts with regular text. Contrasting colors can be used (black and white are the most essential contrasting color combination), as can contrasting image and type sizes. See Figure 12.2.

Complete the Hazardous Waste Disposal Certificate in ***Five Steps***

5. Certificate completed!

4. Schedule an **evaluation** session

3. Complete the **online test**

2. Complete the **readings**

1. **Register** at the Web site

Contact ***Julie Smith*** at ***extension 278*** for more information

FIGURE 12.1 Example of the Alignment Principle
The Five Steps are Aligned to Create a Visual Set of Steps, Drawing the Reader's Eye from Step 1 to Step 5.

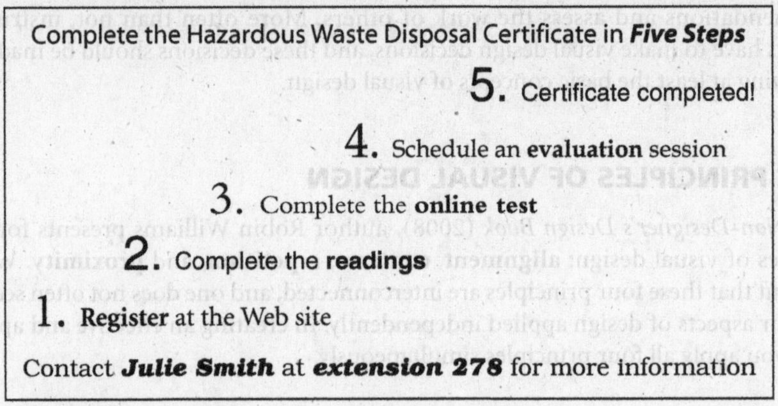

Complete the Hazardous Waste Disposal Certificate in ***Five Steps***

5. Certificate completed!

4. Schedule an **evaluation** session

3. Complete the **online test**

2. Complete the **readings**

1. **Register** at the Web site

Contact ***Julie Smith*** at ***extension 278*** for more information

FIGURE 12.2 Example of the Contrast Principle
This Example Shows Alignment as Well. Vastly Different Type Sizes are Used to Emphasize the Steps. Bold and Italic Text is Used to Draw Attention to Key Information

Repetition

Repetition conveys a sense of deliberate and carefully planned design. Simple elements used over again give the design a unified feeling (for example, a large graphic used on top of a page might be used again at the bottom of the page as a small repeating graphic forming a line). See Figure 12.3.

Proximity

Proximity places together elements that relate to each other, creating one or more "visual units" within the larger design that help organize the information (for example, a picture of a person standing on a scale and text describing weight-loss strategies might be placed very near each other to create one visual unit). See Figure 12.4.

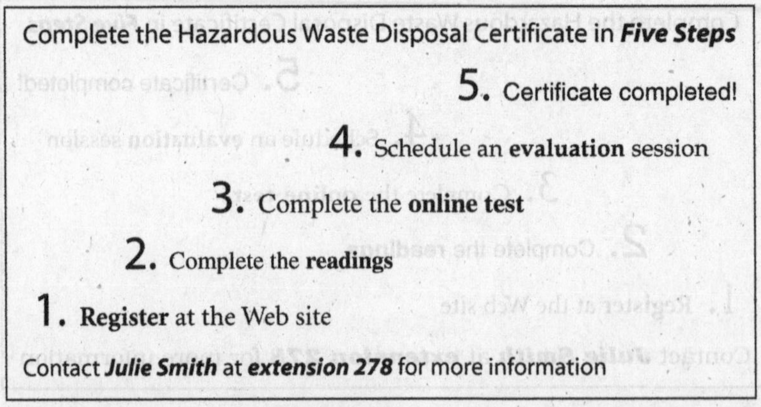

Complete the Hazardous Waste Disposal Certificate in ***Five Steps***

5. Certificate completed!

4. Schedule an **evaluation** session

3. Complete the **online test**

2. Complete the **readings**

1. **Register** at the Web site

Contact ***Julie Smith*** at ***extension 278*** for more information

FIGURE 12.3 Repetition Example
The Example Shows Alignment and Contrast as Well. The Same Typeface is Used Repeatedly for the Step Numbers and the Description of Each Step. The Top Line Typeface is the Same as the Bottom Line Typeface

Complete the Hazardous Waste Disposal Certificate
in ***Five Steps***

5. Certificate completed!

4. Schedule an **evaluation** session

3. Complete the **online test**

2. Complete the **readings**

1. **Register** at the Web site

Contact
Julie Smith at
extension 278
for more information

FIGURE 12.4 Proximity Example
The Example Shows Alignment, Contrast and Repetition as Well. The Information is Grouped into Three Distinct Areas.

VISUAL DESIGN TIPS

Here are a few tips that always seem to make visual displays and print materials more attractive and memorable (see Figure 12.5):

- Do not be timid about "negative space"—the empty or "unused" space within a visual design. It is important to make good use of negative space by resisting the urge to fill it with text or graphics; a page that is completely filled with text and graphics is difficult to read.
- Make use of faces. Human beings are naturally drawn to faces. Think of the billboards and magazine advertisements that attract your attention most quickly. How many have large faces as part of the design? How many cereal boxes designed to attract shoppers' attention have faces on the front? Make use of this by incorporating some type of face graphic as one of the largest elements of your design.
- Use bulleted lists (like this one!) to separate discrete bits of information while simultaneously grouping them together (think of Williams's proximity principle).

TYPE

In visual design, the typefaces that we use to present text are considered to be in one of three categories: serif, sans serif, and decorative. **Serif text** is generally considered the easiest text to read. Serifs are the little tails and squiggles (not exactly the technical terms) that embellish certain typefaces. Serif text is particularly easy to read because the serifs are designed to help the reader identify and discriminate between specific letters. Most newspapers, books, and magazines use serif text for their body copy (body copy is the bulk of the text, as opposed to headlines or callout sections). **Sans serif text** is literally "without serifs" (sans is French for "without"). Sans serif text is the second-most readable type of text and is often used for section headings and captions. Arial and Helvetica are examples of sans serif typefaces. A **decorative typeface** is exactly what its name implies. These are the

FIGURE 12.5 People Tend to Focus First on the Image of a Face, no Matter Whether the Face is Human or Animal, Realistic or Cartoon-like. Use Face Images to Capture the Reader's Attention

fancy typefaces that are most often used to give print materials a specific style or personality. See Figure 12.6.

All too often, people with no training in visual design fall victim to the temptation of overusing decorative fonts. Imagine if you had to read this entire chapter using the Edwardian Script typeface! It would make the chapter considerably less legible. The trick is to recognize that "less is more" when it comes to selecting typefaces. The rubric most commercial artists use is this:

- Use a common, easily recognized, serif typeface for the body of the work (like Times or Times New Roman).
- Break up the body text with headings and captions in sans serif typeface (like Arial or Helvetica).
- Use decorative typefaces sparingly. Only use decorative typefaces for a short title or subheading.

To keep things as legible as possible, always follow the classic rule of KISS (Keep It Simple, Silly). When in doubt, go with the simplest possible typeface choices, and avoid the beginner's mistake of creating a one-page handout by using every single typeface available on your computer!

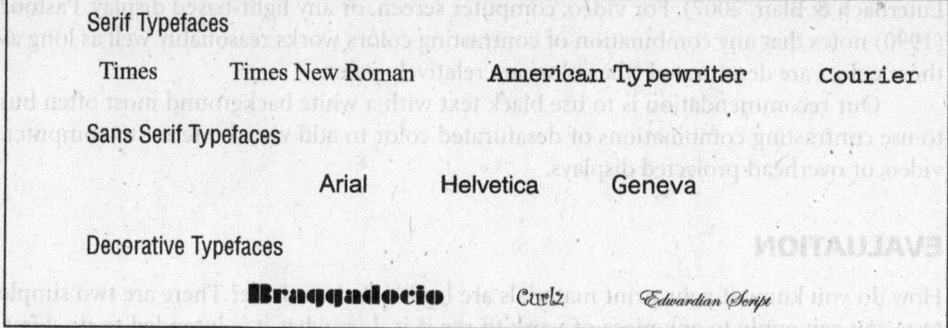

Serif Typefaces
Times
Times New Roman
American Typewriter
Courier
Sans Serif Typefaces
Arial
Helvetica
Geneva
Decorative Typefaces
Braggadocio
Curlz
Edwardian Script

FIGURE 12.6 Examples of Serif, Sans Serif and Decorative Typefaces

COLOR

Color is generally organized into two types of color models: subtractive and additive. These models are based on identifying three primary colors that can be used in combination to create all other colors.

The three primary colors of an **additive color model** are red, green, and blue (this is what is meant by "RGB color"). In an additive model, mixing the three primary colors together at full strength produces white (the presence of all color). This is also called a light model because it explains how colored light behaves.

The three primary colors of a **subtractive color model** are yellow, magenta, and cyan (in elementary school, we usually learn these as yellow, red, and blue). In a subtractive model, mixing the three primary colors together produces black (the absence of color). This is also called a pigment model because it explains how pigments such as paint or ink behave. However, because the pigments are never perfect, mixing the primary colors together most often forms a very dark brown. A true black pigment has to be added to form the color black, which is why we have the **four-color process model**. The four-color process model uses four primary colors: cyan, magenta, yellow, and black (or CMYK—the K stands for "black") in combinations to create all other colors (this is what is meant by a "four-color printing job").

For practical purposes, basic knowledge of these models makes it easier to specify colors in programs such as Photoshop, InDesign, PowerPoint, and Word because the color selectors in these programs are based on these models.

Selecting the Best Text and Background Colors

In designing instructional media, the best text and background colors are those that make the text easiest to read. Studies conducted on the most readable text/background color combinations indicate that black text on a white background is what most people find easiest to read (Brown, Luterbach & Blair, 2007; Mills & Weldon, 1987; Taylor, 1934). However, in studies conducted by Pastoor (1990), subjects expressed a preference for color text/background combinations instead of the traditional black/white combination, claiming it is less monotonous and less of a strain.

Deciding the **polarity** of a visual display is an important design choice. A design may have either dark text with a lighter background or light text with a darker background. In general, it takes a bit more effort to read light text on a dark background (Mills & Weldon, 1987). However, a classic combination that works particularly well for visual display on a computer screen or video monitor is a blue background with yellow text (Brown,

Luterbach & Blair, 2007). For video, computer screen, or any light-based display, Pastoor (1990) notes that any combination of contrasting colors works reasonably well as long as those colors are desaturated (the colors are relatively pale).

Our recommendation is to use black text with a white background most often but to use contrasting combinations of desaturated color to add visual interest to computer, video, or overhead projected displays.

EVALUATION

How do you know if your print materials are legible and readable? There are two simple tests you can apply to any piece of work to see if it does what it is intended to do. First, decide what the most important thing is on any single page of your work and then perform a **squint test** to determine if that most important thing is the most noticeable aspect of the visual design. The squint test is just what it sounds like: Look at the page while squinting hard; whatever you can make out through your blurred vision is the thing that is most noticeable on the page.

A second and equally important test to perform on your work is to hand it to someone who has not been involved in its creation and ask him or her to read it through and tell you what he or she thinks. Try giving it to at least two different types of people: One person who is very similar to the intended audience and one person who is an instructional design peer. Gaining feedback from peers and people similar to those for whom the work is intended can be a difficult process (it can be hard to hear that work you think is perfect may have problems that need to be addressed), but gathering and using this kind of critical feedback is very often immeasurably helpful in creating a truly useful document.

AN EXAMPLE

Figure 12.7 is an example of a handout that follows visual design principles, producing a document that is easy to read and understand. This example was originally published by Brown (2004). If you perform the squint test on this handout, you should see first and foremost a caricature of a person holding a suitcase and the words "Travel Tips."

There is contrast in the size of the decorative typeface used for the words "Travel Tips," the size of the typefaces used for the list of things to remember, and the size of the type used for the body text and the address information below the body text. The graphic image of the person with the suitcase is much larger than the text; this is another form of contrast (the graphic does not "compete" for attention with the text because the two are such different sizes).

Repetition is employed in the bulleted list. The bullets themselves are a form of repetition, as is the use of bold, italicized, sans serif type that is used to highlight the important words in each bullet point.

Almost all the elements that make up the handout are aligned to the left side of the page (a particularly safe and effective alignment strategy). The exceptions are the image of the person holding the suitcase (this graphic is aligned with the title at its top and to some extent with the body text below it). Notice that the graphic itself aligns with the bulleted list; the nose and the extended arm point to the bulleted list.

Information in the handout is divided into separate areas (the proximity principle). The bulleted list, the body text, and the contact information are all separated by negative space. The use of the graphic element is deliberate. The picture is of a person; even if it is a

Travel Tips

Remember to keep in your ***carry-on*** bag:

- Identification or ***ID***
- Copies of your ***prescriptions***
- ***Emergency contact*** information
- ***Destination*** address and phone number

Traveling is stressful for just about everyone. It can be especially stressful if you have a medical condition. Your trip will be safer and more pleasant if you take a few precautions before you even leave your home. Always have copies of your personal identification, your prescriptions, emergency contact information and the address and phone number of your destination in your carry-on bag, wallet or purse. Do not put these items in your checked baggage because baggage is sometimes lost.

For more information on safe traveling, contact:

Travel Right!
PO Box 555
Orlando Heights, NY 55555
(718) 555-1234
www.travelright.org

FIGURE 12.7 An Example that Follows the Principles and Tips Described in This Chapter

highly stylized caricature, it still conveys "human-ness" and takes advantage of the fact that people are drawn to images of faces. The person is carrying a suitcase—an easily recognized symbol for traveling.

FINAL THOUGHTS

One last piece of advice is to do what most visual design professionals do: Look at examples of other designers' work. Visual design is both an art and a science, and there are trends and fashions in the world of visual design that are worth keeping up with. A local supermarket can provide useful information about effective visual design. Companies spend a great deal of money on the packaging of their products. The next time you find yourself in the supermarket, take a few moments to study the signs and packaging used to draw your attention and give you information about the products.

Other groups that spend a great deal of time and money on visual design include magazine publishers and professional Web developers. The next time you are looking at a magazine or professionally produced website, take a moment to look at the page or screen layout in general; see if you can identify the design elements of contrast, repetition, alignment, and proximity. Looking at what the professionals do with a more sophisticated eye may inspire your work.

VISUAL DESIGN AND THE INSTRUCTIONAL DESIGN PROCESS

Communicating effectively is an important part of instructional design, and visual display plays a critical part in most instructional media. Understanding and applying fundamental rules of visual design should help you answer the following questions:

- Is the information presented in a way that is easy to read?
- Is the information presented in a way that is easy to understand?
- Do the instructional materials look professional?
- Is the visual display attractive?
- Does the visual display help the learner comprehend the instructional content?

Summary

Most instructional designers are responsible for some visual design. Even instructional designers who work with commercial artists must often be able to develop preliminary sketches or evaluate visual designs produced by others. Although most instructional designers will not become accomplished commercial artists, they can develop attractive and effective visual designs by following the fundamental rules of visual design.

The four essential principles of visual display are alignment (how the images and text "line up" with each other), contrast (how different graphic elements distinguish themselves from each other), repetition (how graphic elements are used to create a sense of unity in a design), and proximity (how graphic elements are placed to suggest their relationship to other graphic elements). Recognizing and applying these four principles helps to create a professional and pleasing visual design.

Graphic artists use a number of common strategies to create designs that are attractive and easy to read. A few of these strategies include using images of faces to cause the reader to focus (humans are generally predisposed to attend to faces); making effective use of negative space (allowing "blank" space between graphic elements and groupings); and using bulleted lists to group information and make it easy to read.

A visual design that has text requires deliberate choice of typefaces or fonts. There are three basic classes of type: serif, sans serif, and decorative. Serif type is the easiest to read; sans serif is often used for headlines and callouts; and decorative type gives a visual display a unique style but should be used sparingly because it is often difficult to read.

Color is usually described by one of two color models: the subtractive model for print (CMYK) and the additive model for video, computer screens, and overhead projections (RGB). In making color choices, you must first determine the polarity (whether the background will be lighter than the text and symbols or vice versa). The most readable color combination is a white background with black text and symbols.

Other easily readable combinations are any pair of contrasting, desaturated colors.

To evaluate the legibility and readability of a visual design, apply the squint test: Squint hard while looking at the design to determine which elements are the most obvious and prevalent. Another evaluation method is to give the work to both a representative of the target audience and a fellow instructional designer, asking each to respond to the work in general terms.

To develop a better sense of visual design, look at the work of professional designers. Pay attention to visual design used in settings such as a supermarket, and look closely at the designs found in magazines and online at professionally produced websites.

Connecting Process to Practice

1. Develop a preliminary sketch for a single-page handout illustrating the fire safety rule "Stop, Drop, and Roll," and make it appropriate for elementary school children.
2. You are in charge of creating a brochure for a university's graduate program in instructional design/technology. The university's publication services division will complete the design, but they need a description of what you would like the cover of the brochure to look like. Describe in words your idea for the cover.
3. Develop a preliminary sketch for a PowerPoint slide that illustrates a rise in sales related to improved customer service procedures over a three-month period.
4. Take a good look at the front of a professionally produced cereal box or full-page magazine advertisement. On a clean sheet of paper, sketch the design and use colored markers or pencils to identify use of the principles of repetition, alignment, contrast, and proximity.
5. You are in charge of the production of a website sponsored by a local hospital that provides information about the hospital's wellness clinics and workshops. What can you suggest to the design team for the home page design and layout?

Recommended Reading

Clark, R. C. & Lyons, C. (2004). *Graphics for learning.* San Francisco, CA: Pfeiffer.

Lohr, L. L. (2008). *Creating graphics for learning and performance, 2nd edition.* Upper Saddle River, NJ: Merrill Prentice Hall.

Ware. C. (2008). *Visual thinking for design.* Burlington, MA: Morgan Kaufmann Publishers.

Williams, R. (2008). *The non-designer's design book, 3rd edition.* Berkeley, CA: Peachpit Press.

References

Brown, A. (1999). *Strategies for the delivery of instructional design coursework: Helping learners develop a professional attitude toward the production process.* Ann Arbor, MI: UMI Dissertation Services.

Brown, A. (2004). Building blocks for information architects: Teaching digital media production within an instructional design program. *Journal of Educational Multimedia and Hypermedia, 13*(3), 265–281.

Brown, A. (2004). Visual design basics: Creating effective handouts, flyers and brochures. *CMSCOnline: Meet the Experts.* Consortium of Multiple Sclerosis Centers. Retrieved from http://www.mscare.org/cmsc/images/pdf/document_design_brown.pdf.

Brown, A., Luterbach, K. & Blair, H. (2007, June). *Reading in the 21st Century: The challenges of modern media.* Presented at the National Educational Computing Conference (NECC), Atlanta.

Mills, C. B. & Weldon, L. J. (1987). Reading text from computer screens. *ACM computing surveys, 19*(4), 329–358.

Pastoor, S. (1990). Legibility and subjective preference for color combinations in text. *Human Factors: The Journal of the Human Factors and Ergonomics Society, 32*(2), 157–171.

Schriver, K. A. (1997). *Dynamics in document design.* New York: John Wiley & Sons.

Taylor, C. D. (1934). The relative legibility of black and white print. *Journal of Educational Psychology, 25*(8), 561–578.

Williams, R. (2008). *The non-designer's design book, 3rd edition.* Berkeley, CA: Peachpit Press.

INDEX

I

V

W

Y

Z